YORKSHIRE DALES ANGLERS' GUIDE

Youngsters fishing the popular day ticket water, on the River Wharfe, above the weir at Wetherby

YORKSHIRE DALES ANGLERS' GUIDE

by

Laurence Tetley

CICERONE PRESS
MILNTHORPE, CUMBRIA

ISBN 1 85284 260 1
A catalogue record for this book is available from the British Library.

Front cover: The author brings an early season brown trout to the net from the River Wharfe near Bolton Abbey

CONTENTS

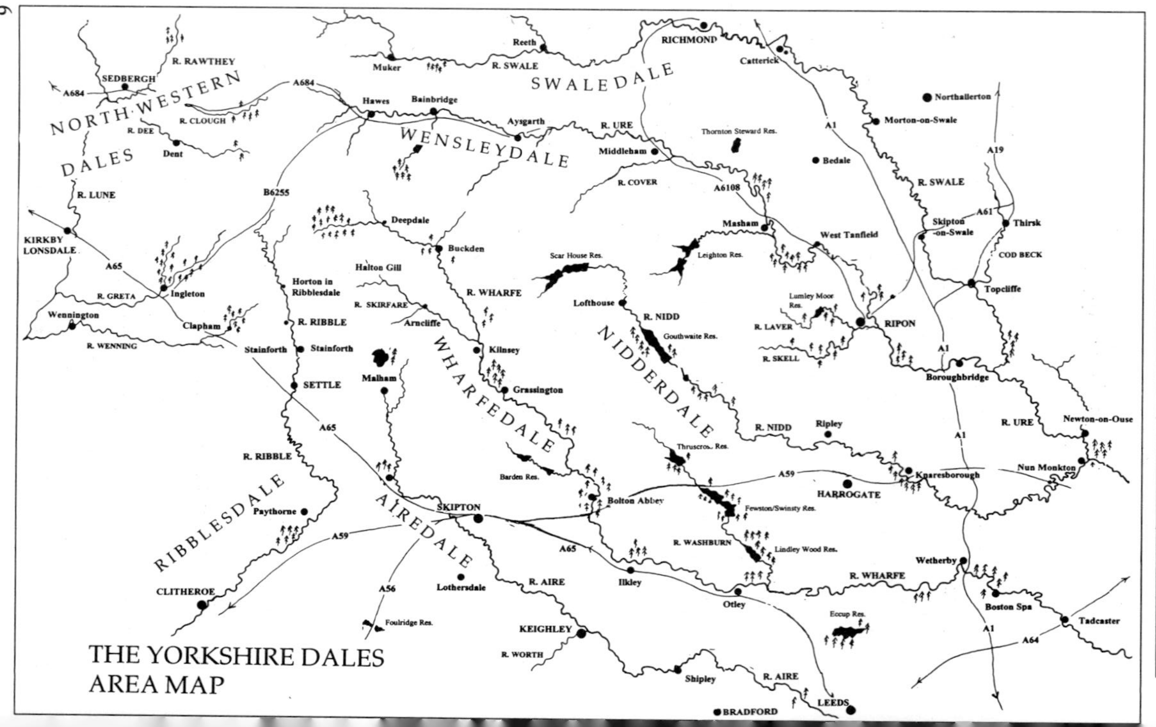
THE YORKSHIRE DALES AREA MAP
SWALEDALE
WENSLEYDALE
NIDDERDALE
WHARFEDALE
AIREDALE
RIBBLESDALE
NORTH WESTERN DALES
Northallerton
Morton-on-Swale
R. SWALE
Skipton -on-Swale
Thirsk
A19
A61
COD BECK
Topcliffe
A1
Boroughbridge
Newton-on-Ouse
Nun Monkton
R. URE
Knaresborough
Tadcaster
Boston Spa
A64
Wetherby
R. WHARFE
HARROGATE
Ripley
Eccup Res.
LEEDS
R. AIRE
BRADFORD
Otley
Shipley
Lindley Wood Res.
Fewston/Swinsty Res.
R. WASHBURN
A59
R. NIDD
Bolton Abbey
Ilkley
A65
KEIGHLEY
R. WORTH
Lothersdale
SKIPTON
Foulridge Res.
A56
Paythorne
CLITHEROE
R. RIBBLE
SETTLE
Stainforth
Malham
Grassington
Barden Res.
Kilnsey
Arncliffe
R. SKIRFARE
Halton Gill
Buckden
Deepdale
Lofthouse
Scar House Res.
Gouthwaite Res.
Masham
Leighton Res.
West Tanfield
RIPON
Lumley Moor Res.
R. LAVER
R. SKELL
Bedale
Catterick
RICHMOND
Thornton Steward Res.
A6108
Middleham
R. COVER
R. URE
Aysgarth
Reeth
Muker
Bainbridge
Hawes
A684
B6255
Horton in Ribblesdale
R. RIBBLE
Ingleton
Clapham
R. GRETA
R. WENNING
Wennington
A65
KIRKBY LONSDALE
R. LUNE
SEDBERGH
R. RAWTHEY
R. CLOUGH
R. DEE
Dent

Introduction

Spread out a map of the Yorkshire Dales, stretch out the fingers of your right hand and place your palm on the National Park. With your wrist pointing towards the River Ouse, each finger now traces a Dale's river, one of the major arteries of Pennine Yorkshire. The shorter River Aire lies to the south beneath your thumb and River Swale to the north, underneath the little finger, with the Rivers Wharfe, Nidd and Ure between. Of course many visitors to Yorkshire will know of the great fisheries on the Swale around Topcliffe, for instance, the Wharfe at Tadcaster, the Ure at Boroughbridge, but few will know of the smaller rivers and tributaries, each of them unique and many of them offering the opportunity to wet a line. Clear streams bubbling from limestone fissures near the famous Stump Cross Caverns mingle to create the River Washburn which, in its tortuous course of only twelve miles, has been dammed four times to create the great reservoirs which store water for the people of Leeds. Two of them, Fewston and Swinsty, already established legends in the trout fishing world, offer the visitor day ticket fishing on some of the loveliest trout water in the country and another, Lindley Wood, is open for season ticket holders. In the north of the region, the diminutive Raydale Beck and tributaries flowing through remote Raydale, high above Lake Semerwater, offer some challenging fishing for wild brown trout in a timeless valley virtually unknown to the visitor. Pen-y-Ghent, affectionately known to locals as a Dales mountain although a mere 694 metres high, dominates the central Dales area. Streams crashing down the spectacular Pen-y-Ghent Gill into diminutive Littondale swell the miniature River Skirfare to create yet another demanding fishery, favoured by the roving fly fisherman.

Many other fine fishing rivers start their lives in the Dales, or touch its borders, before continuing on their relentless passage to the sea. The Ribble, one of the Dales' few salmon fisheries, drains water from the slopes of the great peaks of Whernside, Ingleborough and Pen-y-Ghent before, near Hellifield, turning west into Lancashire. To the north the River Dee, meandering through pastoral Dentdale, and the Clough River tumbling down Garsdale take water from Baugh Fell and Whernside eastwards to Sedbergh, a good base from which to explore the fine fishing opportunities of the north-western dales.

Traditionally Dales trout fishing is about wading in clear streams, swinging a miniature Partridge and Orange wet fly into the inevitable deep pool at the end of a gravely run whilst anticipating the energetic take of a small wild browny. The fish run three, or even four, to the pound, but seem much larger as they perform an aerobatic display that would rival the Red Arrows! If this is what you're after, try any of the upper reaches of our rivers.

But if you're searching for bigger prey, the great reservoirs at Fewston and Swinsty, Scar House and Leighton are the places to head for. The waters may be remote and windswept, but they all hold hard fighting trout which have plenty of room to run when hooked. You'll need strong leaders and good backing to land one of the bigger browns or rainbows from these waters. And then there are the newer waters which, justifiably, continue to make their presence felt. Right across the region, an increasing number of smaller trout waters continue to be created to satisfy the demand for a good day's sport in pleasant surroundings. To the west, in Ribblesdale, there's Helwith Bridge Trout Fishery, to the south, Raygill in Lothersdale, in the east you have a choice, Bellflask and Tanfield, to name but two, and in the north, around Richmond, you have an even bigger choice. All of these purpose built fisheries are famous for the fighting trout that lurk in the clear water. And if you're young and have never caught a trout before, head for Kilnsey Park in Wharfedale. Reserved for beginners, they have a lake full of trout, the tackle to catch them with and an expert to show you how.

But fishing in Yorkshire is not only about trout; the county boasts some of the best coarse fishing in the country, and quite rightly so. The lower reaches of the Nidd below Knaresborough, the Swale below Catterick and the Wharfe below Wetherby are renowned for the quality and size of the barbel, chub, dace, eels and pike that they regularly produce. Few visiting fishermen will not have heard of Topcliffe; the town's name has appeared in the record books for many decades. If you're after barbel and chub, the Swale around Topcliffe is unbeatable and much of the water can be fished on a day ticket. The Ure's also a great river, around Boroughbridge, plus the Nidd around Knaresborough and the Wharfe at Boston Spa and Tadcaster.

If you're a still water angler searching for that juggernaut of coarse fish, the carp, then try the new fisheries in the Vale of York. Many of them are dedicated to carp fishing, although they hold just about everything else. But if you like your carp in bigger waters, try the larger of the Knotford Lagoons, situated alongside the River Wharfe near Otley. It's crammed with carp. Bags of ten to fifteen mirrors a day are not uncommon.

For the ever increasing army of pole fishermen, the Leeds and Liverpool Canal is worth a try. Although it's not strictly in the Yorkshire Dales it does impinge on its borders and has been included in this guide because of the excellent coarse fishing it offers. Then there's the much shorter but no less prolific Ripon Canal with 2 miles of excellent coarse fishing.

Visitors to the Dales cannot fail to be enchanted by the timeless beauty, tranquillity and apparent stability of the area and fishermen are no exception. Please remember though that the National Park is a fragile resource and it is in effect a working farm. Be aware of livestock and close all gates. Don't damage drystone walls to gain access to a remote fishery and try not to add to the erosion of riverbanks. Also remember that the Dales rivers are flood rivers. Keep a wary eye on the weather. A sudden violent storm on the steep sides on Pen-y-Ghent, for instance, will quickly bring the River Wharfe into flood, even in summer, so be very careful when wading.

Wherever and whenever you fish in the glorious Dales, enjoy!

BAITS

Where it is appropriate, some baits have been mentioned in the text but as there is a vast variety of fishing baits currently available the following information has been included to provide newcomers to the sport with an idea as to what can be purchased over the counter and what should tempt fish. Every angler has a favourite bait, one which he feels will always catch fish. In many cases this feeling is simply one of confidence in a particular food. A bait that has always caught fish will naturally be used more often than something which is new and untried. There are of course many traditional baits still in use. For instance at the right time and under the right conditions worms can't be beaten. But did you know there are many different types of worm and they can be bought over the counter in most fishing tackle shops? Another traditional bait, bread, is still very popular. Bread comes in a huge range of varieties all of which seem to tempt fish. What follows is a list of the more popular baits in use today. It is not exhaustive because fishermen are very inventive and constantly try new things, but it may just give you ideas.

Maggots

Probably the best known and most used bait ever. If its use is allowed, the humble maggot is the best bait to try on a new water. Maggots can be used as hook bait either singly or in bunches. They can be used in a swim feeder or mixed in a proprietary ground bait. They're just about as versatile as anything you'll find and they've also undergone changes over the years. Maggots now come in bright colours each with their own devotees. Many carp anglers insist on reds, barbel men often use bronze maggots, some fishermen like them mixed and others use the simple plain white ones. Pole fishermen and match anglers like 'squats' which are the larvae of the house fly. They're much smaller than a standard maggot and on their day there's nothing to beat them. Short and fat 'pinkies' are popular with roach fishermen. Although they're called pinkies they also come in different colours.

Casters

Casters are maggots undergoing metamorphosis. That is, they are changing from the maggot stage into a bluebottle. Sometimes known as 'chrysalis' they're great for tempting most species of coarse fish. Chub, perch and roach love them. Casters vary from white, through orange to a deep burgundy colour and most fishermen have their favourite. The main problem with casters is keeping them in one state. If it's hot and they're in a covered tin you'll soon hear the buzzing of bluebottles. Keep them covered with water: it slows the metamorphosis and stops them floating when you put them on the hook. Use casters singly as hook bait or throw them into a swim as feeder bait. If you do find that they are floating, take off your weights and try them on the surface. At the right time they can be deadly.

Bread

Everyone knows of bread for fishing and it's still a killer. You can use it any way you like and it will attract all kinds of fish including trout. On those warm summer days, floating bread crust is brilliant for carp. Bread paste fished in a back eddy will often bring a big barbel or chub from the depths. Float fished bread flake always attracts perch, roach and rudd in big numbers. Your local tackle dealer will also carry a range of bread punches which are used to compress or shape the bread for hook baits. There's even a range of flavours, such as banana and strawberry, to soak the humble loaf in order to attract the fish.

Hempseed

Hempseed is a firm favourite of match anglers. It seems to attract bream, chub, roach and tench when all other baits fail. You can buy it raw and boil it yourself but it is a messy business. Buy it ready prepared from a fishing tackle shop. It's very versatile: use it as hook bait, loose feed it around a float or mix it with groundbait. It nearly always works.

Sweetcorn

Barbel, carp, chub and tench all love sweetcorn. This is the stuff you buy in cans from a supermarket. In its natural state it's yellow but your local tackle shop will sell it flavoured. It comes in natural yellow, orange and strawberry. They're all killer baits when the fish are in the mood. Use it singly or mixed in a groundbait.

Boilies

This is one of the new baits derived from the humble potato. The exact recipes are closely guarded but 'boilies' are basically marble shaped pieces of potato plus additives. They come in various sizes, the popular ones being in the range 10mm to 15mm. To entice big barbel, bream, carp, chub and tench they come in different flavours. Seafood is popular, as is chocolate. Some fishermen swear by the berries, cranberry and strawberry. Ask in your local tackle shop which flavour is best for your chosen water. (Some fisheries have banned boilies because if they're left on the bank and dry out they can choke wildlife. So take them home.)

Pork luncheon meat

On its day pork luncheon meat outclasses all other baits when you're after the really big fish. Barbel, carp and chub love it and of course if you've got any left you can always put it in your sandwiches.

There are lots of other possibilities most of which will catch fish at some time or another. Trout pellets (not to be used on a trout lake!), Pedigree Chum mixer, Pepperani, Rice Krispies or Coco Pops and corned beef to name but a few. You only need confidence to try them and if they catch fish you'll be hooked as well.

LEGAL

In England and Wales any prospective angler, over 12 years old, who wants to fish for freshwater fish in any water, publicly or privately owned, must first obtain an Environment Agency rod licence, issued by Post Offices. Licences are valid nationally and can be used anywhere in England and Wales. Whilst the appropriate licence allows an angler to fish for salmon, trout, freshwater fish and eels, it does not provide any form of access to a fishery. Having first obtained a licence, an angler must then purchase a fishing ticket, join a fishing club or simply ask a landowner to gain access to his chosen fishing spot. In law the burden is upon the angler to be adequately licensed before starting to fish. Fishing without an

Environment Agency rod licence leaves an angler open to prosecution and a hefty fine.

Apart from the legal aspect, it is important that every fisherman purchases a licence because it is income generated from sales that enables the Agency to continue its work of fishery improvement. The work of the Agency's Fisheries Department includes fishery law enforcement, restocking and monitoring fish stocks, executing fish rescue and improving fishery habitats. The Agency also keeps a continuing watch on abstraction, water levels and pollution.

If you become aware of any pollution incidents please phone the FREE Agency 24 hour hotline 0800 80 70 60 and report it. It is in your interests to keep your fishing waters clean.

Current charges for rod licences are:

Salmon and migratory trout.

Adult season £55.00. Concessionary rate £27.50.
8 day rate £15.00.
Daily rate £5.00.

Non migratory trout, grayling, coarse fish and eels.

Adult season £15.00. Concessionary rate £7.50.
8 day rate £4.50.
Daily rate £1.50.

Concessionary rates, for season tickets only, apply to retired persons receiving a state pension, registered disabled and youngsters between 12 and 16 (inclusive).

The Environment Agency's North East Region is divided into three sub-divisions - Northumbria Area, Dales Area and Ridings Area - with the latter two covering most of the waters in this guide. Yorkshire bylaws apply to both the Dales and the Ridings areas as follows.

Fishing closed seasons (dates are inclusive):

Salmon and migratory trout - November 1st to April 5th.

Non-migratory trout - October 1st to March 24th. These dates apply to the rivers system. Many still water fisheries, holding rainbow trout, are open throughout the year.

Coarse fish and eels - March 15th to June 15th. Again this applies to the rivers system. Many still water coarse fisheries are open throughout the year.

Size limits (measured from the tip of the snout to the fork of the tail):
Barbel - 30cm.
Carp - 25cm.
Bream, chub, grayling, tench and trout - 23cm.
Dace, perch, roach and rudd - 18cm.
Fish less than these limits must not be killed or taken away. Not more than six fish (no more than two bream or tench) may be taken away in any one day without the written consent of the owner or occupier of the fishery. In practice most fishing clubs and private waters insist that all coarse fish be carefully returned to the water unharmed.

Nets:

All landing nets and keep nets must be made of knotless material.

Bait restrictions:

Fish roe may not be used.
Undersized bream, carp, grayling, tench and trout must not be used as bait.
In waters where a close season for coarse fish applies, the only baits which may be used in this period are artificial lure, fly, minnow or worms, except on the following two waters: the River Nidd from the outlet of Gouthwaite Reservoir to 1km downstream of Dacre Bridge, and the River Swale from the waterfall at Richmond to 1.6km upstream of Marske Bridge.

North East Region

Northumbria and Yorkshire Region

Regional Office. Rivers House, 21 Park Square South, Leeds LS1 2QG. Tel: 0113 244 0191. Fax: 0113 246 1889.

Dales Area

Administration Office. Coverdale House, Amy Johnson Way, Clifton Moor, York YO3 4UZ. Tel: 01904 692296. Fax: 01904 693748.

Ridings Area

Administration Office. Olympia House, Geldred Road, Leeds LS21 6DD. Tel: 0113 244 0191. Fax: 0113 211 2116.

Rivers controlled (together with the South Yorkshire area): Aire, Calder, Dearne, Derwent, Don, Esk, Hull, Nidd, Ouse, Swale, Tees, Ure, Wharfe and tributaries.

A few of the north-western fisheries listed in this guide fall under the jurisdiction of the North West Region.

North West Region

Regional Office. Richard Fairclough House, Knutsford Road, Warrington WA4 1HG. Tel: 01925 653999. Fax: 01925 415961.

Central Area

Administration Office. Lostock House, Holme Road, Bamber Bridge PR5 6RE. Tel: 01772 639882.

Rivers controlled: Alt, Calder, Crossens, Douglas, Hodder, Keer, Lune, Ribble, Wyre, Yarrow and tributaries.

Close seasons: Salmon, November 1st to January 31st (except River Eden system - October 15th to January 14th); migratory trout, October 16th to April 30th (except northern region rivers); coarse fish, March 15th to June 15th. No close season for coarse fish in enclosed waters.

NOTES

Returning Fish to the Water

All coarse fishery, and some trout fishery, operators will at some time expect anglers to return fish to the water. In order that a fish is not damaged this should be done with extreme care. Don't remove the fish from the water; leave it in the landing net. Use forceps or pointed pliers and, without touching it, unhook the fish whilst it's still in the net and release it from there. Never take hold of a fish with your bare hands. A fish is a cold blooded animal which can be severely injured by warm human hands coming into contact with its body. The effect is like plunging your hand into scalding water. You wouldn't like it and nor does the fish!

Put and Take

Many of Yorkshire's fisheries operate a policy of "put and take" fishing. This means that the fish stock in a water can be kept at the optimum level if, when fish are removed, a record is made in the "fishing return", the paper which records how many fish have been taken. If it is a rule of the fishery, please fill in the return accurately. On those inevitable blank days, even a NIL return should be made.

The Country Code

Remember that the Yorkshire Dales is in essence a working farm. In your eagerness to get to the bankside make sure that you abide by the simple country code:

- Don't climb over drystone walls. They have the habit of collapsing.
- Close all gates. Livestock should be left where the farmer has put them, not wandering about on the road.
- Park your car properly. Do not obstruct gates or other access points.
- Respect the wildlife habitat. Don't crash through nesting grounds at the edge of waters.
- Never remove birds' eggs from nests.
- Do not leave litter. Take it home.
- Never leave unused bait on the bank. It just encourages the rats which may deposit Weil's Disease.
- Never, under any circumstances, leave unattended baited hooks in or out of the water.
- Before going home make sure there are no baited hooks, or lengths of nylon line, discarded on the bank. Hooks and nylon are deadly to wildlife.

Bankside Designation

Throughout this angling guide the terms right bank and left bank relate to an angler facing downstream observing the river's flow.

Fishery Location

The location of all still water fisheries and Dales towns have been given a map designation based on the Ordnance Survey Landranger series.

Landranger maps are over-printed with a blue grid pattern relating to latitude (horizontal) lines and longitude (vertical) lines. Figures marking the vertical lines, called 'Eastings', increment as they progress east, from left to right. Those of the horizontal lines, 'Northings', increase as they move north, from bottom to top. There are forty vertical and forty horizontal squares giving a grand total of 1,600 squares. In this guide, the map number has been quoted first, followed by three figures for an easting and three more for a northing. The first two figures in each case designate a square and the third number one tenth of that square.

As an example, take Pateley Bridge in upper Nidderdale. Its designation is **OS99:159657**.

OS99 refers to Ordnance Survey Landranger map number **99**.
159 is the easting **15** and the figure **9** shows that Pateley Bridge is located 9/10 easterly inside the square.
657 is the northing **65** with the **7** indicating that the town is 7/10 northerly inside the square.

Ordnance Survey Landranger maps are extremely popular and can be obtained, for a modest price, virtually anywhere. Alternatively, all local libraries carry them.

SAFETY ON THE RIVER BANK

Wading

Wading in the Dales rivers can be difficult, sometimes dangerous, and not just when they're in flood. Because of the water clarity in the upper reaches of rivers like the Wharfe, for instance, the depth is often deceptive. Water which looks to be a few inches deep can often be several feet deep. Some of our rivers tumble over limestone steps which can easily be seen and avoided, but there are other underwater obstructions which can't, particularly when the surface is rippled by the wind. Other rivers, like the upper Nidd, crash down boulder strewn valleys, and when you're concentrating on a trout rising in an eddy behind a boulder it is easy to trip over another one. So do be very careful when wading. Try to read the water. Move slowly and concentrate.

If, however, you're unfortunate and land in deep water, don't panic. Try to bring your feet up to the surface whilst using your hands to paddle and keep your head out of the water. Work with the current, guiding yourself into a quiet eddy and then get out. And don't wade when the river is in flood.

Spectacles

When fly casting, particularly in a strong wind, it's not always possible to tell where the fly is going, so wear some eye protection. It's also just as important when you're ledgering. On those occasions when a ledger weight is stuck fast on the bottom, you're bending the rod and the line is singing under the pressure, be very careful as the weight is likely to shoot out of the water like a stray missile. In instances such as these, there have been cases of hooks spearing an eyeball. Always wear spectacles or sun shades when fishing.

Bank Erosion

In the lower reaches of some Dales rivers (the Swale is a good example) where they follow a twisting course through meadowland, it's possible for the bankside, on the outside of bends, to be seriously undermined. Don't walk too close to the outside edge. The bank may suddenly give way and you'll find yourself in deep water.

Power Lines

Carbon fibre is the new wonder material from which most fishing rods and poles are made. It's ideal. It's strong, resilient and supple, but it's also a good conductor of electricity. That means that if you touch one of the overhead power lines with a pole, your body will make a perfect conductor to earth for the electric current. It's a bit like poking your finger into an electric power socket and the result will be just the same. It's not unknown for fishermen to be killed in this way. If you see any overhead power cables near where you want to fish, give them a wide berth and take heed of the signs, thoughtfully placed on the bankside, to warn of the danger.

Weil's Disease

Leptospirosis, better known as Weil's Disease, can be a killer. Leptospira, the organism which causes the disease, is carried by rats which in turn deposit the bacteria in the stagnant water they urinate in. So it's likely to be encountered in all those places where fishermen like to go: in the quiet water at the edge of a river or pond, in the sloppy mud which always seems to cover the path to the waterside, and in the eddy where you've just dropped your keepnet!

The bacteria finds its way into a human body through any open cut or abrasion or even via the mouth or eyes. In its early stages the disease closely resembles influenza. It's accompanied by a fever, shivering and muscle aches or spasms. Early treatment is vital. Get help immediately. Tell the doctor that you've been fishing and you suspect you may have been near infected water.

But prevention is always better than cure. Don't put your fingers in your mouth or eyes if they've been near suspect water and before you go fishing securely cover any cuts which might come into contact with water.

Blue-green algae

Another dangerous substance lurking in our waters is blue-green algae. The algae are a natural inhabitant of the UK and in still fresh waters they may multiply. Because they like it hot, they're active in the summer months and make their presence obvious by colouring the water a shade of blue-green. These nasty algae ferment to produce a chemical which is toxic to all mammals including man.

Unlike Weil's Disease it's obvious from the water colour that the algae are present. Try to keep away from waters which turn blue-green in the summer. If the problem is brought to the attention of the Environment Agency, the water will be closed and notices informing everyone of the danger will be posted around the infected area.

If you notice a rash on any exposed skin which has been in contact with the algae consult your doctor immediately. Don't drink any infected water.

The Rivers

AIREDALE

Some people view Airedale as a valley of dark satanic mills, with tall chimneys spewing smoke and grime into an already polluted atmosphere. Indeed it once was like that, during the dark days of the Industrial Revolution, but today these are only distant memories. Most of the mills have gone and those that remain no longer poison the air or pour detergent into the river. The River Aire, at least downstream as far as Shipley, is clean once again and even below there it supports some fish stocks. So, thanks to a growing awareness of the environment, the fish are back and well worth pursuing.

Between Malham and Skipton, the river's crystal clear water supports a fine stock of native brown trout and grayling. Below Skipton down to Shipley large shoals of coarse fish make their presence felt and beyond there downstream to Leeds a few hardy fish survive. Below Leeds the river is still a commercial waterway, although the industry is considerably reduced from what it once was, and the water is not as clean as it might be.

Finding the source of the River Aire has always been something of a challenge. On Ordnance Survey maps it's marked as Aire Head, a few hundred yards below Malham village, but there is considerable evidence to support the theory that the Aire actually flows from Malham Tarn and disappears underground into limestone caverns before reappearing at the base of Malham Cove. It then flows through the village to meet Gordale Beck at Aire Head before continuing for a further 50 miles until it joins the River Ouse near Goole. Whatever you believe about its source, there's no doubt that the Aire starts its life near Malham.

Unfortunately a lot of the prime fishing water on the upper river is in private hands. But there is some excellent trout fishing to be had near Skipton and almost all the remainder of the water down to Leeds is available to casual anglers using an Angling Club day ticket. For those expecting to fish for more than a few days it makes sense to buy a moderately priced club season ticket from one of the local fishing tackle shops.

Malhamdale (OS98:902629)

Malhamdale, as Airedale is known in its upper reaches, is a magnet to walkers but offers little to the visiting angler. Although the river here is crystal clear, holding a good head of native brown trout, all the water downstream from Malham through Aireton to Bell Busk is in private hands.

See also Malham Tarn

The Bowland Game Fishing Association controls the rights to about 2 1/2 miles of excellent brown trout fly fishing, on both banks downstream, from Airton Bridge to the limit sign a few hundred yards above Bell Busk. Members only.

Below Bell Busk, from the National Park boundary downstream for about 2 1/2 miles on both banks, the fishing belongs to Coniston Hall Estate and can be fished on a day ticket. Access is from the A65 trunk road from Gargrave to Hellifield. Good pools and long glides are the nature of the river as it winds back and forth through flat fertile grassland. A combination of clear water and prolific insect life provide an ideal environment for the small native brown trout which are not easy to tempt, but well worth the effort. This is classic fly fishing water and traditional Yorkshire Dales patterns will often produce results. Weekly stocking with fish from the estate's hatchery maintains a good head of fish.

Day tickets £9.50 from the Estate Shop, on the A65 near Coniston Cold, between 1000 and 1800 hrs. Outside those hours from the hall. (Tel: 01756 748136)

See also Coniston Hall Lake

Skipton (OS103:990515)

Three fishing clubs control most of the river fishing between Skipton and Keighley. The Bradford City Angling Association has about 2 1/2 miles of excellent fly fishing on both banks from Gargrave weir downstream to the Settle and Carlisle Railway bridge near the A59 river crossing outside Skipton. Then on the left bank from the railway bridge to 500 yards below the road bridge. This excellent water is limited to twenty permits per day for members only. Fly fishing only during the trout season and worm fishing for grayling after August 31st. Size limit 12 inches.

On the right bank from the railway bridge downstream for about 1 1/4 miles to Funkirk Farm and the left bank from the Bradford City AA limit to opposite the farm, the Bradford No.1. Angling Association controls some good mixed fishing for members only. About 400 yards of the right bank through Funkirk farm is also preserved for members of the Bradford City AA.

Approximately 1 mile of excellent mixed fishing on the right bank between Carleton Beck and Carleton Stone Bridge is managed jointly by the Bradford City AA and the Skipton Angling Association. Further downstream, another 2 miles, both banks, below Carleton Bridge, are also controlled by the Skipton AA who issue day tickets to visiting anglers. This is a fine mixed fishery holding some native brown trout supported annually with stocked fish to about 1lb. But the water is mainly fished for the quality chub, dace, grayling, perch and pike that lurk in the streamy water and quiet eddies. Fishing during the trout season is with fly, worm, minnow and spinners only. No keepnets during this period.

Day tickets £4.00, are available from the Hon. Secretary, the Esso Garage on Keighley Road in Skipton (Tel: 01756 793953), K. L. Tackle, Keighley, and Jackson's Fishing Tackle at Earby.

See also Chelker Reservoir, Embsay Reservoir, Foulridge Reservoir, Raygill Trout Fishery, Whinny Gill Reservoir and Winterburn Reservoir.

Cononley (OS103:888470)

About 4 miles of fishing, mainly on both banks, down to Cononley Bridge can be had on a day ticket issued by the Bradford City AA. Fishing on the right bank starts one field below the railway bridge, near Snaygill, and continues down to Cononley Road Bridge. On the left bank, the fishing stretch starts two fields below the railway bridge and, except for one field near Bradley, belonging to the Bradford No.1 AA, extends downstream to approximately 500 yards above Cononley Bridge. It then continues on both banks below Cononley Bridge downstream to the limit sign near Kildwick Bridge.

This is a popular venue for the coarse fisherman. Heavy bags of chub, dace and roach are not uncommon and although the fish tend to be small, the pike fishing is very good, particularly in the autumn.

There are also a few large trout in this water but they tend to be shy. Many years ago this fishery was famous for its grayling but sadly they seem to have disappeared.

Day tickets £3.00, from the start of the coarse fishing season on June 16th, from the Post Office, 2 King Street, Cononley (Tel: 01756 632371) K. L. Tackle and Willis Walker Sports Shop, Keighley.

See Fishing Tackle Shops section.

At the time of going to press, plans have been passed to extend the Aire valley dual carriageway from the roundabout at Kildwick to that at Snaygill. Because this area of Airedale floods badly after heavy rain, extensive engineering work will be needed along the route of the new road. This will undoubtedly have a major impact on fishing along this stretch for some years to come.

Kildwick (OS104:011459)

The Keighley Angling Club controls most of the fishing below the roadbridge at Kildwick. This is another fine stretch of water with long glides and deep pools holding a range of coarse fish including chub, dace, perch, and some pike. There are also fair numbers of trout and grayling. The fishing is on the left bank from about 1/2 mile above the bridge downstream to approximately 1/2 mile below Steeton Bridge. About 3 miles in all. And on the right bank, from the bridge downstream to Sutton Beck. Below the beck for two fields, the fishing is controlled by the Bradford City AA.

Day tickets, from June 16th, cost £3.00, for the Bradford City AA stretch from Cononley Post Office (Tel: 01535 632371), K. L. Tackle and Willis Walker Sport Shop, Keighley. **Day tickets** £2.00, for the Keighley AC stretch, from Keighley tackle dealers, see above. Keighley AC season books and day tickets are also available, in some cases seven days a week, from Barrie's Shoe Repairs, Cavendish Street, Keighley (Tel: 01535 604428), E. Kershaw, Newsagents, Kirkgate, Silsden (Tel: 01535 652370), Noshville Snack Bar, Cononley Lane Ends, P.M. Newsagents, North Street, Keighley, Silsden Boats (Tel: 01535 653675) and Utley Post Office (Tel: 01535 602946).

See also Silsden Reservoir and Whitefield Reservoir

Further down the river at Steeton Bridge, on the A6034, more excellent mixed fishing is available on a day ticket. About 3/4 mile of the right bank, downstream from the bridge to opposite the golf course, belongs to the Bradford City AA. Fishing is by fly, worm, artificial lure or minnow only during the close season for coarse fish.

A further 1/2 mile of really good fishing on the right bank at Utley, near Keighley, is in the hands of the Keighley AC.

Tickets for both these waters from the sources listed above.

Newsholme Dean Beck

The Bingley Angling Club controls some stream trout fishing here at the top end of North Beck, near Goose Eye, east of Keighley. This is challenging fishing on a typical Yorkshire beck. Unfortunately the water level drops severely during the summer. Trout limit size 12 inches. Members only.

River Worth

Hardly worthy of the title "river", this small stream flowing from Haworth Moor to the River Aire in Keighley is often short of water although there are a few good pools holding small native trout. Much of the river is unfished but it is possible to get permission from local farmers. A short stretch of the right bank below the Bronte Caravan Park is available to members of the Keighley AC. No day tickets.

See also Sugden End Reservoir and Teapot Dam.

Keighley (OS104:065415)

Approximately 1 1/2 miles of fishing on the right bank, from the River Worth's junction with the Aire, downstream through Marley Playing Fields to the sewage works, is Keighley AC water and available for fishing on a day ticket. Details listed above. This is a fine mixed fishery producing good roach and chub. Bread, casters, cheese and worm are the popular baits. Use a good strong line as the chub can be large and powerful.

Fishing on the left bank of the river, from the golf club downstream to near Riddlesden Cricket Club, is held by the Leeds and District Amalgamated Society of Anglers for members only. This water is used for match fishing in the summer but a short stretch near the golf club is reserved for non match anglers.

See also Doe Park Reservoir, Hewenden Reservoir, Leeming Reservoir, Linda's Lake, Nunroyd Pond and Robert's Pond.

The Marsden Star Angling Society has the fishing rights to three stretches of the river below the roadbridge at Stocksbridge. Left bank downstream for about 400 yards, known as Laycocks Field, right bank for 100 yards by Ribblesden Cricket Club, and from the old Sandbeds sewage beds downstream to Castlefield Old Mill.

Day tickets £2.00, from fishing tackle shops in Bradford, Earby and Keighley.

Keighley AC controls a short stretch of the left bank from the Airedale Heifer Inn downstream to Southam Garage.

Day tickets from the sources listed above under Kildwick.

Members of the Bradford No.1 AA may fish a stretch of about 1 1/2 miles of the left bank near the A650 road at Sandbeds.

See also Settler Dam and Sunnydale Reservoir.

Bingley (OS104:105395)

By now the Aire is predominantly a coarse fishing water although some stocked trout are still to be had. The best fishing is for chub, dace and roach.

Bingley AC owns the rights to about 1 1/4 miles of both banks, in Myrtle Park, downstream from the Water Bridge to Beckfoot Bridge, also at the Cricket Field on the right bank and about 200 yards downstream from Ravenroyd Private Road sign to the landing stage. Further down at Cottingley, the club holds joint rights, with the Idle and Thackley AA, to the right bank from below Cottingley Water Bridge downstream to the bottom of the rugby field.

Day tickets £2.00, juniors, ladies and senior citizens £1.00, are available from Fishpeople, K. L. Tackle, and Willis Walker, all in Keighley.

See Fishing Tackle Shops section.

See also Coppice Pond.

Starting after the houses on the left bank below Cottingley Bridge downstream for about 3/4 mile the rights belong to the Bradford No.1 AA. Members only.

Saltaire (OS104:139381)

Excellent mixed fishing on both banks for about 2 miles of Saltaire Angling Association water can be had on a day ticket here. On the right bank the fishing extends from Harden Beck downstream to the top of Hirst Mill field, then below Hirst Mill to Salts Mill and then again from below the mill downstream to the A6038 Baildon Bridge. Also on the left bank, with the exception of Robert's Park in Saltaire, from Seven Arches all the way to Baildon Bridge.

Day tickets £2.00 adult, £1.50 juniors and £1.00 ladies, from the Shipley Angling Centre, K. L. Tackle, and Willis Walker Sports Shop, Keighley.

This is an interesting stretch. Deep water above Saltaire weir provides a good home for the large bream which have been known to reach 6lb. This is also a good roach water, with some 2lb fish being recorded. Shoals of small chub and dace are always around above the weir but the trout fishing is better below it.

Members of the Bradford No.1 AA have the right to fish the left bank of the Aire in Robert's Park at Saltaire. No day tickets.

Shipley

There's very little in the river below here, but some anglers do persevere and occasionally have a good day. A short stretch of the left bank downstream from Baildon Bridge belongs to the Unity Angling Club. Members only.

The Idle and Thackley AA also have a short length here. Members only.

See also Chellow Dean Reservoir, Harold Park Lake, Royds Hall Dam, Shelf Dam and Tong Park Lake.

Whilst the river supports a small fish stock, the water below here is hardly ever fished. Local angling clubs don't show much interest in the water, so anyone wanting to try their luck should contact one of the farmers through whose land the river flows.

See also Billing Dam, Clayton Ponds, Larkfield Tarn and Roundhay Park Lake.

NIDDERDALE

The River Nidd is not actually in the Yorkshire Dales National Park, the border of which follows a sweeping curve dissecting Little and Great Whernside to the north, but nobody can deny that it is a Dales river. In the great amphitheatre created by the Whernsides, a host of streams, scurrying down miniature stony valleys, feed the vast Angram Reservoir, the source of the Nidd since Victorian times. Angram, the highest of three reservoirs built to supply clean water to Bradford, and its neighbour Scar House Reservoir give the Nidd a different character to the other Dales rivers. Because these reservoirs control the flow of headwater into the river, effectively smoothing out variations between drought and flood, the Nidd's water level does not change as dramatically as the Wharfe, for instance. But when floodwater crashes along the narrow upper valley it can be both spectacular and dangerous.

Despite holding a large stock of wild brown trout Angram is not open for fishing. However its brother, the equally wild and remote Scar House, is fishable on a day ticket obtainable in Pateley Bridge.

Between the outflow of Scar House Reservoir and Lofthouse village the water tumbles over a rocky river bed, through a compact valley, occasionally disappearing into subterranean caverns, before reappearing and joining How Stean Beck to finally form the infant River Nidd. There's little point in fishing this stretch because for most of the year it appears to be dry and for the rest of the time it's a torrent.

Below Lofthouse, in the area of Nidderdale known as "Little Switzerland", the river cascades over boulders into turbulent pools providing a home for energetic brown trout which rarely grow bigger than 8 inches. Further down the valley, the lovely Gouthwaite Reservoir is home for some rare wildlife but not the fisherman - it is part of a wildlife reserve and fishing is strictly prohibited.

Upper Nidderdale's capital, Pateley Bridge, is a good centre for the visiting angler. Fishing on almost all of the 8 miles between the outflow of Gouthwaite Reservoir down through the village to Summerbridge, is available on a day ticket. Indeed there's fishing on virtually all of the upper River Nidd and the lower section of the river down to its meeting with the River Ouse at Nun Monkton

Pool, close to York.

In its upper reaches, extending downstream as far as Killinghall, the water is a succession of glides and pools holding a stock of native trout and grayling supplemented annually in restocking programmes carried out by local fishing clubs. Because access is limited by badly overgrown banks, it's a difficult water to fish. Indeed, in many places the only access is from the river itself - by wading. For an energetic angler, though, and those not afraid to lose a few flies or floats it is worth the effort.

Below Killinghall, Nidderdale broadens rapidly, its steep sides level off and the river water slows in preparation for its meeting with the expansive Vale of York and the River Ouse. Around here the Nidd increasingly becomes a mixed fishery, its trout and grayling stocks being joined by chub, dace and eels. At Knaresborough the Nidd's waters slow still further to create much deeper glides and pools. It is here that the coarse fish become prevalent and trout are few. Because of the extent of the fishing available in the river and the many lakes that abound in the area, Knaresborough is also a good centre for a visiting angler.

Further downstream the river becomes very sluggish with hardly any noticeable movement as it meanders through meadows on its hesitant journey. It is in these lower reaches at Cowthorpe, Kirk Hammerton and the Monktons that the coarse fishing really comes into its own, and where the big bream, barbel, chub, dace, pike and roach lurk in deep silent eddies beneath sandy banks. Nidderdale has something to tempt almost every angler whatever method is chosen.

Ramsgill (OS99:119710)

The fishing in How Stean Beck is private.

Fishing on both banks from below the beck downstream to the iron bridge at Low Sikes and then on the right bank for a further 1¾ miles belongs to the Leeds and District Amalgamated Society of Anglers for members only. Small trout and a few grayling are the quarry here. It's mainly a fly fishing water with all the traditional Yorkshire patterns doing well, but also trotting a worm down between the rocks usually produces results.

Bradford No. 1 Angling Association holds the fishing rights to about 1½ miles of water between the villages of Lofthouse and

Ramsgill, at Low Sikes, where the road and river meet. On the left bank, the fishing starts three fields above the iron bridge and continues downstream to 1/2 mile above Ramsgill Bridge. Also on the right bank for the further 3/4 mile. Small trout and a few grayling are the fish to try for. Members only. No visitors' tickets.

See also Scar House Reservoir.

Pateley Bridge (OS99:159657)

Virtually all the fishing for 8 miles, on both banks, from Wath downstream to approximately 1/2 mile below the B6451 bridge at Dacre Banks village, is controlled by the Nidderdale Angling Club. Fishing on the left bank starts at the top of the third field below Wath Bridge and extends downstream to Glasshouses Mill, except for a short length at the downstream end of Harefield. The water continues below the Mill down to a point 40 yards above Dacre Bridge, except for short lengths at Crowtrees, the Old Twine Mill, Low Laithe, and Dougill Hall.

On the right bank the fishing continues from the boundary of the field below Gouthwaite Gauge Basin down to the Recreation Ground in Pateley Bridge. Then from the boundary wall at the downstream side of Castlestead to the top of the weir above the sawmill at Dacre and a further three fields below Dacre Bridge. A platform for disabled anglers has been provided on the left bank above the weir at Pateley Bridge.

This is a beautiful stretch of water but in many places it's badly overgrown and difficult to get at. There's good access at a few points, namely Pateley Bridge, Glasshouses, the footbridge near Wilsill, and by the old fire station between Low Laithe and Summerbridge. Float, ledger and fly fishing are permitted on all lengths except for two short 'Fly Only' stretches at Low Green and upstream of Glasshouses Bridge. The trout fishing is from April 1st to September 30th and grayling fishing from June 16th to the end of February. Spinning and minnow fishing are permitted between July 1st and September 30th.

Many local fishermen use float fished maggots to good effect in the pools between the rough water and boulders. Both wet and dry fly fishing give good results. Black Gnats, Greenwells and the local pattern called Treacle Parkin are all good when fished dry or wet. A Treacle Parkin is a Red Tag tying with a yellow tag instead of red.

Early March Browns are good fished wet, as are Partridge and Orange, Waterhen Bloa and Snipe and Purple. When the river's in flood try a lob worm in the eddies. Juniors under 14 must be accompanied by an adult.

Adult day tickets £8.00 and juniors, under 14, £3.00, can be had from the Post Offices in Lofthouse (Tel: 01423 755203), Pateley Bridge (Tel: 01423 711201) and Summerbridge (Tel: 01423 780248), the Royal Oak, Dacre Banks (Tel: 01423 780200) and The Reception at the Riverside Caravan Park, Pateley Bridge (Tel: 01423 711383).

The Bradford No.1 AA holds the rights to fish from two fields on the left bank below Dacre Banks Bridge. Members only.

Below here downstream through Darley to Birstwith, with the exception of a short length at Whitley's Farm, the fishing on both banks is preserved for members of the Harrogate Fly Fishers. Members only. No day tickets.

About a mile and a half along the B6165 road from Summerbridge to Ripley there's a stretch of approximately 600 yards of the river at Whitley's Farm which can be fished for £5.00 a day.

Day tickets. A "fishing" signpost on the right hand side of the road, when driving from Summerbridge, clearly indicates the farm entrance. This underfished water recently gave up two brown trout of nearly 3lb to an angler fishing worm.

From Birstwith downstream to below Hampswaite Bridge, the fishing on both banks is controlled by the local Birstwith Private Angling Club. Members only. No day tickets.

Commencing 1/2 mile below the bridge on the left bank and approximately 100 yards on the right bank downstream to Killinghall, about 2 miles of good fishing belongs to the Knaresborough Anglers Club. Fly fishing and upstream worm only for trout, otherwise single maggot for grayling and coarse fish outside the trout season. Members only.

Ripley. Nidd Bridge (OS104:286597)

In addition to trout and grayling, chub, dace and roach begin to make their presence felt around the Ripley area. A stretch of about 2 miles of the right bank from 300 yards below the A61 road bridge between Killinghall and Ripley downstream to the sewage works is controlled by the Harrogate and Claro Anglers. Members only. No day tickets.

See also Kingsley Carp Water, Prospect Farm Pond and Ripley Castle Lake.

The Knaresborough Piscatorials hold the rights to approximately 1½ miles of the left bank on the Nidd Estate near Nidd village. Members only.

Knaresborough (OS104:348571)

Some of the best day ticket fishing in Nidderdale is to be had around Knaresborough. Barbel over 10lb, chub over 5lb, roach over 2lb and some trout to 3lb have all been landed from the Nidd in this vicinity. There are also large stocks of dace, eels and some pike.

There's even a small stretch of free fishing here. From the High Bridge, the A59 road bridge, upstream on the right bank to one field above Conyngham Hall footbridge, the land is owned by Knaresborough Council and the fishing is free. During the summer months it can be difficult to fish though because of hire boats coming upriver from Knaresborough. The best places to try are where they can't reach, between the weeds and by the islands, where the river teems with small dace, gudgeon, perch and minnows.

Fishing on the right bank, from the Harrogate A59 road bridge downstream for about 1 mile to the Low Bridge, belongs to the Mother Shipton's Dropping Well Estate. Here the Nidd dramatically sweeps round a long bend under Castle Cliffe, drops over a weir and then swings back again. The fishery, on the opposite side of the river to the castle, is flat and tree lined and well constructed roads and paths make access easy from either end of the length. Fifteen fishing pegs, five for disabled anglers, have been provided so there's plenty of room to find the fish, and they are here! Good shoals of chub, dace, gudgeon, perch and roach promise large bags. There are also a few big barbel and some trout, but they tend to be shy. The water is open for fishing from 0930 to 1730 hrs from September 1st to March 14th. No fish to be taken away from the water.

Adult day tickets cost £3.95, senior citizens £3.65, disabled £3.25 and under 18s £2.95, from the entrance gate. For further information telephone the Estate Manager, Bob Johnson (Tel: 01423 864600).

A short stretch of the left bank starting below the Low Bridge is fished by members of the Knaresborough Piscatorials. No day tickets.

Approximately 1 mile of the right bank, from the stile above Birkham Wood downstream to the B6164 Wetherby Road Bridge (Grimbald Bridge), is controlled by the Knaresborough Lido Tent and Touring Caravan Site. The Lido - its name comes from the huge pool formed in the river between two weirs - is very popular with all water users. Swimmers can make the fishing frustrating during the warmer weather but when that happens anglers move above or below the weirs, where the fishing is just as good. It's a fine fishery holding big barbel, chub, and perch and has been stocked with lots of brown trout, some into double figures. These fish can be very greedy and tend to be caught in the early season. Ledgered pork luncheon meat will tempt most of the coarse fish and float fishing the shallower run-off water at the end of the pool is hugely productive. Maggots are the popular bait. The coarse fishing is better in the deeper water above the weir where good bream have been stocked. Below the weirs try a small dead sprat for the pike. Fishing is from March 25th to December 31st. All fish caught must be returned. Keepnets are not permitted. No spinning. No fishing before 0700 hrs.

Season ticket £50.00 for adults and £25.00 for juniors and senior citizens.

Day tickets £5.00 for adults and £3.00 for juniors and senior citizens, from the Lido Caravan Site shop (Tel: 01423 865169). Under 12s fish free when accompanied by an adult.

A short stretch of the left bank above Grimbald bridge belongs to the Knaresborough Piscatorials. Members only.

Nearly 1½ miles of the right bank below the B6164 road bridge downstream to 50 yards above the weir near Goldsborough Bridge, with the exception of a short stretch by the sewage works, at Haugh Farm, is controlled by the York and District Angling Association and can be fished on a day ticket. This is yet another excellent stretch with big barbel being the main quarry. Fish over 8lb are common. The water also contains some good chub, eels, roach and trout. It is open during both the trout and coarse fishing seasons.

Day tickets £3.00 from M.H. & C. Johnson's fishing tackle shop in Knaresborough.

A further 2 miles of good mixed fishing on the right bank

An angler braves the cold spring weather near Hawes in Wensleydale

Fishing a wet fly on the River Wharfe at Barden Bridge near Bolton Abbey

The River Rawthey near Sedbergh. A fine game fishing water with an autumn run of salmon and sea trout

The bridge pool at Topcliffe on the River Swale

downstream from Guy's Crag to near Little Ribston is managed by the local Knaresborough Anglers' Club. Here the river is predominantly a coarse fishery, and an excellent one, but there are still some big trout to be caught.

Day tickets £3.00, £1.50 for accompanied juniors, from M.H. & C. Johnson's fishing tackle shop in Knaresborough, the Ripon Angling Centre and C.J. Fishing Tackle, Harrogate.

Knaresborough Piscatorials hold the rights to approximately 1/2 mile of the left bank near Goldsborough Mill and a prime stretch of nearly 3 miles, also on the left bank, from the new bypass bridge downstream to near Little Goldstone. Members only.

See also Farmire Lake, Farnham Lakes and Knaresborough Lagoons.

Cowthorpe (OS105:426524)

Below the Knaresborough Piscatorial water, nearly 5 miles of fishing, on the right bank, extending from Little Ribston, through Cowthorpe, to one field below Cattal Bridge is owned by the Harrogate Angling Association. Members only.

Traditionally the river in the Cowthorpe area, once able to be fished on a day ticket, was a magnet for coarse anglers searching for specimen barbel and chub. However, anyone wanting to try the water now will have to join either the Harrogate AA or the Bradford No.1. Angling Association who have access to all of the left bank. The fishing starts at the beck, about 2 miles above the weir, and extends downstream for some 5 1/2 miles to 1 mile above Cattal Bridge. This is an excellent venue for anyone who is prepared to join a club to fish it. Renowned for the size and quantity of its barbel and chub, the water also contains large numbers of jack pike which give good sport when float fishing a dead sprat on light tackle in the eddies or the weir pool.

Tockwith (OS105:465525)

The fishing rights on the right bank to a fine stretch of approximately 1 1/2 miles centred on Nethercarr Farm belong to the Knaresborough Piscatorials. Members only.

Continuing downstream from this stretch, the York and District Amalgamation of Anglers has the rights to about 1 mile of the right bank at Skewkirk Hall near Tockwith. The water here is fairly deep and slow with many good eddies and pools of the type favoured by heavy chub. Steep banks make access difficult in places but fishing pegs have been cut down the bankside to improve the situation. Plenty of barbel, chub, dace, roach, perch and pike are all in here for the taking. The best fishing though is for the barbel and chub. Try float fished maggot or casters for the smaller fish, up to about 2lb, or ledgered luncheon meat for the bigger fish. Expect barbel to 8lb and chub to 4lb.

Day tickets £3.00 can be obtained locally from Skip Bridge Garage on the A59 where it crosses the river (Tel: 01423 330365) or the fishing tackle shops in York.

Approximately 3/4 mile of the left bank from Rookery Wood downstream to Mill Lane at Kirk Hammerton is owned by the Wetherby and District AC. Members only.

Continuing downstream for a further 2 1/2 miles on the left bank, from Mill Lane to the railway bridge near Skip Road Bridge on the A59, the fishing is controlled by the Leeds and District ASA. This lovely stretch includes a productive weir pool. The Nidd here winds and twists through meadows, creating the deep eddies which always seem to hold big barbel and chub, and of course the long gravel glides favoured by the smaller fish. Members only.

Further downstream, the Bradford No.1 AA has a good length of mixed fishing on the right bank at Wilstrop Hall, near Skip Bridge, for members only. The water extends from the railway bridge upstream for approximately 2 miles.

Another fine York and District AA water is actually at Skip Bridge. Stretching for 3/4 mile of the right bank between the railway bridge and the old road bridge this short fishery is recognised locally as a fine barbel water. There's very easy access to the water from the good parking in the lay-by on the old bridge.

Day tickets as for the Tockwith length, *see above, also Maran Lakes, Thorpe Underwood Lakes and Thorpe Underwood No.1 Lake.*

Below Skip Bridge, the ubiquitous Leeds and District ASA holds the fishing rights to approximately 1 3/4 miles of the right bank, from the old bridge downstream to the noticeboard on Barnes Farm. It's a good water holding a large stock of barbel, chub, roach and perch and is best fished with maggots on a floating rig or luncheon meat on a ledger. Members only.

Another 1/2 mile stretch of the left bank near Nun Monkton belongs to the big Leeds club.

Day ticket £2.00, juniors £1.00, from the Alice Hawthorne Hotel in Nun Monkton (Tel: 01423 330303). The stretch may be match fished, particularly on bank holidays, so it's best to phone before going.

Below this the Bradford No.1 AA has the rights to about 1 mile of the left bank, known as the Alice Hawthorne water, centred on Milking Lane, Nun Monkton. Members only. No day tickets.

Moor Monkton (OS105:510560)

York and District AA controls about 650 yards of the right bank here for the use of members only.

From about 1/2 mile below the village downstream to its junction with the River Ouse, a distance of about 250 yards of the right bank and a further 1/2 mile of the Ouse, the fishing is controlled by the Leeds and District ASA. It's a length of deep water, slow moving, with a sandy bed ideal for ledgering, particularly in the seemingly bottomless Nun Monkton Pool. Try meat for the barbel and chub. It's also the home of large bream and pike.

Day tickets *see above.* Avoid weekends when the stretch is heavily match fished.

Opposite this water the Bradford No.1 AA holds the right to a productive 1 mile stretch of the left bank either side of Milking Lane in the village. Members only.

See also Carpvale Pool, Hessay Pond, Shipton Lake and The Willows.

NORTH-WESTERN DALES

Dentdale, Garsdale and The Howgills are three great scars in the north-west fells of the Dales National Park down which tumble the rivers Dee, Clough and Rawthey, all major tributaries of the River Lune, one of England's great salmon rivers. As well as being spectacularly beautiful, the three Dales rivers offer individuality and the opportunity to try for one of the autumn salmon as it passes on its way upriver to the breeding grounds.

But above all this is walking country and many of the best walks follow the river's course. Access is therefore relatively easy, but in some places the excessive bankside vegetation can be a problem.

Hundreds of small streams drain the water from Howgills Fells, Baugh Fell, Rise Hill and Whernside into the three rivers causing dramatic changes in their character. In the height of summer the streams can be unfishable because of lack of water until a sudden thunderstorm, clinging to the fells, raises the level to that of a raging torrent. In the late season, September and October, salmon fishermen pray for just such weather to encourage the fish to forge upriver. In winter, flood conditions prevail again making the rivers almost unfishable and the grayling hard to find. If you're staying in Sedbergh you'll discover that each of the three valleys has a different character and each its own devotees.

Further south, Ingleborough, Gaping Gill, Clapham Bents and Bottoms Rig, to name a few, are all names familiar to cavers and walkers who explore the great limestone scar country above Clapham and Ingleton. Anglers of course never venture into this inhospitable area, but it is here that rainwater cascading down the fellsides and falling into subterranean caverns is filtered to produce the crystal clear streams which eventually form the Rivers Greta and Wenning. Both rivers, tributaries of the River Lune and well stocked with brown trout, also have an autumn run of sea trout and salmon. Unfortunately, the salmon are few but the sea trout fishing is excellent, particularly on the Wenning, in September. Much of the fishing is available to the visiting angler.

Pastoral Dentdale and the River Dee

RIVER DEE

Dent (OS98:705870)

Probably the most rural of the three valleys near Sedbergh, Dentdale, which takes its name from its largest hamlet, offers some excellent fishing in the lower reaches for the visiting angler. Alas, most of the fishing on the upper river, above the village, is in private hands but because it's often short of water it is difficult to fish. Occasionally a friendly farmer will give permission to fish; to be certain of wetting a line, though, try the lower reaches where the local angling club manages the water.

The Sedbergh and District Angling Association has fishing rights on both banks for about 2 miles, with a few exceptions, from approximately 1/2 mile below Barth Bridge downstream to near Catholes. See the fishing map in the library shelter, Main Street, Sedbergh. This is great trout and grayling water, best fished with dry or wet fly. The Dee's waters flow quietly through farmland, with long glides between tree-lined banks offering the chance of a good trout. Atlantic salmon do come up the system but the spring run long since disappeared and autumn fish often don't arrive until October. Fishing on all Sedbergh and District AA waters is by fly only until May 1st. Maggots, floats and natural minnow are banned.

Weekly tickets £50.00, and **Day tickets** £10.00, between April and September, can be obtained from Lowis's Country Wear, 45 Main Street, Sedbergh (Tel: 015396 20446). From mid September to October 31st, only **weekly tickets**, costing £100.00, are available.

The massive Prince Albert Angling Society has rights to fishing on the River Dee below Catholes down to its junction with the Rawthey. Members only.

RIVER RAWTHEY
(including RIVER CLOUGH)

Sedbergh (OS97:655920)

The main road from Sedbergh to Wensleydale, climbing the beautiful Garsdale, follows the River Clough to give easy access to the waterside throughout most of the river's length. The Clough is a wild river, hardly worth fishing, above Garsdale hamlet, as it tumbles down the valley from its source near Garsdale Head to its meeting with the Rawthey.

Approximately 1 mile of fishing on both banks of the River Clough, from Danny Bridge downstream, is available on a **Day or weekly ticket** issued from Lowis's Country Wear in Sedbergh, *see above*, on behalf of the local Sedbergh and District AA.

Except for short stretches on both banks at Low Hawgarth and Lowridding, the right bank near Straight Bridge, both banks between New and Millthrop Bridges, the left bank at the Rawthey/Dee junction, the left bank at Holme Farm and both banks below Middleton Bridge to the Lune, virtually all the fishing on 8 miles of the River Rawthey is controlled by the Sedbergh and District AA who issue visitors' tickets from Lowis's Country Wear in Sedbergh. *See above*. A detailed fishing map is exhibited in the library shelter, Main Street, Sedbergh. Similar in character to the Clough, the Rawthey resembles the streamy waters of North Wales and the Lake District. It's a picturesque river, pleasant to fish for anyone who takes the trouble to use traditional wet or dry flies in the water run-offs following the small waterfalls.

A short stretch of about 1/4 mile near Sedbergh belongs to the Prince Albert AS for members only.

Further downstream, close to the Rawthey's junction with the Lune, excellent fishing can be had for a small fee.

Day ticket £2.00, £1.50 for children, from Holme Farm (Tel: 015396 20654). This is a fine stretch of the River Rawthey extending over about 1 mile (except for a small section held by the Sedbergh and District AA) of the left bank, following a long bend across a meadow from the farm.

Holme Farm is an 'Open Farm', a local tourist attraction which offers farm tours, a Roman road and stone age remains, but non of this interrupts the fishing. To find Holme Farm from Sedbergh take the A684 road towards Kendal and on the outskirts of Sedbergh branch left onto the A683 towards Kirkby Lonsdale. In about 3/4 mile, after crossing the Rawthey Bridge, turn sharp left onto a signposted single track road to the farm. After about 2 miles the farm is directly in front of you.

On the right bank, fishing on the last 100 yards of the Rawthey, below the A683 road bridge and about the same distance on the left bank of the River Lune, belongs to the Bowland Game Fishing Association. Members only. This is a great fishery regularly producing good brown and sea trout.

RIVER GRETA
(Including RIVERS DOE and TWISS)

A tributary of one of England's great salmon rivers, the Greta offer some fine late season fishing for migratory fish. It's a flood river which in periods of dry weather can be almost devoid of water. Although the trout only average about four to the pound, they are worth the effort and it is a good river for fly fishing. Most of the traditional wet and dry patterns will take the wild brown trout. Both salmon and sea trout run up the Greta to spawn, but unfortunately not until very late in the season and only then when a good floodwater runs. Spinning is usually the best method to take a fish. Try a Mepps or a quill.

Ingleton (OS98:692730)

Ingleton Angling Association have the rights to some excellent water on the tiny Rivers Doe and Twiss, above the town, and from Greta junction downstream for about 2 miles. Above the town, fishing on the River Doe is from the stepping stones near Beezley Falls and on the left bank from Snow Falls down to Greta Junction. A short stretch at Cravendale, on the left bank above Beezley Falls, is reserved for fly only and season ticket holders only. On the River Twiss, the Association controls both banks from above Keld Head downstream to the Waterfalls Walk entrance. This is rough country - you'll need to be fit and agile to make the most of the fishing on these small rivers. There may be a lot of tourists at busy times because the famous Ingleton Waterfalls Walk Trail follows the River Twiss for much of its course. Fly fishing and season ticket holders only above Thornton Force Waterfall. Sunday fishing is permitted on all this water.

Below the A65 road bridge, Ingleton AA water stretches downstream for about 2 miles to Greta Bank. No Sunday fishing on this water. A length of about 3/4 mile below the sewage field on the left bank is private but the remainder can be fished on a visitors' ticket.

Weekly tickets £35.00, under 16s £12.50.
Day tickets £8.00, for Ingleton AA's waters, from the Hon. Sec., Denbeigh's Newsagent, Main Street, Ingleton (Tel: 015242 41683) and Village Pet Supplies, Station Road, High Bentham (Tel: 015242 62546). Barbless hooks must be used during the brown trout season. No ground bait or maggots allowed. No float fishing before October 1st and no spinning before August 1st.

Burton in Lonsdale (OS97:652723)

Accrington & District Fishing Club controls approximately 2 miles of fishing at Burton in Lonsdale, Wrayton and Cantsfield. Members only.

RIVER WENNING

Very similar in character to the River Greta, the River Wenning, after leaving the limestone country, meanders through fertile meadowland on a westerly route towards its meeting with the River Lune near Hornby. It's a streamy river, small in its upper reaches, with long rocky glides and some deep pools on sharp corners. Salmon do run up the River Wenning but the run has drastically declined over the past decade. There's good fishing here for native brown trout. They're quite small, typically between four and six ounces, but they are hard fighters. Late in the season, there's a good run of sea trout, some as big as 4lb, although they average nearer 2lb. They'll fall to a wet fly fished in the eddies beside the fast water or to the trusty old lob worm.

Clapham (OS98:745695)

Approximately 5 miles of lovely fishing in beautiful surroundings is controlled here by the Ingleborough Estate. The stretch starts at Clapham Beck and extends downstream to Clapham Station railway viaduct. It also includes Austwick Beck, from Waters Farm, and Kettles Beck, from Waters Bridge, down to the meeting of the three becks to form the River Wenning. It's not easy fishing. The water is often very clear and low. It's a traditional fly fishers' water. Use a nymph rod with fine leaders and small flies and fish far off. Be careful not to cast a shadow on the water as the small native brown trout scare easily. Any recognised trout fly will bring results. No wading. No fishing between 2230 hrs and 0600 hrs. No sea trout under 10 inches, and no brown under 8 inches to be killed. The close season for sea trout is September 30th to May 1st, and for brown trout September 30th to March 15th. Tickets are available from the Estate Office in Clapham (Tel: 015242 51302).

Adult season £20.00, week £6.00, no day tickets. Senior citizen £16.00, week £5.00, 14s to 16s £10.00, week £3.00, under 14s, no charge. Reduced rates for village inhabitants.

Below Clapham Bridge, by the railway viaduct, downstream for a short distance on the right bank and extending for about 2 miles of the left bank, the fishing is controlled by the Bowland Game Fishing Association. This stretch also includes part of Keasdon Beck. It's an excellent brown trout fly fishing water with the chance of catching a sea trout late in the year. Members only.

Also on the right bank the Accrington and District FC controls about 1/2 mile of water at Hale Hall Farm. Members only.

Bentham (OS97:650694)

The local Bentham Angling Association controls about 3 miles of fishing on the river. Starting at Waterscale, the association has about

1 mile of water downstream to the railway viaduct. Then, with a few exceptions, both banks downstream from the railway viaduct to High Bentham Bridge and about 1/2 mile on both banks above the road bridge in Low Bentham.

Weekly tickets are £25.00 and £10 for juniors, obtainable from the Hon. Sec., the Post Office, Main Street, High Bentham (Tel: 015242 61650) or the Village Pet Stores, Station Road, High Bentham (Tel: 015242 62546). No day tickets.

The Punch Bowl Hotel owns approximately 3/4 mile of the left bank downstream from the pub below Low Bentham Bridge. This is an excellent stretch of fast water with many good holding pools for sea trout. Try running a worm in the rough water between the boulders, especially when the river is in spate.

Day Tickets £5.00 (Tel: 015242 61344).

There are often escapee rainbow trout, from the Mill Fish Farm, in the river around here. They make for good sport but they can be a nuisance.

The massive Prince Albert AS has fishing on the right bank, opposite the Punch Bowl Inn water, downstream to Ravens Close, where the river meets the road about 1 mile above Wennington. Members only.

Continuing downstream on the right bank and from Clintsfield Viaduct on the left bank down to near Wennington, approximately 1 1/2 miles, the fishing is controlled by the Barnoldswick AC. This is a small syndicate with a fixed membership. No day tickets.

Wennington (OS97:617701)

Wennington Parish Council controls the fishing in the town area. It is free to residents. No tickets for outsiders.

Barnoldswick AC has water upstream from Farrar's Viaduct, below the town. Members only.

River Hindburn

The fishing on this small river is controlled by the Hindburn Trust. It is a syndicate water. No day tickets.

River Roeburn

A very narrow shallow river with little open fishing space to tempt the angler.

RIBBLESDALE

One of the Yorkshire Dales National Park's few salmon waters, the River Ribble flows from the same source as two other great Dales rivers, the Ure and the Wharfe. Whilst they drain the eastern side of Oughtershaw Fell and Widdal Fell carrying the clear water eastwards towards the North Sea, the Ribble flows south and eventually swings west, turning its back on the Dales altogether, as it continues through sedate farmland to the Irish Sea. Like all the Dales rivers, it begins its life as a group of small streams trickling from the wild fell country. High up in the Dales, where intrepid walkers follow the Pennine Way, the waters soon mingle to form Gayle Beck, the infant River Ribble. A further boost comes at Birkwith where water from Cam Beck, only a few miles west of the source of the River Wharfe, joins the diminutive river. By the time it reaches Horton-in-Ribblesdale the river has become fishable, except that is during exceptionally dry summers when it is often reduced to a mere trickle.

At Stainforth the river crashes over spectacular limestone steps, and the steep drop of Stainforth Force, into a deep dark pool below. This is a good place to watch the autumn salmon lurking in the pool conserving energy for the final leap which will take them up the three level waterfall to spawning grounds in the shallow gravely streams of the fells. Sadly, in recent years, the Ribble, like other English salmon rivers, has seen a consistent decline in the numbers of fish returning to spawn from the Atlantic feeding grounds. It is now essentially an autumn river with most of the fish arriving in October. The spring salmon run has all but ceased.

Settle is a good centre for visiting fishermen who fancy their chances of tempting one of the autumn fish. It's also a good place for trout fishing, with many miles of the river open for fishing on a day ticket.

Below Settle, where the river leaves the National Park, it slows down and assumes a winding course through the flat, broad farmland of Ribblesdale. Between here and Long Preston, in the area known as "The Deeps", salmon take refuge and rest on their long journey. Many of them are taken from this area by anglers using shrimp or worms as bait.

At Hellifield the river parts company with the Yorkshire Dales National Park, whose boundary swings east as the river continues south and west. Around Nappa it finally leaves Yorkshire behind and heads across Lancashire to its meeting with the Irish Sea.

Whilst salmon fishing has declined on the Ribble, the trout fishing has improved thanks to intelligent stocking policies carried out by a number of local angling clubs. The average size of stocked brown trout tends to be 12 inches, which is bigger than most of the fish stocked in other Dales rivers. From "The Deeps" downstream there are some coarse fish, mainly chub, to be had but, in the area covered by this guide, the Ribble should not be considered a coarse fishing river. Lots of good grayling and trout are the quarry with the odd salmon making life interesting.

Horton in Ribblesdale (OS98:805725)

Virtually all of the fishing on both banks of the river and its tributaries, from its source downstream to 200 yards below Helwith Bridge, is controlled by the Manchester Anglers' Association for members only. No day tickets. Fly fishing only for trout. After July 15th, spinning for salmon is allowed on the stretch below Horton-in-Ribblesdale Road Bridge.

See also Helwith Bridge Trout Fishery.

A 400 yard stretch of the left bank downstream from the railway bridge and about 150 yards at Cragg Hill belongs to the Lancashire Fly Fishing Association. Members only.

Approximately 3/4 mile of high quality game fishing on both banks above Stainforth Packhorse Bridge is controlled by the Prince Albert Angling Society. Members only. No day tickets.

Fishing from the right bank downstream for approximately 3/4 mile from Stainforth Packhorse Bridge, including Stainforth Force, is available to residents at the Knight Stainforth Hall Caravan Park, Camping and Caravan site.

Tickets are £3.00 during the trout season (Tel: 01729 8222000).

The left bank downstream to the Settle AA water belongs to Norbeck Anglers. Members only.

Summer low water at Staincliffe Falls on the River Ribble near Settle

Settle (OS98:815635)

Excellent trout and salmon fishing can be had here on approximately 7½ miles of water controlled by the Settle Anglers' Association. With a few exceptions, their water extends on the right bank from about ¼ mile below Stainforth Force downstream to 2½ miles below the town to where Rathmell Beck joins the Ribble. And on the left bank, a short stretch at the paper mill and then from Langcliffe Footbridge down through the town to approximately 1 mile below the A65 road bridge. No fishing on a short stretch near Kings Mill.

Weekly tickets £45.00 and **day tickets** £15.00, during licensing hours only, from the Royal Oak Hotel, Market Place, Settle (Tel: 01729 822561). Anglers fishing on a visitors' ticket may use fly only. Members can fish with fly, minnow or worm. There is a daily limit of 3 fish.

Long Preston (OS103:833579)

The water below Settle is highly prized by anglers searching for the salmon that take a rest in the deep water. The fish are not big but they are reasonably plentiful in the late autumn. Most anglers use worm, although some fish are taken on a sunken fly. A number of fishing clubs control the fishing in this area known as "The Deeps".

From below the Settle AA water, on the left bank, the Padiham and District Angling Society controls about 3/4 mile of excellent water. Members only. No day tickets.

Continuing from this downstream past Cow Bridge to Arnford Wood and on the right bank from Wigglesworth Beck down to the limit board about 1/2 mile below the bridge, the fishing belongs to the Bowland Game Fishing Association. Members only. No day tickets.

Below the Settle AA water on the right bank downstream to Wigglesworth Beck, the fishing is controlled by the Staincliffe Angling Club. Members only.

Barrowford Anglers also have a short stretch of fishing here. Again for members only.

Continuing from the Bowland Game FA water below Cow Bridge at Long Preston, approximately 2 miles of excellent fishing for salmon, trout and some chub can be had on a day ticket. The stretch on the left bank downstream to about 1/2 mile above Halton Bridge, at Hellifield, belongs to the Settle Anglers' Association.

Day ticket information *see Settle entry* above.

Fishing on the right bank, with a few exceptions, for approximately the same distance is controlled by the Long Preston Anglers. No day tickets. There's a 3 fish limit and all trout under 10 inches must be returned to the water. Fishing with maggots is prohibited. This is a productive trout fishing water. Following its exit from The "Deeps", the river here is made up of fast glides and deeper pools on the outside of long bends. Fly fishing is best. The fish rise freely to traditional dry patterns, Greenwells, Iron Blue and Black Gnat.

Nappa (OS103:855533)

Below Hellifield most of the fishing is in private hands until the river reaches Guisburn. The Bowland Game Fishing Association controls the fishing on approximately 1 3/4 miles of both banks, except a short stretch of the right bank near the bridge, of the river above Paythorne Bridge. Members only.

The Ribble now turns westwards and leaves the area covered by this guide.

SWALEDALE

Whether you drive sedately down the valley floor from Kirkby Stephen, overlooked by the towering fells, or inch down the precarious road from Hawes over Buttertubs, fighting the gradient all the way, your first impression of upper Swaledale will overwhelm you. However, once your feet are firmly fixed on the valley floor it will come as a surprise to see flat narrow meadows brilliant with spring flowers and dissected by a river which is little more than a stream. In the normal course of things, in its upper reaches, the Swale carries little water. Many of the hundreds of becks, channelling rainwater from the slopes of Angram and Muker Commons into the dale below, are raging torrents for a small part of their life but for the rest of the time they're almost dry. When in flood though they drain the water from vast expanses of high fell territory into a narrow catchment area and consequently the Swale is a river prone to rapid flooding.

Between Muker and Reeth its waters cascade and fall over numerous limestone shelves as it bustles its way eastwards. All the fishing along this beautiful 8 mile stretch is in private hands but the trout which manage to survive in the river's crashing waters are very small anyway. At Reeth the lovely Arkle Beck joins the river and their combined waters begin to slow down as the valley broadens and flattens in anticipation of its approach to Richmondshire.

Past the ancient and modern garrison towns of Richmond and Catterick, the river begins to form its instantly recognisable character. Snaking between high flood banks, its waters become sluggish and deep forming large eddies where the big barbel and chub lurk.

The Swale's great strength lies in its coarse fishing. In the middle and lower reaches, downstream of Catterick, when its waters slow and the river winds snakelike through fertile meadows, huge coarse fish are there for the taking. Indeed it's so popular that many anglers travel the length of the country to ledger luncheon meat at Topcliffe or Cundall, just two of the places where record fish are regularly landed. And there's always talk of the bigger one that broke away and lies sulking in one of the deep pools between sandy banks. Happily nearly all the coarse fishing is available on a day ticket basis.

Muker to Reeth

The river here offers excellent small stream trout fishing but only when there's enough water. Most of the time the river bed is virtually dry. All the fishing is strictly private. If you're staying in upper Swaledale it's best to travel over Buttertubs Pass into upper Wensleydale for some really great trout fishing.

Further downriver, about 1 mile of excellent fly fishing at Marrick Park, by the old priory, is available on a visitors' ticket

Day ticket, £6.00, from Gilsan Sports in Leyburn or Richmond.

This is a fine piece of dry fly water where a Greenwells, Claret Sinner or Olive will take fish. But it is a purist's water, demanding patience and persistence. It's not for the angler who is intent on catching a lot of trout in a short time. Two anglers only per day.

Richmond (OS92:175010)

Richmond and District Angling Society controls, with a few exceptions, nearly 14 miles of prime fishing starting on the left bank 500 yards above Marske Bridge and the right bank 1/2 mile below, downstream to Brompton on Swale. Short stretches on the left bank at Whitcliffe Wood, above Richmond upper bridge, Eastby and Broken Brae and on the right bank near Colburn Beck, are private. Fishing is also allowed on a short stretch of the left bank of Skeeby Beck.

Near Marske the Swale twists and turns through a steep cliff sided valley before finally quietening down into a series of deep long glides with shingle shallows. This is a terrific mixed fishery with trout and coarse fish in abundance. Although it's not possible to scribe a definitive line across the river, it is in the area of Richmond Falls, beneath the Castle walls, where the Swale changes from being a predominantly trout water to a mixed fishery. Above the falls the fishing is mainly for trout which average three to a pound whilst below, shoals of chub and dace abound. The water is also stocked annually with brown trout over 1/2lb. Most anglers use bait - maggots or worms are favourites - but fly fishing often produces good results. Spinning is not permitted. From March 25th to September 30th two trout 10 inches or over may be taken during one session. From June 16th to September 30th two grayling 11 inches or over may also be taken. The water is open all year for coarse fishing.

Weekly tickets £15.00, **day tickets** £5.00, junior and senior citizens half price. Tickets can be obtained in Richmond from Gilsan Sports, the Richmond Angling Centre and the Swaleview Caravan Park. Also from the Darlington Angling Centre.

See also Crab Tree Angling Lake, Dalton Fields Lake, and Langlands Lake.

Catterick (OS99:240980)

On the left bank, from the end of the Richmond and District AS water at Brompton on Swale, stretching for about 1/2 mile, good fishing is available on a day ticket from Broken Brae Coarse Fishery Lake alongside the river.

Day tickets £5.00, are available at the lakeside. The water is predominantly a coarse fishery with lots of chub and dace to be caught from the streamy water.

See also Broken Brae Coarse Fishery and Lakeside Fisheries.

Good coarse fishing on about 500 yards of the left bank, downstream from the railway bridge, on Skeeby Beck belong to the Richmond and District AS. The Society also owns about 150 yards of the left bank of the Swale above Catterick Road Bridge.

Day tickets as for Richmond entry. *See above.*

Downstream of Catterick village the Swale turns south and begins its characteristic meander through flat meadows. This is where the good coarse fishing begins. There are several stretches near here available to the visiting angler. Commencing below the Richmond and District AS water, about 1/3 mile of good fishing on the right bank downstream of Catterick Road Bridge belongs to the Bridge House Hotel (Tel: 01748 818331).

Day tickets £3.00, during opening hours only.

Below the Bridge House water on the right bank, the Leeds and District ASA holds the rights to around 1 1/2 miles of top class water and three lakes.

Day tickets £2.50 from H.J. Winkinson's cafe and newsagents opposite Swale Lane, on the A6136 in Catterick village.

This stretch, including the Angel Hotel water, offers something for everyone. The trout and grayling are still here in large numbers so it is sometimes worth trying a fly. Good shoals of chub, dace and roach make the float fishing exciting and there's the chance of a big barbel. Below here the fishing is private, belonging to the RAF.

See also Catterick Lakes, Ellerton Park Lake and Green Lane Pond.

The fishing on the right bank below the RAF water, opposite Kiplin Hall, for 1 mile downstream to Langton Bridge, plus a very short stretch of the left bank, is managed by the Richmond and District AC.

For ticket details see above entry for Richmond.

Great Langton (OS99:295965)

Good fishing on approximately 3½ miles of both banks below Langton Bridge is in the hands of the Kirkby Fleetham Angling Club. Strictly private. Fly fishing members only. Membership is restricted to local residents.

See also Langton Ponds and Kiplin Hall Trout Lake.

Below here the river begins a twisting course between steep flood banks, a characteristic which continues until it reaches the Ure. The water slows right down creating deep pools and the long shingle glides beloved of big barbel and chub.

Bedale Beck

In its upper reaches, this tiny water offers little scope for wetting a line, but further down access can be had using a cheap day ticket.

A stretch of about 1 mile on both banks, centred on the villages of Patrick Brompton and Great Crakehall, belongs to the Crakehall Angling Club. Village residents only. No outside members. No day tickets.

Further downstream, for several miles before it joins the River Swale at Leeming, the beck does provide some limited fishing for trout and small coarse fish, mainly chub, dace and roach. But the fishing is not as good as that to be had on the river.

See also Shield Fly Fishing Lake and Thorpe Perrow Lake.

Leeming (OS99:295895)

The fishing on both banks of Bedale Beck, from the A1 road

bridge down to Leeming Bar sewage works and then the right bank down to its junction with the Swale, excepting two fields upstream of Leeming Bridge, is controlled by the Black Ox Angling Club.

No Day tickets

Season ticket costs just £5.00.

See Angling Clubs section.

See also Roleith Fishery, Jenkins Lake and Olde Mill Lake.

Morton-on-Swale (OS99:324917)

About 5 miles of prime water on the left bank from Morton bridge downstream to near Ash Tree Farm can be fished on a day ticket.

Day ticket from the Northallerton and District Angling Club. These cost £3.00 and are obtainable locally from the Morton Auto Services, Tel: 01609 775342, next door to the Swaledale Arms in the village. Also from the Northallerton Angling Centre Tel: 01609 770140.

The Leeds and District Amalgamated Society of Anglers holds the rights to approximately one mile of excellent mixed fishing on the right bank from Cross Lane Farm downstream to where Bedale Beck joins the Ure. It's a good stretch for trotting a worm or luncheon meat in the pools beside the gragel glides to pick-up a barbel or chub. Members only.

Further downstream, also on the right bank, the Bradford No.1. Angling Association has stretches at Gatenby, from the beck downstream for about 4 miles to near Low Swainby Farm. And also on the left bank from the beck near Far Fairholme down through Maunby to Stubthorpe House. Members only. Open all year. This is a fine fishery. Expect heavy bags of barbel, chub, dace, eels and the odd bream. Swim fed maggots or ledgered luncheon meat generally take fish. A further 1$^{1}/_{2}$ miles of the right bank at Pickhill, centred on Scarborough House Farm, is reserved for members only.

On the right bank, from below the Bradford No.1 AA water at Low Swainby Farm downstream for 1$^{1}/_{2}$ miles the fishing is in the hands of the Idle and Thackley AA for members only.

On the left bank at Maunby, the Middlesbrough Angling Club controls about 1$^{1}/_{2}$ miles of excellent water from near Rush Farm downstream to the railway bridge.

The Leeds and District ASA also have the rights to approximately 500 yards of fishing on the left bank by the disused airfield upstream of Skipton-on-Swale. Members only.

Continuing downstream from this stretch, the Knaresborough Piscatorials have about 1 mile of fishing. Members only.

Skipton-on-Swale (OS99:365798)

In this area the Swale is arguably the best coarse fishery in the north of England. The fish are very big. Barbel average 5lb, with many over 10lb, chub of 3 to 6lb are common, the bream can reach 4lb and roach top 2lb, so as you can imagine it's a great water. Unfortunately a lot of the fishing stretches on the Swale can be heavily match fished at weekends leaving little room for pleasure anglers. It's always best to check before buying a ticket.

The Thirsk Angling Club holds the rights to some fine fishing here on the left bank from the road bridge downstream for about 1/2 mile and the right bank from the old railway bridge down to Baldersby St James.

Day tickets cost £3.00, from the Thirsk Anglers' Centre.

See also Woodland Lakes.

Fishing from the right bank above and below the road bridge, downstream to the old railway cutting, belongs to the Brighouse Angling Association. Members only.

Bradford No.1. AA has a short productive stretch of the left bank near the piggeries at Catton. Members only.

Below here on the right bank, the Baldersby Park Estate offers mixed fishing on approximately 2/3 mile of water through the park. Leeds and District ASA control the fishing.

Day tickets £2.00 or £1.00 for juniors, from the Black Bull Caravan Park, near Topcliffe Bridge, *see below*, and the fishing tackle shops in Leeds.

Topcliffe (OS99:400760)

Topcliffe is without doubt the Mecca for coarse fishermen, many of whom make the weekly pilgrimage to this quiet village in search of specimen coarse fish. And they find them in the river's deep quiet corners, long glides and eddies which all provide a perfect breeding ground for strong fighting fish. Possessing sandy banks and a gravel bed, the river here lends itself to ledgering. Pork luncheon meat is still an outstanding bait for big fish as are lob-worms, and the chub continue to like cheese. Thanks to a recent stocking policy shoals of big bream also lurk in the deep waters around Topcliffe. Roach, the traditional king of coarse fish, also grows big here.

On the left bank, above the famous weir, a 750 yard length belonging to Salmon Hall Farm, named in the days when salmon were the main quarry here, is available for fishing.

Day ticket, £1.00, from the farmhouse (Tel: 01845 577273). No Sunday fishing. The water is match fished on some days.

There's more Leeds and District ASA water here. The club holds the rights to two excellent lengths straddling the weir. About 1/2 mile of the right bank, continuing from their Baldersby Park stretch, is for members only, and about 3/4 mile of the left, known as "Lister's", can be fished on a visitors' ticket.

Day tickets £2.00 or £1.00 for juniors, from the Black Bull Caravan Park near Topcliffe Bridge (Tel: 01845 577219), Topcliffe Post Office (Tel: 01845 577517) and fishing tackle shops in Leeds/Bradford area. Open all year. The water is often match fished on the left bank above the weir.

Continuing from the Leeds and District ASA water on the right bank downstream for about 1/2 mile to the road bridge, the fishing belongs to the Black Bull Inn Caravan Site. Many regulars consider this short stretch to be the best in Topcliffe. Specimen barbel and chub are regularly landed from this stretch. The water is pegged (33 pegs) but it is mostly used by pleasure anglers.

Day tickets £4.00 from the Black Bull Caravan Park Office adjacent to the bridge, or alternatively tickets can be bought from the bailiff on the bank. No night fishing.

Another pub in the town, the Angel Inn, owns the fishing rights on about 1/3 mile of the left bank downstream from below the Black Bull Caravan Site to the new bypass road bridge. Open all year.

Day tickets £4.00 from the Angel Inn (Tel: 01845 577237). Fishing 0730 hrs to dusk only. No night fishing.

Further down, the Idle and Thackley AA control the fishing on two fields for members only.

Below the road bridge on the right bank, where the river runs alongside the road, the fishing is controlled by Asenby Parish

Council for local residents only. No visitors' tickets.

Continuing below this stretch for about 1/2 mile downstream to the new A168(T) bypass bridge, some great fishing belongs to the Bradford No.1 AA. Members only.

See also The Oaks Fisheries.

Cod Beck

A small lazy stream flowing sedately from its source near the border of the North Yorkshire Moors National Park through Thirsk to join the River Swale at Topcliffe, Cod Beck provides some excellent fishing. In its upper reaches the water is shallow and clear making the fishing difficult for indigenous small brown trout and grayling. However, it is worth the effort because the fish are wild and acrobatic when hooked. The Thirsk Angling Club has the fishing rights on a productive mile of the left bank at Spa House near the town. Fly fishing only.

Day tickets £4.00 from the Thirsk Anglers' Centre. Another mile near here is reserved for members only.

Further downstream, near Topcliffe, the tiny beck begins to resemble a mini River Swale but although it is a mixed fishery the fish are not as large as those in the main river.

Good fishing can be had on a stretch of about 4 miles of the right bank near the town, at Richmond Farm. Fishing rights belong to the Thirsk AC.

Day tickets are £3.00, from the Thirsk Anglers' Centre.

Try trotting a worm in the deep water in one of the eddies beneath the sandy banks to tempt a chub or roach. The Club also has approximately 3 miles of the right bank at Gristhwaite Farm for members only.

Further downstream the Bradford City AA has fishing rights on about 3 3/4 miles of both banks down to the beck's junction with the Swale. Members only. Fishing by fly, worm, artificial lure and minnow only allowed during the coarse fish close season. No keepnets.

Back on the Swale, below Topcliffe the fishing is controlled by local farmers who mostly issue tickets to visiting anglers.

Cundall (OS99:425725)

Water extending downstream on the left bank for about 2 miles and some 3 3/4 miles of Cod Beck at Topcliffe Manor Farm is controlled by the Bradford City AA for members only.

Below the A168 road bridge at Topcliffe on the right bank downstream for about 1/2 mile, some prime fishing belongs to the owners of Sheephills Farm (Tel: 01845 577377).

Day tickets cost £3.00 from the farm. Sheephills Farm entrance is signposted left off the Topcliffe to Cundall road. Cars are permitted on the riverbank. No fishing before 0800 hrs.

Further downstream, the Cundall Lodge Farm offers about 1 mile of fishing on the right bank and Cundall Hall Farm has an adjoining length of 1 mile.

Day tickets cost £3.00 for adults and £1.50 for under 14s from the Cundall Lodge Farm (Tel: 01423 360203). Cars can be taken to the water's edge.

Day Tickets, £3.00, can be had from Cundall Hall Farm (Tel: 01423 360678).

Park in the stackyard next to the river. Both these lengths are outstanding and fish well throughout the season, but they are very popular and get busy at weekends.

Approximately 800 yards of fishing on the left bank above and below the weir at Crakehill, and about 1 mile of small stream fishing on Sessay Beck, is controlled by the Thirsk AC for members only.

Helperby (OS99:438701)

Fishing on the left bank commencing at Fawdington Beck opposite Cundall Hall Farm and extending downstream for approximately 1 1/2 miles to a point 1/2 mile above Thornton Bridge is available on a

Day ticket £2.50, from Plowman-Render Grocers, Main Street, Helperby (Tel: 01423 360685).

There's good access to the river here which runs alongside the road. Open during the coarse fishing season.

Outside Brafferton, by Thornton Bridge on the Helperby to Cundall road, the Brafferton Manor has fishing rights on the left bank for about 1/4 mile upstream and 3/4 mile downstream of the bridge. This is a great water with many swims suited to big barbel and chub.

Day tickets £2.50, can be obtained at the Oak Tree pub in Helperby (Tel: 01423 360268).

See also Brafferton Carp Lake.

Again on the left bank, a stretch of about 1/4 mile from the footbridge in Helperby downstream can be fished on a

Day ticket £2.50, from Plowman-Render. *See above.*

About 2 miles of the right bank downstream from Helperby swing bridge is controlled by the Leeds and District ASA for members only.

Further down the river, on the left bank, a 3/4 mile stretch of water at Myton Grange Farm is open for fishing on a visitors' ticket.

Day ticket £3.00, from the farm.

Entry to the water is via the farmyard where cars can be parked. It's a lovely stretch of typical Swale water. Long twists and turns beneath sandy banks create eddies in which lurk some of the biggest chub and barbel in the river. Try the ever popular luncheon meat or a piece of boiled potato, the forerunner of the modern boilie, on a ledger rig.

Leeds and District ASA members fish about 1/2 mile on both banks of the river, starting about 50 yards above the footbridge at Myton village, down the first fence below. Members only.

Finally, on the left bank below the village down to the river's junction with the Ure and extending a further 1 1/4 miles of that river, the fishing belongs to the Bradford No.1. AA. Members only.

WENSLEYDALE

More than any of the others, Wensleydale is Yorkshire's internationally famous Dale. The generic name of the world renowned cheese has seen to that by having its name at the front of every supermarket shelf from Wensleydale to Wollongong in Australia. Then there's that famous Masham brewery! And also Alf White, better known as the veterinary James Herriot, who did his bit by making the lower Dale prominent in his magical writings about Yorkshire's characters and their animals. Whilst it's true that most visitors are drawn to Wensleydale to view the many tourist attractions, Hardraw Force, Aysgarth Falls and of course Herriot country, many others come for the fishing which is some of the best in the county.

Beginning life as a multitude of small streams bubbling from the limestone strata of Lunds Fell, the sparkling waters flow south and then east through classic upper fell country to near Appersett where Cotter, Widdale and Hardraw becks give the fledgling river substance. From here it meanders, turns, falters, tumbles and falls eastwards along the fertile valley floor, its volume steadily swelling with further water from the River Bain, Apedale and Bishopdale becks and the River Cover, before turning south near Masham.

Wensleydale is the centre of a family of Dales each with its own character and each with its own speciality fishing possibilities. Centred around Hawes, for instance, the local angling club issues visitors' tickets for around 14 miles of fishing on the River Ure plus some really challenging fishing in the smaller dales on Cotterdale Beck, Duerley Beck, Hardraw Beck and Widdale Beck. Further down at Bainbridge another local club issues tickets for about 10 miles of fishing on the main river, the River Bain, and the wonderful Raydale streams above Lake Semerwater. Indeed down to Aysgarth the trout and grayling fishing is unsurpassed and most of it is available to a visiting angler.

In its upper reaches the River Ure, not as turbulent as some of its neighbours, meanders along the flat narrow valley. But it does have its moments, suddenly crashing over flat limestone shelves into deep pools, many of which hold the possibility of big trout. At Aysgarth its waters fall over craggy steps and through a steep gorge

Manchester angler Chris Pitts braves the spring winds at Hawes and takes a fine 2lb brown trout for his trouble

before slowing down to enter the quickly broadening dale. Trout and Grayling predominate but chub and barbel begin to make their presence felt as the river further slows its progress around Wensley, the village that gives the Dale its name. Access to fishing is not easy between here and Ripon as most of the water is in the hands of syndicates, but at Ripon, a town situated on three rivers, the Ure, the Laver and the Skell, the fishing is excellent and almost completely open to visitors. By now the river is a good mixed fishery, its broad long reaches holding barbel, chub, dace and some pike, and its gravely glides offer fine fly fishing opportunities for trout and grayling. It's worth trying a big bushy dry fly in these glides for the chub. Hook one and they're real rod benders!

Below Ripon downstream through Boroughbridge to its junction with the River Swale, the Ure is essentially a coarse fishing river and nearly all of its banks are accessible for fishing by visiting anglers. There are specimen roach and perch in addition to the record barbel, bream, chub and pike to be caught in any of the fisheries listed along this stretch. It's also possible to hook the odd salmon, but don't count on it.

As a fishing venue Wensleydale can't be beaten. The higher reaches provide some of the finest trout fly and worm fishing in the whole country, its lower reaches the best of coarse fishing, and if the fish are not biting just sit and admire the spectacular scenery to make the outing worthwhile.

Hawes (OS98:872899)

There are no better centres for a visiting trout fisherman than here or further downriver at Bainbridge.

Virtually all the fishing around Hawes is in the hands of the local Hawes and High Abbotside Angling Association. They have rights to around 16 miles of the upper River Ure, Cotterdale Beck, Duerley Beck, Hardraw Beck (except above Hardraw road bridge), Snaizeholme Beck and Widdale Beck. That's virtually everything from the Ure source, near Lunds, downstream to Borwins Farm, just off the A684, about 2 miles below the town.

Weekly tickets £24.00 and **day tickets** £8.00 (50% concession for over 65s and 12 to 16s) can be bought in Hawes from Lowis's Country Wear, Riverside House, Town Foot (Tel: 01969 667443), Brown Moor Caravan Park (Tel: 01969 667338), The Gift Shop, Main Street, and The Board Hotel, Market Place (Tel: 01969 667223). Also, from September 30th, **grayling only tickets** can be had from the same sources, season £10.00 and for the week £5.00 (50% concessions apply).

Most of the water is easily accessible from a road, but please be careful how you gain access. Use styles only. Don't park across gates or paths. And remember, this is sheep country, no dogs allowed. A good road from Appersett skirts Widdale Beck. Although it's a bit of a hike to Snaizeholme Beck, it's worth it because of the acrobatic small trout it holds. From the centre of Hawes take the road climbing over Oughtershaw Side into Langstrothdale for easy access to the good fishing in Duerley Beck in Sleddale. For the more energetic fisherman a small steep road into Cotterdale provides access to even more challenging fishing on Cotter Beck. Fishing in the becks can be strenuous but extremely rewarding. They hold truly wild brown trout that are easily 'spooked' by a badly placed fly or footfall. Small dry or wet flies fished in the rough water often bring success. Try fishing wet with a Snipe and Purple, Waterhen Bloa or Partridge and Orange, or a dry Greenwells. A Sturdy's Fancy usually does the trick with the grayling. When there's some floodwater about, a worm fished in the deeper pools close to the bank should bring quick results.

Trout in the main river, which is stocked twice a year, are generally bigger than those on the becks, typically 3/4lb, but they're no less energetic. The Ure around here winds lazily through meadowland, but be careful when wading because there are sudden changes in depth as the water flows over submerged gullies with little surface indication. The pool at 'Halfway', between Appersett and Hawes, is very dangerous. It's an inviting pool, but it's deep, up to 10 feet in places, and it shelves suddenly, so be careful.

Fishing is permitted seven days a week. No groundbaiting. Maggot fishing only after June 15th.

See also Blackburn Farm Trout Fishery.

Bainbridge (OS98:934902)

This is another excellent centre for game fishing. The Wensleydale Angling Association has the right to fish on about 6 miles of the main river continuing from the Hawes water at Borwins Farm downstream, through the town, to Worton Bottom. Their rights also extend to 2 miles of the River Bain which drains Lake Semerwater and joins the Ure at Yorebridge, and a further 2 miles above the Lake in delightful Raydale.

Tickets, weekly £12.00, **daily** £6.00, are available in the town from the Post Office (Tel: 01969 650221), The Village Shop, and the Rose and Crown (Tel: 01969 650225). Also from the Kings Arms in Askrigg (Tel: 01969 650258), and the Victoria Arms at Worton. Outside the trout season, **Grayling only tickets** are also available, **season** £7.50 and **day** £3.00.

Like the river at Hawes, the water here holds bigger trout, up to about 1 1/2lb, which rise freely to dry fly. Many of the fish are stocked but they soon become acclimatised and don't surrender to the first fly they see. No maggots or spinning permitted.

RIVER BAIN

Because it falls some 60 feet from the outflow of Semerwater to its meeting with the Ure, the River Bain is a difficult water to fish. It's popular with worm fishermen though and can be rewarding; the wild brown trout are energetic when hooked. Much of the fishing, except for that listed below, belongs to the Wensleydale AA.

For **ticket** *information see above.*

Fishing on about 1/2 mile of the left bank and 1 mile of the right bank downstream of the road bridge over the outflow from Semerwater is in the hands of the Richmond and District Angling Society.

For **tickets,** *see entry under Richmond.*

Compared with the Bain, Raydale Beck and the delightful streams flowing into Semerwater are very sedate. In summer they are gin clear and success demands very careful tactics. Don't be afraid to kneel and cast to the tiny 'dimple' rises under the trees. Try worming when the water is coloured following heavy rain. Day tickets are issued by the Wensleydale AA, *see above.*

See also Semerwater Lake.

Further down the Ure, at Worton, the Bradford City Angling Association controls approximately 3/4 mile of fishing on both banks downstream from the bridge to the weir and approximately 440 yards of the right bank. Fly fishing only is allowed during the trout season plus worming during the coarse season. Members only.

Aysgarth (OS98:885011)

More Bradford City AA here. The club has about 4 miles, mostly both banks, of really good trout and grayling fishing, on the left bank from approximately 500 yards above the stepping stones downstream to the noticeboard near the iron bridge, and on the right bank from about 500 yards above the stepping stones downstream to approximately 900 yards above the iron bridge. Members only. No spinning during the trout fishing close season.

Fishing tickets can be obtained for a stretch of about 1 mile owned by the Richmond and District Angling Club. The fishery is on the right bank from the footbridge, outside the town on the A684 Bainbridge road, upstream for approximately 1 mile. This is a good stretch of trout and grayling fishing. Any method except spinning is permitted. The fishery is easily accessible from the road. There's a daily limit of three fish over 10 inches.

Day tickets £5.00 from fishing tackle shops in Richmond.

A short stretch of nearly 1/4 mile of the right bank near Wensleydale's major attraction, the Aysgarth Falls, belongs to the Palmer Flatts Hotel (Tel: 01969 663228).

Day tickets £2.50 from the hotel.

This is an interesting fishery. Some parts, particularly along the Falls, are difficult to get access to, but it is worth the effort. A careful angler using fly or upstream worm can have a great day catching trout up to 1 1/2lb here, but do be wary of the limestone outcrops. They can be very slippery when wet and it's a long way to the bottom of the Falls! **Not recommended for young children.**

Redmire (OS98:046913)

Several miles of excellent fishing on both banks, from just below Aysgarth, downstream are owned by the Bolton Estate. There are no visitors' tickets.

Season tickets costing £120.00 can be had from the Bolton Estate Office, Wensley, Leyburn (Tel: 01969 622303).

See also Thornton Steward Reservoir.

RIVER COVER

This attractive little river starts its life near upper Nidderdale on the northern slopes of Little Whernside. Numerous tiny streams cascade down Cow Side Moor's steep gradient to slowly mingle with others from North Moor to create this diminutive river. It then continues for 12 miles, from Woodale, through delightful Coverdale to join the River Ure near Ulshaw, Middleham. Coverdale is still an important cross-Dales route with the precipitous road from Kettlewell in central Wharfedale climbing Whernside before plunging into the fertile grazing land of Wensleydale. In its upper reaches, where few fish survive, the river is minute, falling into the valley as a series of waterfalls and rocky pools. Below Gammersgill the Dale starts its transition from rough moor to pastoral scenery and the river settles peacefully into a series of slow turns and deep pools, some of which hold trout weighing about a pound.

Much of the fishing is in private hands, even in the upper reaches where in summer the water is so low that the fishing can be virtually impossible. Because of the lack of water there's little point in trying to fish the river above West Scrafton anyway, although local farmers do sometimes give permission to a polite request for access.

Further down, between West Scrafton and Coverham Abbey, the fishing is controlled by a syndicate who don't issue visitors' tickets. However below the Abbey for approximately 1½ miles on both banks downstream to Cover Bridge, on the A6108, good trout and grayling fishing can be had on a day ticket. *See below.*

Ulshaw (OS99:145872)

Tickets for this water, belonging to the East Witton Estate, cost £2.00, for fly fishing only, and are issued from the Cover Bridge Inn, East Witton (Tel: 01969 622115), alongside the river.

This is a small water, very shallow in places with the odd deep pool, especially on the sharp bends. When the water is low it is classic dry fly stalking water. Fish with fine leaders and far off to a 'spotted' rising fish. The trout tend to be small but they are hard fighters and worthy of the chase. When the river is carrying floodwater try a wet fly under the trees.

Below Cover Bridge the fishing is private, belonging to the Danley and Jervaulx Fly Fishers. No day tickets.

Middleham (OS99:127878)

Back on the River Ure, some of the best fishing for barbel, chub, grayling and trout on the middle reaches can be had in the Middleham 'Deeps', about 1 mile upstream from Middleham Bridge. The chub particularly are worth trying for. Try a dry fly, a big one, and you'll need a strong leader because the fish can reach 4lb and the takes will be weighty. There are also local rumours of autumn salmon lying in the deeps but they're substantiated only by the occasional fish taken over many years of fishing.

Fishing rights on some fine stretches of the river here belong to the Leeds and District ASA. Members may fish both banks, starting 1 mile above the iron bridge down to the beck on the left bank about 100 yards above the bridge and to the limit board about 200 yards upstream on the right bank. The day ticket water, on the left bank, commences one field above the bridge and runs downstream to the stone wall a mile below.

Day tickets £2.00 or £1.00 for juniors, from the White Swan Inn, Middleham (Tel: 01969 622093) during licensing hours only, and from the fishing tackle shops in Leeds. Ticket holders must be accompanied by a member.

This mixed fishery, open throughout the trout and coarse fishing seasons, is a fine stretch regularly producing barbel to 8lb, chub to 4lb and trout to about 1$^{1}/_{2}$lb. It also holds dace, grayling, roach and pike. Maggot is the popular bait for the smaller fish whilst ledgered worm will account for good barbel and perch.

Below here, with the exception of a field at Broughs Farm, the Bradford No.1. AA controls about 1$^{1}/_{2}$ miles of fine fishing on the right bank downstream to one field short of Ulshaw Bridge. Members only.

On the left bank at Spennithorne, the Knaresborough Piscatorials hold the rights to a length of about 1,000 yards. Members only.

From here downstream, through Masham and West Tanfield, to Ripon most of the fishing is in the hands of local syndicates and associations, none of whom issue day tickets. However, those anglers wanting to join a local club will find that the fishing is excellent all along this stretch.

At Kilgram Bridge members of the local TAA fish the left bank above the bridge whilst anglers from the Buck Inn Fly Fishers Club enjoy exclusive rights on the right bank below the bridge.

Masham (OS99:223809)

Either side of Masham, the famous Yorkshire brewing town, the fishing is owned by the Swinton Estate which offers a limited number of **season tickets** to fish approximately 2 miles of the right bank above and below the Masham Angling Club water and 3 miles of the tiny River Burn. Details from the Estate Office, Swinton,

Patiently waiting for a bite at Knaresborough Lido on the River Wharfe

Overlooked by Kilnsey Crag, an angler tries for an early season rainbow trout

The fishing's good right in the heart of Skipton, on the Leeds and Liverpool Canal

Masham (Tel: 01765 689224).

The local Masham Angling Club controls good mixed fishing on about 3 miles of the middle section of the Swinton Estate water on the right bank near the town.

Season tickets only, from the River Keeper, Mr A.R. Proud, Park Street, Masham (Tel: 01765 689361). *See Angling Clubs section.* This is a fly fishing only water. Only anglers are permitted at the water. No water sports enthusiasts!

On the left bank upstream of the town the Yorkshire Fly Fishers' Club control about 2 miles of the prestigious Clifton Castle Water. Members only. Long waiting list.

See also Leighton Reservoir.

At West Tanfield the local Tanfield Angling Club controls about 5 miles of fishing on both banks through the town. Tickets for members' guests only. Waiting list for membership.

Further downstream at North Stainley, the Ripon Piscatorial Association holds the rights to about 1 mile of fishing on the right bank from Sleningford Caravan Park downstream to the Gutter below Stainley Bank Gorge. Members only.

Across on the left bank, members of the Knaresborough Piscatorials can fish about 1½ miles of river at the Norton Conyers Estate. No day tickets.

See also Bellflask Trout Fishery and Tanfield Lodge Lake.

Ripon (OS99:312712)

Ripon, a town built on three rivers, the Ure, the Laver and the Skell, plus many ponds and a canal, is an excellent centre catering for all types of fishermen. There are two local angling clubs, both of whom issue temporary tickets as well as season membership to both local and visiting anglers. The River Ure here is a good mixed fishery with fine barbel, chub, dace, grayling and trout to be had. Barbel can run to 8lb, the chub to 5lb and the occasional wild brown trout can reach 3lb.

See also Brickyard Carp Fishery, Racecourse Lake, Roger's Pond and Queen Mary's Ponds.

Approximately 4½ miles of the left bank of the river from Nunwick Beck, a mile above North Bridge on the A61, downstream to Newby

Hall boundary fence, and about 4 miles of the right bank starting a few hundred yards above North Bridge downstream to opposite Newby Hall is controlled by the Ripon Piscatorial Association. This is a really good water with the large broad sweeps, shallow runs and deep pools favoured by big barbel and chub. Float fished or ledgered sweet corn and luncheon meat will tempt both these strong fighting fish. Chub will also rise to a large bushy palmer-tied dry fly. Brown is usually the best colour.

Tickets, week £12.00 and **day** £4.00, are obtainable from the Ripon Angling Centre, (Tel: 01765 604666), Ure Bank Caravan Site (Tel: 01765 607764), the Station Hotel, North Road (Tel: 01765 602140) and R.E. Wain and Son, Newsagents, 82 Bondgate (Tel: 01765 602742).

The other local group, the Ripon Angling Club, controls some good fishing on the right bank above the town. Their stretch commences at Spinney Wood and continues downstream for about 1 mile to the site of the old bridge, near South Parks. Fishing is by any method.

Day tickets £5.00 (limited to two per day) can be obtained from the Ripon Angling Centre. These tickets also cover trout and grayling fishing on the Rivers Laver and Skell.

See also the Ripon Canal.

RIVER LAVER

Hardly worthy of the title river, the Laver is a tiny stream starting its life on Kirkby Malzeard Moor, approximately 12 miles west of Ripon, and flowing 14 twisting miles to join the River Skell on the outskirts of the town. Much of its course is through thick woods making access to the fishing difficult. This is another water demanding small stream tactics. Patience and careful methods are needed to get a result. The Laver holds many small wild brown trout and some grayling but they're not easy to catch.

The Ripon Piscatorial Association controls approximately 6 miles of fishing on both banks downstream from Hencliffe Wood, Winksley to the Military Bridge at Clotherholme.

Weekly tickets £12.00 and **day tickets** £4.00 from the same sources as for the River Ure fishery, *see above*. Ripon Piscatorials also control the fishing on a further stretch of approximately 1,000 yards continuing downstream to Bishopton Bridge. Members only.

See also Lumley Moor Reservoir.

The fishing downstream from Bishopton Bridge to the junction with the River Skell is in the hands of the Ripon Angling Club.

Day tickets costing £5.00 (two only per day) are available from the sources listed for River Ure day tickets. *See above.*

Fly fishing only until after June 15th when any method, except spinning is permitted.

RIVER SKELL

The second most important of Ripon's three rivers, this streamlike river has its source on the slopes of Dallow Moor high above Gouthwaite Reservoir in upper Nidderdale. Because, during its course of approximately 10 miles from Sell Gill to join the River Ure at Ripon, this diminutive river flows alongside Fountains Abbey in Studley Park, it is probably one of the most photographed of Yorkshire's waters, often appearing in calendars. In common with its cousin the River Laver, the Skell is tiny and in summer fishing is hampered by a shortage of water and an excess of vegetation. It does however provide some challenging fishing for trout and grayling, particularly on the stretch above Studley Park. Fishing on the upper reaches above the Abbey is unfortunately in private hands but below there day tickets can be obtained.

Day tickets £5.00 (two only per day) for fly fishing on the river, from its junction with the River Ure upstream for about 5 miles to near Studley Park boundary, can be obtained from the Ripon Angling Centre.

Fishing is best in the lower reaches near the town where many larger stocked trout come upstream from the River Ure but it is heavily fished by local youngsters, particularly following a re-stocking!

Back on the River Ure, downstream at Newby Hall. Approximately 1 mile of the left bank from Newby Hall weir downstream to where the combined Bradford club's water starts at Brampton Farm and about $^{1}/_{2}$ mile of the right bank above and below the weir are available to day ticket holders.

Tickets £3.50 for this excellent mixed fishery are obtainable from the Newby Estates Office (office hours only, Tel: 01423 322583) or the ticket office on the gate.

This water is well stocked with barbel, chub, dace and roach. Try sweetcorn ledgered in the weir pool for quick results, but generally float fish maggots in the fast water below the pool are best for the dace and chub.

On the right bank, some excellent fishing can be had on a

Day ticket, £3.00, from Westwick Hall Farm (Tel: 01765 677293).

The fishing starts below the weir at Newby Hall and extends downstream for about $1^{1}/_{2}$ miles to Roecliffe Grange.

Continuing from the Westwick Hall Farm water, around $^{1}/_{2}$ mile of good coarse fishing on the right bank near Roecliffe is in the hands of the Bradford City AA. The fishing starts at the limit sign in Cherry Island Wood and runs downstream to the middle of Roecliffe Wood. Fly, worm, artificial lure and minnow only to be used during the coarse fish closed season.

Day tickets £3.00 from The Rod and Backpack, Boroughbridge.

The club also owns a short stretch, for members only, above the caravan field in Roecliffe.

Commencing at Brampton Hall Farm on the left bank and stretching downstream for about 2 miles, under the A1 Boroughbridge bypass bridge to the boat slipway at Langthorpe, the fishing is in the hands of the Bradford City AA. Part of the water is controlled jointly with the sister club, the Bradford No.1 AA.

Day tickets £3.00 from The Rod and Backpack fishing tackle shop, Boroughbridge, for fishing on the Bradford City AA water only, not the joint Bradford No.1 AA water which is occasionally booked for matches.

This is a fine stretch. Sandy banks and a sandy river bottom make it ideal for ledgering luncheon meat for the big barbel and chub that lie in the deep eddies. Or try trotting maggot or a chunk of cheese along the edges of the glides for chub.

Below this stretch, in front of the houses, downstream to the old railway embankment, the fishing is private.

Continuing downstream from the embankment to a point level with the end of the island, the fishing is free. Don't forget to get an Environment Agency rod licence.

Boroughbridge (OS99: 395671)

Boroughbridge is yet another excellent centre for the visiting fisherman. A number of clubs, most of whom issue visitors' tickets, control the fishing rights to miles of the river above and below the town.

On the right bank above the weir, the Boroughbridge Marina (Tel: 01423 322011) permits all year round fishing inside the marina and, during the season, on the river bank.

Day tickets £2.00.

One of the best stretches in the town belongs to the Boroughbridge Social Angling Club and may be fished on a visitors' ticket.

Day ticket, £3.00, from The Rod and Back Pack (Tel: 01423 324776) and the Three Horseshoes pub (Tel: 01423 322314).

The fishing is from both banks from the weir downstream to the road bridge. It contains some fine barbel and chub, particularly in the weirpool. Try float fishing a piece of luncheon meat in the swim below the salmon ladder.

The Boroughbridge and District Angling Club has the rights to extensive fishing, mostly on both banks, above and below the town. Upstream of Boroughbridge, the club has rights on both banks above the A1 Road Bridge and on the right bank below, down to the marina.

Day ticket, £3.00, for weekday fishing only, from The Rod and Back Pack in Boroughbridge.

Day tickets, £3.00, for the Harrogate and Claro Conservative Angling Association water can be obtained from The Rod and Back Pack, Boroughbridge, and C.J. Fishing Tackle, Harrogate.

The fishery virtually encircles Milby Island. The water, partly on the river and partly on the canal, starts on the left bank at the bridge and extends downstream to the canal entrance. It then doubles back on itself along the canalside of the island for about half the distance back to the bridge. On the river section, there are lots of chub and dace for the taking. Try a maggot trotted between the streamer weed below the bridge or for the barbel try ledgered sausage or meat in one of the pools. Maggots, pinkies or squats are king on the canal for the roach.

There's a short stretch belonging to the Unity Angling Club on the canal offside from the Harrogate and Claro water to the road bridge. Members only.

See also Raskelf Lake.

Commencing a short distance below the town road bridge, on the right bank, and extending downstream for nearly 2 miles to Aldborough, the Boroughbridge and District AC controls the fishing rights.

Day tickets £3.00 from the Rod and Back Pack in Boroughbridge. No Sunday fishing.

This is one of the best stretches on the river. It's great for most kinds of river dwelling coarse fish and there are some trout. Not many, but those that are in the water are big! Occasionally one of the bigger trout falls to worm or maggot.

See also Aldborough Pond and Roecliffe Brick Ponds.

The Leeds and District ASA owns the fishing rights on a really good, although short, stretch of the right bank at Aldborough village. The fishing starts below the Boroughbridge and District AC water and continues downstream for 15 peg lengths.

Day tickets £2.00 for adults and £1.00 for juniors from The Rod and Back Pack in Boroughbridge, The Angler Inn at Dunsforth (Tel: 01423 322537) and the many tackle shops in the Leeds/Bradford area.

Below this water the Boroughbridge and District Angling Club controls about 1 mile of the right bank and 1½ miles of the left bank, at Ellenthorpe Lodge downstream to the river's junction with the Swale at Ellenthorpe Ings.

Day tickets £3.00 from The Rod and Back Pack in Boroughbridge. No Sunday day ticket fishing.

Another brilliant water. Long deep glides with swirling eddies full of barbel, bream, chub, dace and roach. Pork luncheon meat, the old faithful, works wonders here. Try ledgering a chunk on the edge of one of the deep glides and watch out for a vicious take.

Continuing downstream, again on the right bank at Lower Dunsford, there are two stretches, one of approximately 1 mile just above the village and another 2 miles from Holbeck Drain down to their Aldwick fishery, controlled by the Leeds and District ASA. For **day ticket** information, *see above*.

A short stretch between these waters is controlled by the Knaresborough Piscatorials. Members only.

There's more Leeds and District ASA on the left bank about 1 mile upstream and downstream of the toll bridge. For **day ticket** information *see above*. Above the toll bridge, on the left bank, the water is reserved for pleasure anglers. No match fishing.

See also Grafton Mere, and Staveley Lakes.

RIVER OUSE

Below Aldwark Toll Bridge at Ouseburn, the River Ure unceremoniously becomes the River Ouse. The Ouse is a big river which has been dredged to allow navigation by the bigger boats from the marinas near York. They often stop overnight in Nun Monkton Pool. However, the boats don't seem to affect the quality of the fishing. Perhaps the fish need to be woken up occasionally by a passing boat!

The Ouse can be very deep, up to 18 feet in places, so be careful if you choose to wade. And remember it is a flood river, at times carrying huge volumes of water from the Dales rivers. But it is a good river to fish. It's clean, fast flowing, with good deep pools and a sandy bottom. It holds a good stock of trout and a large variety of coarse fish. Barbel and chub grow to be monsters and they are easily tempted with the usual baits. Try ledgering the ever popular sweetcorn for one of these specimens, or maggots and a swim feeder will make short work of the big roach. There are also some good bream lurking in the deeper water. Much of the Ouse is heavily match fished at weekends and during bank holidays. If possible check before going.

Both the Aireborough and District AA and the Bradford No.1 AA have the fishing on two stretches of about 1/4 mile of the right bank and a lake, at Thorpe Underwood. Members only.

There's some good Leeds and District ASA water on the left bank, but this time for members only, starting 3/4 mile below Aldwark Bridge and, with a few small exceptions, continuing downstream for 2 miles to the beck at Newton on Ouse.

Linton on Ouse (OS100:500603)

One of the best fishing spots around here is on the left bank at Linton Weir and Lock. The stretch starts at the weir, including the pool, and runs downstream for about 250 yards. It's full of fish. Big bags of bream are not uncommon, the perch run to 4lb, the pike to 20lb and there are good roach and tench. There are even some trout and grayling and the odd salmon. The fishing belongs to Linton Lock Leisureways who welcome fishermen and caravaners to the site (Tel: 01347 848010).

Day tickets are £2.00 plus a £1.00 parking charge, from the shop. And to get out into the huge weir pool, boats can be hired at £10.00 a day.

The York and District AA have the right to fish a nice stretch of the right bank from the fish pass at Linton Weir downstream for about 3/4 mile to Kyle Beck.

Day tickets £3.00 from the Post Office at Nether Poppleton (Tel: 01904 794351) and York fishing tackle dealers.

More Leeds and District ASA water on the right bank, starting at Thorpe Underwood Hall. The fishing extends downstream to Widdington Hall. Members only. Then from below Linton Weir at Kyle Beck, the water continues downstream to Nun Monkton.

Day tickets £2.00, juniors £1.00, for the Nun Monkton water can be obtained at the Alice Hawthorne Inn in the village (Tel: 01423 330303).

Day tickets are also available for the Leeds and District ASA Nidd Mouth fishery from the Skip Bridge Service Station. *See Nidderdale entry.*

See also Oak Tree Leisure Angling.

Nun Monkton (OS 105:506578)

Facing the River Nidd at Beningbrough Park, the York and District AA control approximately 2 miles of some of the best fishing on the river. This is lovely water holding big barbel and chub. Shoals of bream, roach and perch swim in the deep quiet eddies at the sides of powerful streamy runs. There are some very big pike in the deep water of Nun Monkton Pool where the Nidd joins the Ouse. Try laying a dead silver sprat on the sandy river bed and be patient.

Day tickets £3.00 from the Post Office at Nether Poppleton (Tel: 01904 794351) and York's fishing tackle dealers.

Further downriver, the Knaresborough Piscatorials control about 1/2 mile of fishing on the left bank near Overton village. Members only.

See also Shipton Lake.

York and District AA control the fishing on three lengths of the left bank near Overton. The water extends downstream from the village to a point just above the railway viaduct. It's a nice water but it can be heavily match fished at weekends.

Day tickets £3.00 from the fishing tackle dealers in York.

Nether Poppleton (OS105:560547)

Facing this water at Nether Poppleton the Leeds and District ASA have a nice stretch of water beginning at the lower end of the village, just above the railway bridge and extending downstream on the right bank for approximately 400 yards.

Day tickets £2.00, juniors £1.00 from Skip Bridge Service Station (Tel: 01423 330635) and the fishing tackle shops in Leeds.

See also The Willows.

Below the Leeds water, from Pipe Hole extending downstream on the right bank for about 3 1/2 miles to the entrance to the Lido, the fishing belongs to the York and District AA.

Day tickets £3.00 from one of York's fishing tackle dealers.

Further downstream on the left bank, approximately one mile, from the bungalow to the old jetty of Rawcliffe Ings and Clifton Ings, of York and District AA water is available for fishing on a visitors' ticket.

Day ticket, £3.00, from York fishing tackle dealers.

WHARFEDALE

Upper Wharfedale, where a myriad crystal streams tumbling over the steep inclines of Oughtershaw Side and Cam Fell combine to form this internationally famous trout fishing river, is actually called Langstrothdale. This bleak, often remote, section of Wharfedale is part of the great limestone scar country, beloved of fell walkers, where the bleached skeletal bones of the Pennines pierce its slender peaty skin. It is here, where hill farmers eke out a precarious living, sure footed sheep scale the fell sides in search of food and kestrels soar in the stormy sky, that the Atlantic clouds roll in and drop heavy rain to swell the infant river. There is little in this barren area to tempt the fisherman. The few trout that do inhabit the deep pools gouged beneath waterfalls are often very small, although they are easily caught.

At Beckermonds, Oughtershaw Beck meets the inappropriately titled Green Field Beck to create the infant river. From here, in close company with the Dales Way and the difficult road connecting Wensleydale with Wharfedale, its waters flow easterly through Langstrothdale to Buckden where it turns south. It is still a small clear stream tumbling and falling along limestone ledges into foaming pools as it continues past farmsteads and hamlets with magical names like Deepdale, Yokenthwaite and Hubberholme on the start of its 60 mile journey to join the River Ouse below York. This is native wild brown trout country where the fish run about four to the pound and the very occasional half pounder is talked about as if it was a monster.

Further swelled by the waters of Cray Gill, a short distance below Hubberholme, the river turns south to flow into Wharfedale proper. Like all the Dales, Wharfedale is unique. Sandwiched between steep fell sides, its flat fertile valley floor, providing some respite from the worst winter weather for grazing animals, seems to confuse the baby river which meanders, almost doubling back on itself at times. This is classic small stream fly fishing country where the winter floodwater, crashing along gravely glides, has gouged deep runs around the outside of river bends. A dry fly fished on the glides or a wet fly swept through the deep water beneath overhanging banks often brings instant results. Below Buckden the native brown trout become a little larger. About three to the pound! However stocked fish can weigh a pound or better. There are also some big grayling, but they are timid and not easy to find.

At Kilnsey the Wharfe is joined by its baby brother the Skirfare, itself a fine game fishing river. Because of the stocking policies of local fishing clubs below here the trout get larger, typically averaging a pound with some even bigger. Grayling are more in evidence too but sadly, for whatever reason, the legendary shoals of big Wharfe grayling have long since disappeared.

At Linton, near Grassington, the river drops some 20 feet down a spectacular limestone ladder sandwiched in a limestone gorge. Not only does this natural phenomenon attract tourists, it is also a magnet for fishermen who come here in the hope of luring one of the huge trout that legend has it live in the dark green turbulent water below the falls. Occasionally a native brown trout weighing several pounds falls prey to a worm but they are few and far between. Linton Falls, like the river's other big tourist attraction The Strid on the Duke of Norfolk's Estate at Bolton Abbey, are attractive but extremely dangerous especially when the rocks are wet. So if you're fishing anywhere near the waterfalls be careful.

Below Bolton Abbey Estate the Wharfe is calmed by many stone weirs built across it to channel water into the woollen mills which, in the nineteenth century, thrived along its banks. A few mills still exist, mainly as flats, but most have gone. The weirs remain though and the deep water which they hold back is a haven for shoals of fish, excellent places for a fisherman to use a worm on a float or ledger rig.

Around Ilkley the chub begin to make their presence felt, many of the fish being in excess of 3lb. They often fall to fly although most anglers prefer to fish for them using the more traditional float rig and a large lob-worm. Above the weir at Otley it is common to see large shoals of chub and roach cruising in the summer sunshine. Floating bread crust is a method worth trying but take care as the fish are easily scared.

By the time the Wharfe reaches Wetherby coarse fish have become predominant, mainly chub, roach, dace and some pike. The few trout that are left are large but not really worth the effort of trying to catch them. By Boston Spa the river becomes lazy, meandering between fairly high flood banks. Here it is primarily a coarse fishing water renowned for the quality and size of its fish.

Good barbel can be found in the water below the town and shoals of bream occupy the slower water. There are tales of salmon accidentally being caught here by fishermen ledgering for chub and barbel. Indeed, a decade ago a Leeds angler fishing for chub landed a 5lb specimen cock fish. Whilst the fish was not large for a salmon it does provide proof that the water is clean enough to support this finicky migrant. Close to Tadcaster the river becomes tidal but is nonetheless a fine coarse fishery. Ulleskelf is a good centre for anyone looking for heavy keepnets full of dace, chub and barbel with the occasional flounder or eel.

Throughout its length the River Wharfe provides excellent fishing, a surprisingly large amount of which is accessible on a day ticket basis. Whether you're a serious trout or coarse angler, or a fly or float fisherman, the Wharfe has something for you.

Langstrothdale (OS98:840800)

Although there are some small trout to be caught from the infant river along Langstrothdale, this beautiful area is probably of greater interest to the artist or photographer than a serious fisherman. The minor road from Hawes and Wensleydale into Wharfedale is separated from the river by only a few yards of sheep shawn grass offering perfect stopping places and play areas for families. On a sunny day there's hardly a stretch of water that's not paddled in, swam in or floated on by young children. For the determined angler though day tickets can be obtained to fish a number of small scattered stretches controlled by the Kilnsey Angling Club. One stretch is on the right bank from lower Greenfields downstream to the small new bridge at Deepdale. Another is near Raisgill and another further downstream on Cray Beck. Full details of tickets and access can be had from Ken Wharton, the Keeper at the Tennants Arms, Kilnsey.

See entry under Kilnsey.

It's best to fish this water with a dry fly. Some visiting fishermen use north country patterns tied in size 18 to 20 but locals lay a size 12 sedge in the pools beneath the waterfalls and get a surprising number of takes. Best times to try it are outside the main holiday periods in spring or autumn when there is more water in the river. This can be very difficult fishing but it is rewarding if only for the

The infant River Wharfe in Langstrothdale

spectacular surroundings.

Buckden (OS98:942772)

This is where the real fishing starts. Bradford City Angling Association controls about 2 miles of fine river fishing mostly on the right bank downstream from the road bridge and a few selected fields above. The water here is gin clear and the river has a pebbly bottom making it ideal for fly fishing or running a worm under the few overhanging bushes. Small native brown trout stocks are annually supplemented with stocked fish to about 1lb. Fly, worm, artificial lure and minnow are the permitted methods and two fish over 12 inches may be taken in one fishing day.

Day tickets £3.45, from Dalegarth Holiday Cottages on the B6160 road to Kettlewell on the outskirts of Buckden village.

The fishing on the left bank downstream below the road bridge is private.

Kettlewell and Kilnsey (OS98:970722 & 975679)

Approximately 7 miles, mainly both banks, of prime trout fishing, stretching from 1 mile above Starbotton down to 2 miles below Kilnsey, at Netherside, is controlled by the Kilnsey AC. Easily accessible from the B6160, it is excellent fly fishing water boasting long gravely glides alternated with deep pools. A good stocking policy, below the stepping stones near Kettlewell, ensures that trout of about 1½lb are plentiful with some fish reaching 2lb. Above the stepping stones, the river is not stocked and all the fish are wild browns. Kilnsey AC water will appeal to the early season traditional wet fly fisherman and the dry fly purist who likes to fish 'fine and far off'. That is with fine leaders and long casts. In season a dry Greenwell's Glory can be a killer or alternatively anything tied in black, with white wings. For the wet fly fisherman a traditional early March Brown fished in the deep pools beneath overhanging trees will catch fish. Fly fishing only. Limit three brace over 10 inches.

Day tickets £20.00 and **weekly tickets** £100.00 are available, between 0900 hrs and 1000 hrs, for this stretch on the River Skirfare and the Wharfe in Langstrothdale, from Ken Wharton at the Tennants Arms, Kilnsey (Tel: 01756 752301). No tickets on bank holidays or Sundays.

See also Kilnsey Park Trout Fishery.

RIVER SKIRFARE

Rising in the spectacular walking country around Pen-y-Ghent, the Skirfare flows for approximately 8 miles through Littondale to join the Wharfe near Kilnsey. Above Arncliffe, the shallow clear water makes fishing very difficult and the fish are small. Try using fine points on long leaders and very small flies. Both brown trout and grayling grow to about 6 to 9 inches but they are generally nearer 6 than 9!

Arncliffe (OS98:932720)

Fishing on about 2 miles of water above and below the village, down to Hawkswick, and most of Cod Beck is owned by The Falcon Inn at Arncliffe. This lovely stretch of well-keepered water is free to residents at the Inn.

Day tickets, £7.00, are also issued to visitors. No Sunday fishing. (Tel: 01756 770205 for further information.)

Below the Falcon water,

Day tickets £20.00, for fishing on the Skirfare can be had from the Keeper at the Tennant Arms in Kilnsey.

See above.

Grassington (OS98:004640)

This is a good base from which to explore Wharfedale and its fishing. Extending from below the Kilnsey water at Chapel House Farm downstream to Linton, most of the water is preserved by the Linton Threshfield and Grassington Angling Club.

Day tickets £16.00 and **weekly tickets** £55.00 for visiting anglers can be obtained at the Grassington Post Office (Tel: 01756 752226) and the Black Horse Hotel (Tel: 01756 752770) in the market square. These tickets also include fishing on the small Captain, Linton and Threshfield Becks. Fly fishing only and no Sunday fishing. The trout fishing season is April 1st to September 30th and the grayling only season October 1st to February 28th. **Weekly grayling only tickets** cost £20.00 and **daily** tickets are £4.00.

This is a very varied stretch of the river. Below Netherside Hall, in the "Ghaistrills", the Wharfe crashes through a mini gorge with steep limestone sides making access difficult but worthwhile. For the adventurous angler large native trout can be tempted with a sunken fly. But be careful as limestone is very unforgiving, particularly when wet. Above the road bridge the water calms as it flows along gently sloping ledges. On the left bank a large meadow offers easy access.

Below the village at Linton, the river tumbles spectacularly down deep clefts in the limestone strata, through a succession of large pools and finally falls into a seemingly bottomless lagoon. This is the home of large trout but they're not easy to tempt and clambering about on the rocks is dangerous. Fishing, on about 500 yards of the left bank from the lower weir downstream to one field below the falls, is managed by the Saltaire Angling Association who don't issue visitors' tickets. However, the annual subscription is a mere £16.00, cheaper than some day tickets!

See the Angling Clubs section.

Burnsall (OS98:032615)

With a few minor exceptions, the fishing from both banks from

Linton Falls, Grassington

A lovely spring day by the two weirs on the River Wharfe at Linton

Linton Stepping Stones downstream for 6 miles through Burnsall to Barden Bridge is in the hands of the Appletreewick, Barden and Burnsall Angling Club. This is a beautiful varied stretch of water but unfortunately it suffers from its location either side of this most popular Dales village. The fishing in the turbulent waters about 1/2 mile above the bridge is excellent. Below the river bridge, the large field, virtually circumnavigated by the Wharfe, is used as a massive overflow car park and consequently on hot summer days the river teams with bodies. However ignoring this section of the water, below the car parking field downstream to Barden Bridge some fine trout, to about 2lb, and the occasional grayling are to be had. Fly fishing only and a three brace daily limit.

Day tickets £18.00, half price for juniors, and **weekly tickets** £90.00 from The Red Lion Inn (Tel: 01756 720204), The Fell Hotel in Burnsall (Tel: 01756 720209), and Burnsall Post Office (Tel: 01756 720232) for the period June 1st to September 30th except for weekends in June. **Grayling tickets** are available, £5.00, for the period November 1st to January 31st.

A stretch of about 1/2 mile on the left bank near Appletreewick village is owned by the Bradford City AA and preserved for members only. Access is via the caravan field where the owner charges for parking. Fly, worm, artificial lure and minnow only.

See also Barden Moor Reservoirs.

Bolton Abbey Estate (OS104:072540)

Probably the best known fishing water on the Wharfe, this 5 mile stretch of river running through the Duke of Devonshire's Bolton Abbey Estate is well managed, keepered and stocked but it suffers from public access. Stretching from Barden Bridge in the north to Kex Beck, about 1/2 mile below Bolton Bridge, in the south, the river flows through beautiful country and past several tourist attractions. Indeed the Estate Office advises anglers against booking tickets on Sundays and bank holidays. But don't be put off as the tourists tend to congregate around the famous attractions, the ruins of Barden Tower, The Strid, Cavendish Pavillion and of course Bolton Priory. Stay clear of these areas and the fishing is excellent. This is a put-and-take fishery where, depending upon the numbers indicated in daily fishing returns, hard fighting brown trout up to 1 1/2lb are stocked regularly.

Fly fishing only using barbless or debarbed hooks. No lures. Two fish over 10 inches long may be taken in one day. All other fish to be returned carefully to the river. The trout fishing season is April 1st to September 30th and grayling June 16th to December 31st.

For day and weekly ticket fishermen the 5 miles is divided into six bookable beats as follows:

No.1. Barden Beat. Barden Bridge to the Strid. This is a very popular beat. It's productive and there's good parking at Barden Bridge.

No.2. Strid Beat. The Strid to Cavendish Wooden Bridge. A challenging beat mainly contained within Strid Gorge. It's good fishing for the energetic. Parking at Cavendish Pavillion.

No.3. Cavendish Beat. Cavendish Wooden Bridge to Ungain Deep. A lovely stretch of water. One of the best but part of it is alongside the car park and it can be noisy.

No.4. Priory Beat. Ungain Deep to Priors' Pool. The one often seen in photographs because it straddles the abbey ruins. This is a fine stretch but keep clear of the busy stepping stones as the pool below is very dangerous.

No.5. Bolton Bridge Beat. Priors' Pool to Old Bolton Bridge. Yet another very popular beat. It offers excellent fishing in the long glides right down to the old bridge. Good parking by the bridge.

No.6. Beamsley Beat. Old Bolton Bridge to Kex Beck. There's easy access from the B6160 road to Addingham but this is probably the least fished water. It's a good length for the dry fly fisherman.

There's a limit of two rods per beat or a party of four may book one beat. The beat system applies until 1500 hrs after which day and weekly ticket holders are permitted to fish anywhere. Season ticket holders are not limited to one beat, they may fish anywhere. It's advisable to book in advance. The Estate Office is open Monday to Friday from 0900 hrs to 1700 hrs (Tel: 01756 710227).

A **season rod** costs £230.00 and a **junior season rod** is £20.00. **Grayling only tickets** (October 1st to December 31st) cost £10.00. Season and grayling tickets from the Estate Office only.

Fishing is permitted between 0900 hrs and one hour after sunset. A

A day ticket fisherman tries his luck on number 5 beat at Bolton Abbey

variety of day and weekly tickets can be obtained from the Estate Office or at weekends from the Information Trailer in the village car park between 0900 hrs and 1000 hrs, thereafter at the Post Office (Tel: 01756 710331).

An **adult day ticket** costs £14.50, a **junior** (16s and under) £7.00 and a **junior accompanied by an adult** £3.00. A **weekly adult ticket** is £60.00 and a **junior** £25.00.

Addingham (OS104:078498)

Commencing below the Bolton Abbey water, extending on the right bank downstream to Addingham weir and on the left bank from Kex Beck down to the start of the Bradford No.1 Angling Association stretch at Stephen Bank, the Addingham Angling Association controls fishing on a very good stretch of about 3 miles. Approximately two-thirds of the length is classic Dales stream water with long gravely glides interspersed with deep pools. The bottom third, immediately above Addingham upper weir, is the deep slow moving water favoured by bait fishermen when ledgering for large trout and grayling. Addingham AA operates a good

An angler sits quietly by the lower weir pool at Addingham

stocking policy to keep brown trout stocks high. Fish average about 1lb with a scattering of larger fish depending upon water conditions.

Day tickets £6.00 from the Addingham Post Office in the Main Street (Tel: 01943 830331). The post office is closed on Wednesday afternoon and Sunday.

Water on the left bank above Addingham weir for about 1/2 mile, at Stephen Bank, and below for about 1 1/2 miles, is controlled by the Bradford No.1 AA for members only.

The Bradford City AA manages a short stretch, for members only, on the right bank from 250 yards above the suspension bridge to 50 yards below. Then one field behind Addingham Parish Hall.

Fishing rights on a good stretch of water, on the right bank, for a few hundred yards above and 1 1/2 miles below the lower weir at Addingham's Low Mill, and a short stretch above and below the weir on the left bank, belong to the Bradford No.1 AA. This stretch, easily accessible from the A65 which comes close to the river here, includes the productive weir pool behind the old mill. Members only.

Fishing on a 2 mile stretch starting below the Bradford No.1 AA water, from where the A65 trunk road comes close to the river, and extending downriver on both banks through Ilkley Golf Club property for about 2 miles, belongs to the Myddleton Angling Club for the use of members only.

Ilkley (OS104:117480)

An easily accessible good quality fishery managed by the Ilkley Angling Association extends for about 2 miles from the new bridge, by the Parish Church, downstream on both banks to the stepping stones at Denton. Stocked annually with brown trout, the water also holds a good head of grayling, dace and chub. Coarse fish are now beginning to make their presence felt particularly in the deep pools on river bends. This is traditional Yorkshire Dales small river fishing. The club permits the use of worms and maggots in addition to fly fishing. Good chub to about 3lb are common and, as they are likely to rise to a fly, a fairly strong leader is needed. Try a big bushy dry fly, or a float fished worm, for the chub.

Day tickets £6.50 from the Tourist Information Office inside the Public Library (Tel: 01943 436226), in Railway Station Road and Runnymeade Newsagents on Leeds Road (Tel: 01943 607406). Members only on Sunday and there is a limit of four fish over 11 inches.

Fishing on the left bank from Bow Beck, below the stepping stones, downstream for about 1 mile and on the right bank from the iron road bridge to the end of Ben Rhydding Sports Club fields is controlled by the Bradford No. 1 AA for members only.

Below here on the left bank, Bradford City AA members may fish a short stretch of about 1 mile downstream from Hundwith Beck. No day tickets.

Burley in Wharfedale (OS104:165465)

There's a stretch of about 600 yards, on the right bank, here alongside the main A65 trunk road at Burley, facing the Little Chef restaurant, which has traditionally been known as "free fishing". Of course there is no such thing as free fishing, but most people fish this stretch without hindrance. Don't forget, though, that you must have a rod licence issued by the Environment Agency.

See Legal section

One field on the left bank at Askwith is fished by members of the Airborough and District Angling Association. Members only.

The Bradford City has AA have about 3/4 mile of fishing for members only on the right bank from the weir down to Greenholme Mills.

Further downstream at Askwith, the Airborough and District AA has a short productive stretch of the left bank for members only.

On the right bank below the weir at Greenholme Mills is the start of the West Riding Anglers' length running down to the new bypass. Members only. The club, which also controls fishing further downriver at Harewood, only accepts new members by invitation.

Otley (OS104:202456)

Commencing below the West Riding Anglers' water at Burley, the Otley Anglers own the fishing on both banks down to the site of the old upper weir, with the exception of a short stretch of free fishing near the road. Members only. No tickets.

The free fishing is on about 1/4 mile of the right bank alongside the A660 trunk road to Ilkley. Don't forget your Environment Agency rod licence.

See Legal section

Below here the Bradford No.1 AA manages two good lengths of streamy water for members only. One length, on the right bank, starts below the free fishing stretch and extends downstream for approximately 1/2 mile behind the mill and the other on the left bank, from the Otley Anglers' water limit, downstream for 1 mile past the sailing lakes. Fly fishing only on the top half of this water during the period March 15th to June 15th.

Further down the Otley Angling Club manages 3 miles of good mixed fishing, on the left bank, from just above Otley Bridge and from the bridge on the right bank, downstream to the confluence of the River Washburn. Members only. No day tickets.

The fishing on both banks of the River Washburn from the outflow of Lindley Wood Reservoir downstream to its junction with the Wharfe belongs to the Farnley Estate. Season tickets only.

For information see the entry for Lindley Wood Reservoir.

See also Fewston and Swinsty Reservoirs, Knotford Lagoons and Yeadon Tarn.

Approximately 5 miles of fishing from the left bank from below the River Washburn downriver through Pool to just below Castley Beck, $1^{1}/_{2}$ miles below the viaduct, is owned by the Leeds and District Amalgamated Society of Anglers who issue day tickets. No fishing from the island by the paper mill. No fishing in one small field near Arthington weir. This is a top bait fishing water with lovely long glides suitable for trotting a maggot and many deep pools for ledgering. There are some good dace and chub in this stretch which also holds grayling and trout as well as a few perch. No wading between March 25th and May 31st. No night fishing. From here downstream coarse fish begin to take over. The few trout which remain are generally very large and difficult to catch.

Day tickets, £2.50, are available from the petrol station at Pool Bridge (Tel: 0113 2842105), Angling & Country Sports in Otley (Tel: 01943 462770) and most of the fishing tackle shops in the Leeds/Bradford area.

Below this water, the small Huby Angling Club has approximately 3 miles of water for members only. Fly fishing only. No day tickets.

Several miles of fishing on the left bank between the Nunnery and Netherby Sands and the right bank between Rougemont and Netherby is owned by the Harewood Estate and leased to the West Riding Anglers. No day tickets. Members only.

Fishing in the lakes on Harewood House Estate is private.

Below Netherby, at Kearby Town End, approximately 900 yards of the left bank is fished by members of the Idle and Thackley AA jointly with the Bingley AC. This is an excellent water holding good barbel, chub, grayling and trout. The Wharfe is lovely here, with long glides over a stony bottom making it ideal for trotting a float rig. All the usual baits score, but try sweetcorn for the barbel and chub and the trout will always come for a fly. Only trout may be removed. Limit two per day, over 12 inches.

Approximately $^{1}/_{2}$ mile of good fishing on the left bank near Whitewell Farm about $^{1}/_{2}$ mile upstream of Linton road bridge is controlled by the Leeds and District ASA. Members only.

One and a half miles of the right bank at Moor End Farm is fished by members of the Knaresborough Piscatorials. No day tickets.

Wetherby (OS105:405480)

The River Wharfe below Wetherby is a renowned coarse fishing venue favoured by visiting anglers. In addition to the large shoals of chub and dace, some good barbel, bream and roach begin to show themselves around here. Whilst the Wharfe does not produce huge pike, fish in the region of 10 to 12lb are common.

The fishing from Linton Bridge at Collingham extending for 1½ miles on the right bank, except for about 350 yards in Collingham Wood, to Wetherby Weir is preserved by the Wetherby and District Angling Club and available on a day ticket. Also, approximately ¾ mile on both banks below the weir downstream to the sewage works for members only. This is a popular fishery with lots of coarse fish and a few trout to be had. It can be difficult to fish in the summer, though, especially in the playing fields and close to the swimming pool.

Day tickets, £1.50, for the water above the weir can be obtained from the Esso Service Station on the York Road (24 hours), newsagents in Collingham, Lower Wharfe Angling Centre and J.T. Rodgers, fishing tackle shop in Leeds. Any legitimate bait or lure is permitted and the limit for takeable trout is 11 inches. Use barbless hooks only.

Boston Spa

Downstream of Wetherby, the Wharfe is primarily a coarse fishing water holding fine stocks of barbel, bream, roach, chub, dace and pike. The trout have not completely disappeared though and a number of the local angling clubs stock annually with both trout and grayling but the few fish which remain tend to be elusive. Trout fishing is better below the weir. There are also some reports of salmon being caught here, one even falling to a float fished maggot, but it's mainly for the barbel and chub that anglers visit the Wharfe between Boston Spa and its confluence with the River Ouse.

The Bingley AC have just over a mile of good fishing at Wray Wood near here. Members only.

Approximately 1½ miles of fishing on both banks starting about 1 mile below the weir at Flint Mill and extending downstream through Boston Spa to Firgreen Beck belongs to the Boston Spa

Angling Club for members only. Another stretch of the right bank continuing for nearly 2 miles from just above the old gasworks to Newton Kyme is also Boston Spa AC water and can be fished on a day ticket.

Day tickets £2.00 from Lower Wharfe Anglers in Boston Spa and Kirkgate Anglers in Leeds.

There's a limit of three takeable fish. Two trout over 12 inches plus one grayling or vice versa. Early season is best on this water with the favourite baits for chub, dace and bream being maggots, pinkies or casters. Luncheon meat or boilies do well with the barbel and chub.

The same baits also bring success on about 2 miles of really productive water on the left bank, centred on Eastdyke Village, belonging to the Leeds and District ASA. The river here twists and turns, gouging some wonderful deep eddies beneath sandy banks. It's a great water for barbel. Non members must be accompanied by a member.

Day tickets £2.50 from the Bay Horse, Tadcaster (Tel: 01937 832299), K Westmoreland, Newsagent, 5 Commercial Street (Tel: 01937 832397) and the Lower Wharfe Anglers, Boston Spa (Tel: 01937 844260).

Tadcaster

A short stretch of the left bank from the town downstream for 200 yards belongs to the Britannia Inn on Tadcaster Bridge.

Day tickets £1.50 from the Inn (Tel: 01937 832168).

Continuing downstream from this stretch the local Tadcaster Angling and Preservation Society controls a mile of fishing on the left bank down to the sewage plant outlet and 1¾ miles of the right bank from the town road bridge downstream, under the bypass, to Grimston Park.

Day tickets, £2.00, can be obtained in Tadcaster from K. Westmoreland, Newsagent (Tel: 01937 832397) and the Pet Shop on Tadcaster Bridge, and the Lower Wharfe Anglers in Boston Spa.

Continuing downstream on the left bank for a further 1½ miles from the sewage plant, the Leeds and District ASA controls some fine fishing. They also fish the right bank from above Kirkby Wharfe village downstream to about ¼ mile below the railway bridge at

Ulleskelf and approximately 1/2 mile of the left bank below the bridge down into the tidal stretch.

Day tickets £2.50 for the water below the railway bridge from The Crown Inn, Bolton Percy (Tel: 01904 744255) and Lower Wharfe Anglers in Boston Spa.

This is a semi-tidal fishery containing large stocks of the usual coarse fish plus flounders and eels. However, the flounders tend to be more prolific below Ulleskelf. In common with most tidal rivers the banks around here are steep and can be slippery, especially at low water.

See also Sandwath Lake.

Ulleskelf

Continuing below the Tadcaster A and PS water, the Leeds and District ASA has fishing on the right bank for about 1 1/4 miles downstream to Ulleskelf Railway Bridge. The Society also has the fishing opposite on the left bank for approximately 1 1/4 miles down to a point some 500 yards above the bridge and on a stretch of about 1 mile of the left bank downstream from the railway bridge.

Day tickets £2.50 from The Ulleskelf Arms, School Lane, next to the railway bridge (Tel: 01937 832136) the Lower Wharfe Anglers, Boston Spa, and the Leeds tackle dealers.

And finally a short stretch of the right bank at Ryther, by the splendidly named Mucky Lane, is held for members only by the Castleford and District Society of Anglers Clubs.

Still Waters

This section lists 87 still water fisheries ranging from the vast Pennine reservoirs to tiny mill dams. Somewhere in this list you should find just the water you're looking for. There are brown and rainbow trout and virtually every species of coarse fish swimming in remote tarns, quarry lakes, huge reservoirs, park lakes, ex-gravel pits and purpose built fisheries, right across the area. There are fisheries with single lakes, multiple lakes, shallow lakes, deep lakes, clear water or peaty water. In fact there's almost any combination that you could want.

Where the fishery is a day ticket water comprehensive details have been included not only of the ticket prices and stock but also the ease of access, the quality of the banks, fishery facilities and, where possible, full information on the baits or flies which normally bring success. If the still water is fished as a members-only fishery, a description is given to assist readers who anticipate joining the appropriate fishing club to get access to the venue. Fishing is not permitted on a few of the listed waters. They have been included because they exist and in order to save you wasting your time finding out that you can't fish them anyway!

All the waters are listed alphabetically and the position of all the day ticket fisheries is indicated on the fishing maps.

Coarse Fishing Still Waters

Aldborough Pond, Boroughbridge.	Season tickets only.
Brafferton Carp Lake, Helperby.	Day tickets.
Brickyard Carp Fishery, Ripon.	Day tickets.
Broken Brae Coarse Fishery, Catterick.	Day tickets.
Carpvale Pool, Moor Monkton, York.	Day tickets.
Catterick Lakes, Catterick.	Day tickets.
Chellow Dean Reservoir, Bradford.	Season tickets only.
Clayton Ponds, Leeds.	Day tickets.
Coppice Pond, Harden, Bingley.	Season tickets only.
Doe Park Reservoir, Denholme.	Day tickets.

Ellerton Park Lake. Catterick.	Day tickets.
Farnham Lakes, Knaresborough.	Season tickets only.
Foulridge Reservoir, Foulridge, Colne.	Day tickets.
Grafton Meres, Boroughbridge.	Day tickets.
Green Lane Pond, Scorton, Catterick.	Day tickets.
Harold Park Lake, Bradford.	Day tickets.
Hessay Pond, Hessay, York.	Day tickets.
Hewenden Reservoir, Cullingworth, Bradford.	Season tickets only.
Jenkins Lake, Northallerton.	Day tickets.
Kingsley Carp Water, Starbeck, Harrogate.	Day tickets.
Knotford Lagoon, Otley.	Day tickets.
Langton Ponds, Great Langton.	Day tickets..
Larkfield Tarn, Rawdon, Leeds.	Season tickets only.
Linda's Lake, Keighley.	Season tickets only.
Nunroyd Pond, Guiseley, Leeds.	Season tickets only.
The Oaks Fisheries, Sessay, Topcliffe.	Day tickets.
Oak Tree Leisure Angling, York,	Day tickets.
Olde Mill Lake, Northallerton.	Season tickets only.
Prospect Farm Pond, Harrogate.	Day tickets.
Queen Mary's Ponds, Ripon.	Season tickets only.
Racecourse Lake, Ripon.	Day tickets.
Raskelf Lake, Raskelf, Boroughbridge.	Season tickets only.
Ripley Castle Lake, Ripley, Harrogate.	Season tickets only.
Robert's Pond, Keighley.	Season tickets only.
Roecliffe Brick Ponds, Boroughbridge.	Season tickets only.
Rogers Pond, Ripon.	Day tickets.
Roleith Fishery, Northallerton.	Day tickets.
Roundhay Park Lake, Leeds.	Day tickets.
Royds Hall Dam, Bradford.	Day tickets.
Sandwath Lake, Church Fenton.	Season tickets only.
Semerwater Lake, Bainbridge.	Day tickets.
Settler Dam, Morton, Bingley.	Season tickets only.
Shelf Dam, Bradford.	Season tickets only.

Shield Fly Fishing Lake, Crakehall, Bedale.	Day tickets.
Shipton Lake, Shipton by Benningbrough.	Season tickets only.
Staveley Lakes, Boroughbridge.	Season tickets only.
Sugden End Reservoir, Keighley.	Day tickets.
Teapot Dam, Keighley.	Season tickets only.
Thorpe Perrow Lake, Bedale.	Day tickets.
Thorpe Underwood Lake, Boroughbridge.	Day tickets.
Thorpe Underwood No.1 Lake, Boroughbridge.	Season tickets only.
Whinny Gill Reservoir, Skipton.	Day tickets.
Whitefield Reservoir, Keighley.	Season tickets only.
The Willows, York,	Day tickets.
Woodland Lakes, Thirsk.	Day tickets.
Yeadon Tarn, Leeds.	Day tickets.

Trout Fishing Still Waters

Barden Moor Reservoirs, Skipton.	Season tickets only.
Bellflask Fishery, East Tanfield.	Day tickets.
Billing Dam, Rawden, Leeds.	Day tickets.
Blackburn Farm Trout Fishery, Hawes.	Day tickets.
Chelker Reservoir, Skipton.	Season tickets only.
Chellow Dean Reservoir, Bradford.	Season tickets only.
Coniston Hall Lake, Coniston Cold, Skipton.	Day tickets.
Crab Tree Angling Lake, Richmond.	Day tickets.
Dalton Fields Lake, Richmond.	Day tickets.
Embsay Reservoir, Skipton.	Day tickets.
Farmire Trout Lake, Knaresborough.	Day tickets.
Farnham Lakes, Knaresborough.	Season tickets only.
Fewston & Swinsty Reservoirs, Blubberhouses, Skipton.	Day tickets.
Helwith Bridge Trout Fishery,	Settle. Day tickets.
Kilnsey Park, Skipton.	Day tickets.
Kiplin Hall Trout Lake, Great Langton.	Day tickets.

Lakeside Fisheries, Catterick.	Day tickets.
Langlands Lake, Newsham, Richmond.	Day tickets.
Leeming Reservoir, Denholme.	Day tickets.
Leighton Reservoir, Masham.	Day tickets.
Lindley Wood Reservoir, Otley.	Season tickets only.
Lumley Moor Reservoir, Ripon.	Season tickets only.
Malham Tarn, Malham.	Day tickets.
Maran Lakes, York.	Day tickets.
Raygill Trout Fishery, Lothersdale, Skipton.	Day tickets.
Scar House Reservoir, Pateley Bridge.	Day tickets.
Settler Dam, Morton, Bingley.	Season tickets only.
Shield Fly Fishing Lake, Bedale.	Day tickets.
Silsden Reservoir, Silsden.	Season tickets only.
Sunnydale Reservoir, Morton, Bingley.	Day tickets.
Tanfield Lodge Lake, West Tanfield, Masham.	Day tickets.
Thornton Steward, Leyburn.	Day tickets.
Thorpe Underwood Lake, Boroughbridge.	Day tickets.
Tong Park Lake, Shipley.	Day tickets.
Whinny Gill Reservoir, Skipton.	Day tickets.
Winterburn Reservoir, Gargrave.	Season tickets only.

ALDBOROUGH POND

Location (OS99:386659)

From Boroughbridge take the road to Aldborough. The pond is at the bottom of Low Close Lane.

Fishery Controller

Boroughbridge and District Angling Club. *See Angling Clubs section.*

Water and Stock

One small pond holding a good stock of coarse fish.

Ticket Prices

Season tickets only. *See Angling Clubs section.*

Fishery Rules

Barbless hooks only. No keepnets.

BARDEN MOOR RESERVOIRS

Location (OS104:035566)

From Skipton take the road to Embsay. Continue through the village towards Eastby. Approximately 1½ miles after the village, at the road's summit, Lower Barden reservoir is on the left.

Fishery Controller

Appletreewick, Barden and Burnsall Angling Club. *See Angling Clubs section.*

Water and Stock

There are two large reservoirs here, Upper Barden, which is private, and Lower Barden containing wild and stocked brown trout.

Ticket Prices

Members only. *See Angling Clubs section.*

BELLFLASK FISHERY

Location (OS99:296773)

From West Tanfield village, take the road towards Wath. Continue through East Tanfield, and after about ¾ mile, turn right down a track to the lake. Drive slowly down the lane because it passes through a wildlife preserve.

Fishery Controller

Brian Morland, Bellflask House, Bellflask Fishery, Wath Road, East Tanfield, Ripon HG4 5LW (Tel: 01677 470716).

Water and Stock

A 10 acre gravel pit holding rainbows, averaging 2½lb with some into double figures, and a few browns.

Ticket Prices

Season tickets £450.00. Day tickets £20.00 for 4 fish, then catch and release is permitted. No half days or concessions. Advance booking advisable.

Opening Times

All year from 0800 until 2000 hrs or dark, whichever is the earlier.

Description

Bellflask, a 10 acre ex-gravel pit situated alongside the River Ure, is a great water for the stalking fly fisherman. The water is gin clear and it's very deep, dropping away to around 25 feet in places but the banks have been sensibly landscaped to give good cover. The lake is situated on an 80 acre wildlife estate with abundant vegetation providing a breeding ground for rare birds. It's also a rich source of insect life, much of which gets blown onto the water and consequently the trout grow-on quickly. Currently, the record rainbow trout is a magnificent 19lb 12oz. It's worth trying a black tadpole in the margins to tempt one of the big cruising trout. Use a strong leader. When hooked these fish make the most of the deep water, taking you down to the backing. For lure fishermen, the old saying "bright day - bright fly" is worth sticking to on this water. Try a Cat's Whisker on a bright day or Black Chennile when it's dark and grey. The raft in the centre of the lake is for nesting terns and is not a fish cage as one would expect. All the bank-space is open for fishing but the owners request that anglers are very careful where they tread. Many rare birds nest near the water's edge.

After reaching your limit, catch and release fishing is permitted but only if barbless hooks are used and the fish are gently unhooked whilst still in the net.

A coarse fishery is also planned for the site

Best flies

Drys: In season Daddy-Long-Legs and May Fly. Anytime, Iron Blue Dun, Greenwells or any of the Wulffs.

Wets: Early season, Invicta, Claret and Orange.

Nymphs: Caddis Gold Head, freshwater shrimp or any of the buzzers.

Lures: Appetiser, Black Chenille, Cat's Whisker, Viva or Montana.

Fishery Rules

Fly fishing only. No wading. No dogs.

Facilities on Site

Car park. Toilets.

BILLING DAM

Location (OS104:215395)

From Leeds take the A65 road towards Yeadon, continue through Horsforth to Rawdon. Turn right into Well Lane. Go over the crossroads, by the side of the Emmott Arms public house, and follow the road to the fishery.

Fishery Controller

Mr A. Aldridge, 1 Alexander Terrace, Yeadon, Leeds (Tel: 0113 2504363 (day) and 0113 2505951 (evening)).

Water and Stock

A 2 acre lake holding brook, brown, golden and rainbow trout.

Ticket Prices
Full day £16.00 for 4 fish. Half day £7.00 for 1 fish, £9.00 for 2 fish and £11.00 for 3 fish. Catch and release permitted after reaching limit.
Opening Times
March 15th to December 31st, from 0800 hrs until dusk.
Description
A very attractive small dam set in a wooded area on the outskirts of the village. There's good access to all the banks that have been carefully planted with shrubs and trees to improve the insect life. The lake supports a large stock of quality trout averaging 2 to 3lb with many fish running into double figures and some up to 20lb. It's an interesting fishery because it holds brook trout and golden trout in addition to the usual browns and rainbows. It's also a traditional fishery where nymphs usually do well in the water which, although it drops away to 15 feet, is clear enough to spot the fish. Casting to individual trout often brings results. Try a weighted black tadpole for the cruising fish. On a warm summer evening try a dry fly, a white moth or similar will take fish. For lure fishermen anything in black with a green or orange beard, like a Viva or a Montana, is good. Use strong leaders, because the fish run hard and fast when hooked.
Fishery Rules
Barbless hooks only. Minimum of 6lb leader point. 15 rods only per day.
Facilities on Site
Car park. Toilets.

BLACKBURN FARM TROUT FISHERY

Location (OS98:876892)
From Hawes take the A684 road towards Bainbridge. Turn first right into East Gayle Lane, the road to Gayle. The fishery is signposted about 200 yards on the left past the Bainbridge Ings Camping Site.
Fishery Controller
Gill and Bryan Moore, Blackburn Farm, Gayle, Hawes DL8 3NX (Tel: 01969 667524).
Water and Stock
One spring-fed man-made lake of approximately 1 acre containing rainbow trout.

Ticket Prices

Day Ticket £11.00 for 3 fish, and half day £8.00 for 2 fish. Six rods only per day so it's advisable to phone before going.

Opening Times

Open all year from 0730 until 2030 hrs or dusk whichever is the sooner.

Description

Created by damming a small beck, this pretty lake sits on the southern fellside of Wensleydale and, as well as offering excellent fishing, it commands magnificent views of the upper dale and Hawes. The beck supplying the lake, and the trout farm, with clear water also brings in abundant aquatic life to encourage the fish to grow-on quickly. This is not a big fish water, but there are lots of trout averaging a couple of pounds and they are free feeders. Good fly hatches, particularly in the evening, mean that it's a fine dry fly and nymph water so there's no need to bring a sinking line. Try black buzzers or pheasant tail nymphs during the day. In the early morning or evening try a dry Black and Peacock Spider, a Grey Duster or White Moth. Catch and release fishing is permitted after a limit has been reached. Return fish carefully to the water.

Fishery Rules

No lures. Barbless hooks only.

Facilities on Site

Car park, toilets, camping facilities, farmhouse bed and breakfast. Environment Agency rod licences for sale.

BRAFFERTON CARP LAKE

Location (OS99:440704)

From Boroughbridge take the road towards Helperby. At Thornton Bridge over the Swale, turn right. Just before Helperby village take a left on a signposted road to the fishery. In about 250 yards turn right and follow the dirt road across a field.

Owner

Mr David Falkener, Brafferton Manor Farm, Helperby, York YO6 2PD (Tel: 01423 360402).

Water and Stock

One small lake holding a good stock of carp (common, leather and ghost) to 20lb, bream, roach and tench.

Ticket Prices
Day £5.00, senior citizen £4.00 and evening (after 1600 hrs) £4.00. Under 12s and ladies sharing a peg fish free.
Opening Times
All year from dawn to dusk.
Description
As the name suggests this is primarily a carp water. There are some nice fish to be had up to about 20lb. The recently excavated lake lies in a hollow across a field. The unmade track from the farm buildings to the lake will be difficult to navigate in wet weather. However, once at the bankside, access all around the oval shaped lake is good to the 20 plus fishing stages that have been built. The water has a uniform depth of around 8 feet dropping to nearer 10 feet in the middle. Bream, roach and tench have been stocked, but it is for the carp that most anglers come to this water. On the right day it's not unknown to land 10 or 15 fish in a session. They like sweetcorn, pork luncheon meat and, in the summer, will come to the surface for bread crust. Maggots are always worth a try for the other coarse fish. The tench respond well to sweetcorn.
Fishery Rules
No boilies. No keepnets.
Facilities on Site
Small parking area near lake.

BRICKYARD CARP FISHERY

Location (OS99:340747)
From Ripon take the A61 road towards Thirsk. Pass over the river and climb Hutton Bank. After a further 1½ miles on the left, turn into the lane signposted to the fishery.
Fishery Controller
Michael Scawthorn, Brickyard Fishery, Hutton Moor, Ripon (Tel: 01765 640666).
Water and Stock
Currently, two lakes holding carp (Common, Mirror, Ghost, Koi and Crucian), golden rudd, gudgeon, perch, roach, and tench.
Ticket Prices
Day ticket £5.00 from 0700 hrs to dusk, or £3.50 after 1600 hrs. From October 1st until March 31st day ticket prices reduce to £4.00. Obtainable on site or from the Ripon Angling Centre, Ripon

(Tel: 01765 604666).

Opening Times

All year from 0700 hrs until dusk.

Description

The two lakes have been excavated from a series of spring-fed brick ponds and are attractively landscaped with flat banks giving easy access from the car park. A peninsula extending two-thirds of the way across the large pool creates a U shape and is a popular spot for fishing. There are 34 marked fishing pegs on this lake and a further 16 on the smaller one to the left. Currently a third lake is being created to increase the number of fishing pegs.

Everywhere flat grassy banks give easy access and some young bankside vegetation provides a little cover. Both lakes vary in depth from 3 feet to around 6 feet and, being spring fed, the water is clean and moderately clear. A lot of mid-range carp have been stocked and there are fish up to 15lb. For anyone not interested in carp, try maggots, casters of hemp for the shoals of perch, roach and rudd. They're plentiful and active feeders.

Once the pools were used as rearing ponds for ornamental fish, many of which remain and have grown bigger. Don't be surprised to hook a Ghost of Koi carp. These gold fish run to about 10lb and can make a dull day interesting.

Fishery Rules

No night fishing. No boilies. One rod only per angler. Barbless or microbarb hooks only. No dogs.

Facilities on Site

Car park, toilets, fishing hut with snack facilities.

BROKEN BRAE COARSE FISHERY

Location (OS99:211997)

From Catterick village take the A6136 road north. Just over the River Swale bridge turn left onto the B6271 road to Richmond. The fishery lies approximately 1 mile beyond Brompton-on-Swale on the left-hand side of the road.

Fishery Controller

Clive Simpson, Broken Brae Farm, Eastby, Richmond (Tel: 01748 825647).

Water and Stock

A small man-made lake of about 4 acres teeming with bream, carp, gudgeon, perch, roach, rudd and tench.

Ticket Prices

Day ticket £6.00, juniors and senior citizen £4.00 and half day £4.00. Obtainable on site. Separate ticket needed to fish the River Swale.

Opening Times

Open from dawn to dusk, April to December.

Description

About 6 years old, this attractive 4 acre man-made lake, set in attractive countryside, has settled down quickly to become a favoured venue for coarse fishermen looking to catch fish. Although the fish are small, they are plentiful, around 10,000 crucian carp, roach and rudd have been stocked, and heavy catches are the order of the day with some fishermen catching 30lb weight. The water is clear and fairly shallow in the margins, where lilies and rushes grow, dropping away to over 14 feet at the lake's centre. There's plenty of aquatic life in the pond to ensure that the large fish stock is maintained. Fishing is from one of 50 easily accessible marked pegs. As you would expect, perch, roach and rudd form the majority of catches for those people using maggot or caster. Of the bigger fish, the bream up to 7lb, carp to 15lb, and tench to 6lb will all take bread, worm or luncheon meat. Carp anglers will be disappointed, however, that night fishing is not permitted.

Fishery Rules

Barbless hooks only. One rod only. No pets on site. No night fishing. No ground baiting. Junior anglers under 12 must be accompanied by an adult. The following baits are banned: all nut baits, live baits, gorge baits, anline dyed maggots and unboiled seed baits.

Facilities on Site

Car park and toilet.

CARPVALE POOL FISHERY

Location (OS105:508564)

Follow the A59 from the A1 junction towards York. About 2 miles after crossing the River Nidd at Skip Bridge, turn left at a sign indicating Moor Monkton village. Follow this road for about a mile and turn left at the sign leading to the fishery and car park.

Fishery Controller

K. & M. Whincup, South View House, Church Lane, Moor Monkton YO5 8LA (Tel: 01904 738249).

Water and Stock

One 4$^{1}/_{2}$ acre pool heavily stocked with carp, bream, chub, crucian carp, eels, golden orfe, gudgeon, perch, roach, rudd and tench.

Ticket prices

Day tickets, March 1st to October 31st, £6.00 and November 1st to February 28th, £5.00. Senior Citizen, day £5.00. Children, 13 and under, £4.00. Half day after 1500 hrs £4.00. Tickets must be booked in advance. Don't just turn up and expect to fish.

Opening Times

All year from 0700 hrs until dusk.

Description

Excavated in 1990, the fishery has now become established and a firm favourite with coarse fishermen. A continuing policy of bank maintenance has ensured that all the 51 fishing pegs are easily accessible and attractive to fish from. Each peg is constructed of timber with a gravel hard standing providing a good base from which to set up a complex rig. Thoughtfully constructed, with peninsulas and islands, this interesting fishery is something of an oasis in the flat land which surrounds it. The bankside vegetation is growing well to give some shade on the hottest days and some protection from the wind. There are huge fish stocks of everything except barbel, pike and zander. The carp average about 2$^{1}/_{2}$ to 3lb with some fish in the 15lb bracket and they are very lively. And if you can interest one of the shoals of big bream or chub, you'll have a good day. All baits are permitted so it's a good place to try your home brewed favourite!

With a maximum of 30 rods a day and 51 pegs to fish from there's always plenty of room to move around and find the fish. Anglers must pre-book before going as the whole lake is occasionally used for match fishing.

Fishery Rules

No keepnets or carp-sacks. Fishing only from the designated gravel platforms. Barbless or microbarb hooks only to be used. No fish to be removed. Maximum 30 anglers per day.

Facilities on Site

Car park and toilets.

CATTERICK LAKES

Location (OS99:239996)

In Catterick village turn right, facing the church, into Swale Lane (leading to Brough meadows). In about 1/4 mile take the signposted car track across the fields, for 1/2 mile, to the lakes which lie alongside the River Swale.

Fishery Controller

Leeds and District Amalgamated Society of Anglers. *See Angling Clubs section.*

Water and Stock

Two lakes of varying size holding thousands of bream, carp, chub, perch and roach.

Ticket Prices

Season fee: *See Angling Clubs section.*

Day ticket £2.50 from H. & J. Wilkinson's cafe and newsagents shop opposite the entrance to Swale Lane.

Opening Times

All year. Dawn to dusk.

Description

Access is easy and the fishing is good. Although the lakes are exceptionally well stocked they cannot be classed as a specimen water. Whilst there are carp to 20lb, particularly in the larger lake, generally the fish tend to be small for their species. In 1988 the lakes were extensively stocked with approximately 1,000 roach and 600 bream by Yorkshire Water. Later the club transferred other stock, 400 mixed species plus more carp to 20lb from other waters in the Leeds area. Big mixed bags are not uncommon here. Try the usual baits. Maggots and caster will account for the perch and roach. For the bream, carp and chub try boilies, worm or bread.

Fishery Rules

No night fishing.

Facilities on Site

Car park.

CHELKER RESERVOIR

Location (OS104:055515)

Take the A65 road from Skipton towards Otley. After approximately 2 miles the reservoir lies alongside the road on the left.

Fishery Controller

Bradford Waltonians' Angling Club. *See Angling Clubs section.*

Water and Stock

A large windswept reservoir containing brown trout. Chelker is a holding lake for water extracted from the River Wharfe near Addingham. Consequently the water may be coloured and its level will vary.

Ticket Prices

Season tickets only. *See Angling Clubs section.*

CHELLOW DEAN RESERVOIR

Location (OS104:117347)

From Bradford city centre, follow the signs to the Royal Infirmary. Continue along Duckworth Lane into Pearson Lane. The entrance to Chellow Dean is on the right at the next crossroads.

Fishery Controller

Bradford No.1 Angling Association. *See Angling Clubs section.*

Water and Stock

Fishing is in the top one of two small reservoirs which look more like park lakes. They both hold trout and coarse fish.

Ticket Prices

Season Tickets only. *See Angling Clubs section.*

Opening Times

Open all year, sunrise to sunset.

Facilities on Site

None.

CLAYTON PONDS

Location (OS104:255382)

From Leeds city centre, take the A660 road towards Bramhope and Otley. At the roundabout on the Leeds Ring Road, turn left to Horsforth. In about 1½ miles turn right into Clayton Wood Road. Continue down this road to the lakes.

Fishery Controller

Fox and Hounds Angling Club.

Water and Stock

Two small ponds holding bream, carp, eels, perch, roach and tench.

Ticket Prices

Season tickets £10.00 adult and £3.50 for juniors. Day tickets £2.00 adults and 0.75p for juniors. Obtainable from Abbey Match Anglers and Headingly Angling Centre in Leeds. *See Fishing Tackle Shops section.*

Opening Times

All year from dawn to dusk.

Description

The bottom lake is the deepest at 18 feet and the favourite, if it's carp you're after. The top lake drops away to about 10 feet towards the middle. Access is easy to all the bankspace with trees on one side to give some shade in the summer months. Bream are the best bet. Both lakes have been well stocked with fish in the 1½lb bracket and many have grown on to over 4lb. The fish are not big but they are avid feeders and bags of 20 and 30 fish are not uncommon. Fish up to 2lb make the perch and roach fishing exciting. Most anglers use maggots. Sweetcorn is a good bait for the tench. The carp are mostly small but there is a sprinkling of double figure fish to make the effort worthwhile. Try small boilies but use them sparingly.

Fishery Rules

No night fishing.

Facilities on Site

Small car park.

CONISTON HALL TROUT FISHERY

Location (OS103:895558)

Approximately 5 miles north-west of Skipton on the right-hand side of the A65, the road to "The Lakes".

Fishery Contact

Anyone on the estate or in the shop (Tel: 01756 748136 or 749551).

Water and Stock

One mature 24 acre lake holding brown and rainbow trout between 1½ and 7lb. Also approximately 2½ miles of the River Aire. *See separate entry in Airedale.*

Ticket prices

Day ticket £15.00. Four fish limit. Boats (4 available) £5.00 per day extra. Book boats in advance.

Opening times

Every day dawn to dusk during the trout season.

Description

This is an attractive lake nestling in a compact valley below Coniston Hall House on the 1,200 acre estate near Skipton. The lake is kept stocked with both brown and rainbow trout from the estate's own hatchery and because of the prolific aquatic life they grow to maturity very quickly. Coniston Lake is deep, providing ample space for fish to run hard when hooked. It is not uncommon to be stripped down to the backing by a large brown as it heads for the bottom. Use fairly substantial leaders with a tippet of around 5lb. Dry and wet fly only is permitted with most of the traditional patterns performing well. Dry fly fishing from one of the estate's boats by the trees usually gets results. Try tugging a sedge in the ripple, even in the early season - it usually brings a curious rainbow from the bottom. Traditional wets such as Partridge and Orange fished in the margins will take fish.

Popular flies

Wets. Partridge and Orange, Snipe and Purple, Black & Peacock Spider, Red Tag and Mallard & Claret.

Drys. Any time - Hawthorn, Black Gnat (with white wings) and Greenwell's Glory. In season - Daddy-long-legs, Mayfly and Sedges.

Nymphs. Caddis, Gold Ribbed Hares Ear and buzzers.

Fishery Rules

Dry and wet fly fishing only. No lures.

Facilities on Site

Restaurant, tea room, shop, toilets and a smoke room for curing trout.

COPPICE POND

Location (OS104:215395)

From Bingley take the B6429 road towards Harden and Cullingworth. About 2/3 mile outside Bingley, turn right into St Ives Estate. The pond is on the left.

Controller

Bingley Angling Club. *See Angling Clubs section.*

Water & Stock

A small clear water pond holding bream, carp, roach and tench. The fishing for bream and carp is particularly good.

Ticket Prices

Members only. *See Angling Clubs section.*

Fishery Rules

No carp over 4lb to be kept in nets. Limited night fishing.

Facilities on Site
None.

CRABTREE ANGLING LAKE

Location (OS92:172053)
From Richmond take the B6274 to Gilling West. Turn left in the village onto a road signposted with a green sign on the right-hand side of the B6274. Follow this track to the lake on the right.
Fishery Controller
Stan and Barbara Willis, Crab Tree House Farm, Gilling West, Richmond DL10 5JD (Tel: 01748 850158).
Water and Stock
One 2½ acre man-made lake regularly stocked with both browns and rainbows of 1½lb, with some double figure fish.
Ticket Prices
Day ticket £16.00 for 4 fish, £12.00 for 3 fish. A 4hr or evening ticket is £8.00 for 2 fish, from 1700 hrs to dusk. A father and son ticket is £4.00 extra, plus 1 extra fish. Special prices for senior citizens and disabled anglers.
Opening Times
Open all year. Fishing dawn to dusk.
Description
This irregularly shaped lake, with islands, was excavated several years ago since when it has matured into a popular fishery. It lies in a secluded area, well away from main roads, providing a quiet day out in the country. There's a good stock of full tailed fish to be caught with a minimum weight of 1½lb, many in the middle range and some into double figures. The fishery record rainbow is 14lb 11oz and, the brown, a fine fish of 3lb 8oz.

It's not a deep lake so you won't need the lead cored lines popular on other fisheries. The deepest water, about 8 feet, is near the islands and is favoured by the bigger fish. Lure fishing is not permitted. It's primarily a dry fly and nymph water. Try pheasant tail nymph or a small goldhead. There's a small hill to climb back to the car park, but disabled anglers may take cars down to the water's edge. A disabled fishing platform has been provided but wheelchair access would be difficult across the grassy bank.
Fishery Rules
Barbless hooks only. No returning fish until bag limit reached. No

lures. Maximum hook size 10 short shank. Fishing return required.
Facilities on Site
Car park, fishing lodge, toilet, disabled fishing platform, disabled vehicles permitted on lakeside.

DALTON FIELDS LAKE

Location (OS92:113092)
From Richmond, take the Ravensworth road and after about 3½ miles turn to Gayles. Continue through the village to Dalton. In about 1 mile turn right to Dalton Fields Farm.
Fishery Controller
Richmond Angling Centre, 8 Temple Square, Cravengate (Tel: 01748 822989) and Northallerton Angling Centre, 3 East Street (Tel: 01609 773398).
Water and Stock
A 3 acre lake holding a good stock of rainbow trout of various sizes.
Ticket Prices
Day tickets £10.00 and evening tickets £6.00, from the angling centres shown above. Four rods only per day.
Opening Times
All year from 0800 hrs until dusk.
Description
The lake is very shallow and is only fishable in the spring after which excessive weed growth makes casting and retrieving a fly virtually impossible. In the early months, though, some good sport can be had on most of the surface and sub-surface flies. Try black or green buzzers for a good day.
Fishery Rules
No night fishing.
Facilities on Site
Car park.

DOE PARK RESERVOIR

Location (OS104:073340)
From Keighley, take the A629 road to Denholme. In the centre of the village, turn left down a small road to the Denholme Sailing Club and the reservoir.
Fishery Controller
Bradford City Angling Association. *See Angling Clubs section.*

Water and Stock
A 20 acre reservoir with a good stock of bream, carp, chub, eels, perch, pike, roach, rudd, tench and trout.
Ticket Prices
Day tickets £3.00 from K. & M. Pearson, Newsagents, 1 Station Road, Denholme (Tel: 01274 832881), and from the fishing tackle shops in Bradford and Keighley. Some tickets can be obtained from the reservoir keeper's house but not in the early morning.
Opening Times
All year, weekdays 0700 hrs until 1 hour after sunset. At weekends and bank holidays fishing starts at 0900 hrs.
Description
A typical "tooth" shaped Pennine reservoir offering some good coarse fishing. Access to the banks is good, except on the west side where fishing is not allowed. Bream is the target fish for many anglers who use casters, maggots and corn to good effect. The fish are not big, averaging about 3lb, but they are plentiful. Doe Park is a favourite with pole fishermen who fish the margins for tench, averaging about 4lb and in the shallower area at the top end near the feeder stream. If you can find them, there are some very big pike. A dead bait laid well out in the deeper water should attract one of these old fish. It's a deep reservoir susceptible to winds but there's plenty of room to move around the 70 fixed fishing pegs. Denholme Sailing Club shares the water but they rarely interfere with the angling.
Fishery Rules
No fishing from the dam wall or from the western bank. No access to the reservoir grounds before 0630 hrs on weekdays and 0830 hrs at weekends and bank holidays.
Facilities on Site
Car park.

ECCUP RESERVOIR

Location (OS104:295415)
From Leeds take the A61 towards Harrogate. Turn left at Alwoodley Gates. In 1½ miles turn right into the reservoir grounds.
Fishery Controller
Yorkshire Water, 32/34, Monkgate, York YO3 7RH.
Water and Stock
A huge drinking water supply reservoir, holding trout and coarse

fish.

Ticket Prices

No fishing.

ELLERTON PARK LAKE

Location (OS99:255980)

Take the B6271 from Brompton-on-Swale near Catterick, to Bolton-on-Swale. About 2/3 mile past the village turn right onto the road signposted Ellerton Park. In about 400 yards the entrance to the park is on the right.

Fishery Controller

Mr J. Thompson, Ellerton North Farm, Scorton, Richmond (Tel: 01748 811373).

Water and Stock

One 60 acre lake with a stock of most coarse fish including carp, perch, pike, roach and tench.

Ticket prices

Season tickets £40.00, day tickets £2.00, available at the entrance kiosk or from the bailiff on the bank.

Opening Times

All year. Monday to Friday 0730 until 2130 hrs. Saturday 0730 until 2000 hrs and Sunday 0800 until 2000 hrs.

Description

This is a massive landscaped lake forming part of the leisure area Ellerton Water Park. The fishing can be difficult, not only because anglers have to share the water with other users, water skiers, divers and boaters, but because it is in a wildlife preservation area and the cormorants eat many of the smaller fish. The fish that do survive, however, tend to be fairly big and they have a lot of space to live in. The lake is over 60 acres and up to 30 feet deep in places so don't expect to find the fish first time. It'll take some practice, but when you do, you'll have a good day. For instance, the carp run to 30lb and they have a taste for most of the proprietory baits. Unusually for this area, the pike fishing is excellent. Fish can reach 30lb so it's worth dead baiting alongside the reedy margins. Try pinkies, squats or hemp to attract one of the large shoals of roach.

Fishery Rules

No exclusions as long as anglers act sensibly.

Facilities on Site

Car park, toilets, water-sports changing rooms, and a caravan park.

EMBSAY RESERVOIR

Location (OS104:000566)

From Skipton, take the road to Embsay. In Embsay village, 2 miles north of Skipton, turn left at the Elm Tree Inn and follow the road to Embsay Crag. The road ends at the reservoir.

Fishery Controller

Skipton Angling Association. *See Angling Clubs section.*

Water and Stock

One mature 26 acre reservoir holding rainbows and wild browns in the range 3/4 to 5lb.

Ticket Prices

Season ticket: *See Angling Clubs section.*

Day ticket £7.00 for 2 fish, £4.00 for accompanied juniors. Available from the Hon. Sec; the Paper Shop, Main Street, Embsay (Tel: 01756 792810), the Esso Garage on Keighley Road, Skipton (Tel: 01756 793953), K. L. Tackle in Keighley, and Jackson's Fishing Tackle, Earby.

Opening times

Every day between March 25th and October 31st. Dawn to dusk. In future the water may remain open all year.

Description

Set in a beautiful position, beneath Embsay Crag, high above Airedale, the reservoir inevitably suffers badly in the wind. However, fishing is permitted on every side, except the dam wall, so it is possible to move and get the wind at your back. Fishing is usually best on the moor side away from the small sailing club that shares the water and uses the central area. The water is peaty coloured, although it's quite clear and good for spinning or lure fishing. The trout are mostly wild and tend to be acrobatic when hooked. They can also be large. The record brown trout was a beautiful fish of 3lb 4oz and the best rainbow was 6lb 12oz. Fishing is by fly, minnow and spinning giving a range of methods to suit most tastes. Worm fishing is best on the side below the crag.

Popular flies

Wet. Anything in black usually with a flash of orange or green.

Dry. Red Tag, Wake fly and Brown Palmers. In the evening white patterns can be lethal.

Fishery Rules

Fishing by fly, minnow and spinning only. No fishing from the dam wall. Maggots are banned.

Facilities on Site

Car park and toilets.

FARMIRE TROUT FISHERY

Location (OS99:339601)

From Knaresborough take the A6055 road towards Boroughbridge. On the outskirts of the town turn left into Scriven Lane and follow this road, towards Farnham, for about 2 miles. The fishery is clearly signposted on the right.

Fishery Controller

Bob McDougall, Farmire Trout Fishery, Farnham, Knaresborough HG5 9JW (Tel: 01423 866417).

Water and Stock

One 5 acre ex-gravel pit lake situated in 12 acres of natural land. The clear water contains predominantly rainbow trout weighing a minimum of 2lb with some reaching double figures. There are also a few browns.

Ticket Prices

Full season £450.00 (any day). Weekend season £275.00 (nominated day).A one day booking of the whole lake, £250.00. Day tickets £18.00 for 4 fish, half day or evening £12.00 for 2 fish. A sporting ticket is £13.00. Catch and release permitted after limit is reached. Three boats are available at £10.00 extra. Each boat can safely accommodate two anglers.

Opening times

Open all year, except for the Christmas and New Year holidays. Fishing is from 0800 until 2000 hrs in the summer and 0800 hrs until dusk in the winter.

Description

This beautiful fishery, created about fifteen years ago by well known northern angler and author Brian Morland, now operates a policy of providing a good day's fishing for sporting anglers in pleasant surroundings. A flooded ex-gravel pit, the lake is set in natural scrubland providing a breeding habitat for wildlife and an abundant fly life for the lake's trout. The water is heavily stocked with around 1,200 to 1,300 full tailed fish averaging 2lb. About 20% of them are over 7lb and there are some big doubles. Fish grow-on very quickly and soon become strong fighters. Expect fish between

4lb and 6lb and use substantial leaders.

Fishing is only allowed from fourteen angling platforms, strategically placed around the lake, and because only twelve rods per day are allowed there's always room to move. Three sensibly designed high quality boats, suitable for two anglers each, give access to the centre of the lake from the four mooring sites. There's easy access to three sides of the lake by gravel paths. The fourth side is left unfished.

Because it is such a deep lake, dropping away to 30 feet in places, even alongside some of the fishing platforms, many anglers ignore the surface feeding fish and use sinking lines to go deep. But often a fairly large dry fly, like a Grey Duster or Walker's Wake fly, will tempt one of the surface trout and they can be large. They'll also take with a bang, so use a good leader. Nymphs work well in the surface film. Pheasant Tail, Green nymph or buzzers all take their share of fish. For anyone using a sinking line try the flashy type lures, lots of orange, yellow, black or white marabou often does the trick.

The current fishery record is a splendid rainbow of 17½lb.

A catch-and-release system is in operation for all ticket holders. After reaching a limit, fish may be carefully unhooked whilst still in the net and released. Never touch fish with bare hands.

For wheelchair bound disabled anglers this water is unique. A regular fisherman here, Jack Shaw, has kindly donated a 'wheelie boat' and the fishery owner Bob McDougall has provided an access ramp. This purpose-built wheelie boat, known as the PINCO Boat Mobile, is recommended by the English Disabled Fly Fishers for use by wheelchair bound anglers. Mr Shaw, who has first call on the boat, has kindly offered its use to other disabled anglers. Phone in advance to book the boat.

Fishery Rules

Fly fishing only. Barbless hooks only. Use the landing nets provided by the fishery. Unhooked fish to be returned carefully. Maximum size of hook size 8. Fishing only from designated platforms. One angler only per platform. No dogs. No firearms.

Facilities on Site

Car park, heated fishing hut with free tea or coffee, toilet, disabled fishing platform and boat, flies for sale.

FARNHAM LAKES

Location (OS104:350595)

From Knaresborough take the B6055 road towards Boroughbridge. The lakes are about 1½ miles from the town centre on the left-hand side of the road.

Fishery Controller

Harrogate and Claro Conservative Angling Association. *See Angling Clubs section.*

Water and Stock

Two huge gravel pits. A 40 acre lake holding a good stock of coarse fish and a 20 acre lake holding trout.

Ticket Prices

Season tickets only. *See Angling Clubs section.*

Fishery Rules

Not known.

Facilities on Site

None.

FEWSTON AND SWINSTY RESERVOIRS

Location (OS104:188538)

The trans-Peninne route A59 crosses the end of Fewston Reservoir at Blubberhouses. From here take the road to Otley, up the steep hill by the side of the church. In about 1½ miles turn left towards Timble village. Take the next left for about 1 mile and the Swinsty Moor Fishing Office and car park are on the right.

Fishery Controller

Yorkshire Water, Recreations Department, 32/34 Monkgate, York YO3 7RH. Swinsty Moor Fishing Office and keeper, Ray Bell (Tel: 01943 880658).

Water and Stock

Both of these beautiful 153 acre reservoirs contain browns, averaging about 1½lb, and rainbows averaging 3lb. There are also many double figure fish and even some reaching 20lb.

Ticket Prices

Day ticket £9.00 for 4 fish. Concessionary tickets for state pensioners, disabled anglers and unaccompanied children under 15, £8.00, also for 4 fish, and evening tickets, from 1600 hrs May 1st until August 31st, £6.00 for 2 fish. Children under 15 fishing with a parent or grandparent may fish free. In this case a single limit of 4 fish applies.

All tickets must be purchased from vending machines at the Swinsty Moor Fishing Office and you'll need a supply of one pound coins. Tickets must be purchased separately for each reservoir.

Opening times

Daily from the Saturday preceding March 25th through to November 30th inclusive. No brown trout to be taken after September 30th. Fishing is permitted from 0730 hrs until dusk. Actual fishing times are promulgated in the fishing office at Swinsty Moor.

Description

Two of the four reservoirs in the Washburn valley, Fewston and Swinsty are undoubtedly the jewels in the crown of Yorkshire Water's Recreations Department and a magnet drawing anglers from all over the country. There is easy access to both waters, plenty of open bank space, wooded picnic areas and most importantly, lots of hard fighting trout. Despite being very similar each reservoir has its own band of devotees, which is just as well because the choice of which one to fish must be made before buying a ticket. Access is not quite as easy to Fewston Reservoir which is generally preferred by anglers who like to fish away from others. Favourite spots on Fewston are near the top end where the River Washburn flows in, on the southside near the wall and by the overflow. No fishing is permitted from any of the dam walls.

Swinsty draws anglers with families who come for a day out. A delightful picnic area is situated at the water's edge at Stack Point, near where a road dissects one arm of the reservoir. Also here, in the area known as Swinsty Lagoon, there are fishing facilities for disabled anglers who are permitted to use worm as well as fly. Unfortunately the area tends to dry out in summer as the water level drops. The western corner by the dam wall is a favourite hot spot particularly in summer when the water level has dropped below the overflow. Fishing is not allowed in the marked conservation area at the end of Swinsty where it meets the outflow from Fewston. The area around Stock Point can be productive, especially when a westerly wind blows.

Both reservoirs are strictly fly fishing only. Use good strong leaders because full tailed fish of 15lb are stocked weekly. Get into one of these on such a big water and you'll know about it! The wind can be a problem but there are miles of bank space so it's easy to get it at your back. In the wind try a Walker's Wake Fly or a muddler.

All colours of buzzers do well. The current rainbow record is 13lb taken from Fewston.

Fishery Rules

Fly fishing only. No fishing from any dam wall. Barbless hooks only. After September 30th only rainbow trout may be taken. Thigh waders and wellingtons only - no chest waders.

Facilities on Site

Car parks are situated at Swinsty Moor fishing office, Stack Point Picnic Site and just off the A59 at Blubberhouses near the top end of Fewston Reservoir. Toilets are located at Swinsty Moor fishing office.

FOULRIDGE RESERVOIRS

Location (OS103:885418)

From Skipton take the A59 road towards Guisburn. At Broughton turn left onto the A56 road to Burnley. In about 6 miles, just through Foulridge village, you'll find the reservoirs situated alongside the road. Continue to the next roundabout and turn right. Next right takes you to the car park by the dam wall.

Fishery Controller

British Waterways. Contact Alan Astin (Tel: 01282 867116).

Water and Stock

The trout fishing in the top reservoir belongs to the Colne Angling Association. No day tickets. Fishing is permitted in the 80 acre lower reservoir which holds bream, carp, perch, pike, roach and tench.

Ticket Prices

Day ticket £3.50 from the bailiff on site. Start fishing and he'll find you.

Opening Times

Dawn to dusk during the coarse fishing season.

Description

Although Foulridge (pronounced Foalridge) reservoir depth varies between 6 and 30 feet it is a supply reservoir for the Leeds & Liverpool Canal and consequently the water level changes dramatically. During very dry summers the reservoir can be virtually empty but British Waterways never permit the level to fall below a point where fish stocks would be affected. This big water, lying in lovely countryside high in the Pennines, suffers badly in the wind but it is possible to get shelter by moving round the banks. It's certainly worth a visit if bream is your target fish because there are a lot of them in here with fish reaching over 4lb. The roach don't grow very large but there are plenty of them. Carp to about 6 or 7lb are also common, but they can be a bit shy. Fishing near the dam wall is the favourite place and ledgering is the favourite method. Caster, red maggots, redworm and sweetcorn all take fish. Some locals like the new flavoured boilies for the bream and small carp.

Fishery Rules

None.

Facilities on Site

Limited car parking near the dam wall and on the A56 road.

GOUTHWAITE RESERVOIR

Location (OS99:135685)

Upper Nidderdale, 3 miles north-west of Pateley Bridge.

Owner

Yorkshire Water, 32/43, Monkgate, York YO3 7RH.

Water and Stock

A large, relatively shallow, picturesque reservoir holding wild brown trout.

Description

No fishing. This beautiful reservoir is part of a nature reserve and access is not permitted. It is a favourite with bird watchers.

GRAFTON MERES

Location (OS99:410635)

Take the B6265 road from Boroughbridge south towards York. In about 2 miles turn right to Grafton. Take the next left into the village. Prospect Farm is on the right in approximately 1/2 mile. From here continue downhill to the T junction. Turn right and, on the outskirts of the village, turn left onto a single track road leading to the car park.

Fishery Controller

Roger Naish, Prospect Farm, Grafton, Boroughbridge (Tel: 01423 322045).

Water and Stock

Two lakes, one of 2 1/2 acres holding carp to 23lb and Wels catfish to 12lb, and another one of 3/4 acre with bream, crucian carp, golden orfe, perch, roach, rudd and tench.

Ticket Prices

Day ticket £6.00. Two rods per angler.

Opening Times

Dawn to dusk during the coarse fishing season.

Description

Forming part of a conservation project on the farm in 1986, the two lakes were created in what has become an area of outstanding beauty. Carp Lake, the largest of the two, holds a good stock of carp in the 5lb to 8lb region and many others exceeding 20lb. Wels catfish growing to over 12lb, an interesting addition to the lake, seem to like the water and give good sport. Try luncheon meat or corn for both the carp and the catfish. Use strong lines as both fish are strong fighters boring deep into the water. Fishing is from eighteen specially built platforms only.

Tench are the main quarry in the smaller lake which also contains a mixed bag of other coarse fish. An attractive addition to the lake, the golden orfe, can often be seen sunning themselves in the summer. They're not easy to catch though. Fishing is from nine comfortable platforms. Both lakes have rapidly become popular so it's advisable to book in advance. It's also possible to stay on site in bed-and-breakfast accommodation or in a cottage but carp anglers will be disappointed that night fishing is not permitted.

Fishery Rules

No night fishing. No ground baiting. No keepnets. Barbless hooks only. No wading.

Facilities on Site

Toilet, car park, holiday cottages and B & B accommodation.

GREEN LANE POND

Location (OS93:260026)

From Catterick village take the B6271 road towards Scorton. Go through the village and take the A1263 road towards Teeside and Yarm. Turn left onto a farm track about 1/2 mile beyond derelict buildings marked "four wheel drive auctions". There's a sign mounted on a tree advertising the lake and a caravan site.

Fishery Controller

Mr and Mrs Taylor, Green Lane Farm, Scorton (Tel: 01325 378643).

Water and Stock

One small lake approximately 1 1/2 acres and two small ponds, all holding a good head of bream, mirror carp to 20lb plus, pike, roach, rudd and tench.

Ticket prices

Day ticket £4.00 from the farmhouse.

Opening Times

All year. Dawn to dusk.

Description

Quietly situated in the corner of a small meadow, these attractive lakes provide some good coarse fishing. The wooded area along one side of the larger lake makes a good windbreak when the weather is rough. The water's usually coloured but it doesn't seem to bother the fish which are happy to take sweetcorn, casters, hemp seed or the ubiquitous maggot. If you can locate a shoal of bream on the feed, heavy bags are not uncommon. Many anglers come here after the carp, which average about 8lb with some fish over 20lb. They readily take boilies, worms or bread, as do the tench. Pinkies are the bait to tempt the roach. In the summer when the sun is on the water, try a floating crust for the carp. It's a method which often interests the bigger fish and it's an exciting way to fish.

Fishery Rules

Barbless hooks only. No keepnets. No groundbaiting.

Facilities on Site

Car park and camping.

GRIMWITH RESERVOIR

Location (OS99:060641)

From Grassington take the B6265 road towards Pateley Bridge. In about 3½ miles, just past Dibbles Bridge, turn left onto the track leading to the reservoir. There is a car park at the end of the track.

Fishery Controller

Yorkshire Water, 32/34, Monkgate, York YO3 7RH.

Description

This appropriately named reservoir sits in a remote bleak area high on the side of Hebden Moor commanding spectacular views across Wharfedale. There are nature trails in the fells around it and sailing on it but alas there is no fishing permitted in it!

HAROLD PARK LAKE

Location (OS104:149290)

From Bradford city centre take the Huddersfield Road to Odsal Top. Then follow the Halifax Road. Turn left into Cemetery Road and Harold Park is on the left.

Fishery Controller

Bradford No.1 Angling Association. *See Angling Clubs section.*

Water and Stock

A small park lake holding most kinds of coarse fish.

Ticket Prices

Day tickets, adults 70p and juniors 35p from Wibsey Angling, High Street, Wibsey.

Opening Times

Open all year, sunrise to sunset.

Description

This is a typical raised, stone terraced park lake, rectangular in shape with a small island at one end. It contains a surprisingly good stock of coarse fish including roach, rudd and perch in large numbers and a few small jack pike. Best baits are maggots and bread. Try laying a silver sprat on the bottom to attract the pike. Access is very easy and the banks are all solid.

Facilities on Site

Toilets.

HELWITH BRIDGE TROUT FISHERY

Location (OS98:810682)

From Settle take the B6479 road towards Horton-in-Ribblesdale and Ribblehead. At Helwith Bridge, where the road turns sharp right, turn immediately left on the Austwick Road. Go over the rail and river bridges and take the first left into an old quarry. The fishery is clearly signposted.

Fishery Controller

David Oversby, 10 Laburnum Cottages, Ingleton, via Carnforth LA6 3EY (Tel: 015242 41694).

Water and Stock

An ex-gravel pit of approximately 4½ acres containing mainly rainbow trout averaging 2½lb with some browns.

Ticket Prices

Adult day ticket £14.00 for any 8 hours (3 fish), ½ day £10.00 for any

5 hours (2 fish) and evening ticket £6.00 for any 3 hours after 1700 hrs, (1 fish). Boats available at £1.00 an hour. Sporting tickets £9.50 for any 8 hours, no fish and £5.50 for any 4 hours. Casting lessons £14.00 per hour.

Opening Times

Season from March 7th until November 9th. Fishing is permitted from dawn to dusk.

Description

Attractively situated on the right bank of the Ribble, and overlooked by Pen-y-Ghent, this ex-gravel pit has matured into a fine trout fishery. There's one circular lake on the site with easy access to all the bankspace, although the path is fairly high above the water on the quarry side away from the fishing hut. In common with most ex-gravel pits the water is gin clear making this a good fish stalking water. Most fishermen use sinking lines and lures to get down to the fish but there is usually a good rise that is worth fishing to. In the evening try a big bushy white fly in the surface ripple and be prepared for a savage take. Similarly a Walker's Wake Fly or a sedge does well when skittered across the surface in the wind ripple. Most colours of lures take rainbows. Try something fairly large and black when it's overcast. In the sunny weather a white marabou does well. Buzzers, in any colour, are a favourite here. Fished in the surface film they can be deadly but the takes will be gentle. Other flies worth trying are Black and Peacock Spiders, Olives, any colour of Cat's Whiskers and Black Ghost. The record rainbow is 10lb but there are bigger fish lurking in the deeps.

Fishery Rules

Fly fishing only. Barbless hooks only.

Facilities on Site

Car park at the lakeside and toilets.

HESSAY POND

Location (OS105:509530)

Take the A59 from the A1 towards York. In about 2¼ miles, after crossing the River Nidd, turn right at a cross roads to Long Marston and Hessay. In about a mile, at a T junction, turn right and park on the grass verge. The lake is in the field to your left.

Fishery Controller

Mr Wilkin, Holly House Farm, Hessay, near York (Tel: 01904 738204).

Water and Stock
One man-made lake of approximately 2 acres holding a variety of coarse fish.
Ticket prices
Day tickets £3.00, evening tickets £1.50, available on the bank.
Opening Times
Dawn to dusk during the coarse fishing season commencing June 1st.
Description
This attractive lake sits in a large meadow. The water is fairly clear and there's good tree cover around one side. Reeds growing in one end provide interesting fishing spots for those people after the bream, carp and tench which are here in good numbers. It also contains some good pike in the mid range 5lb to 15lb with others tipping the scales at over 20lb. Best bait is a silver sprat fished on a ledger out near the weeds. Best coarse fish weights are bream 10lb, carp 10½lb and tench 6½lb. Other fish include silver bream, eels, perch and roach. They're not large but they are plentiful and on a good day heavy bags can be taken. There's no restriction on baits. Try maggots or pinkies to attract the bream. Small boilies and luncheon meat will take the carp and tench. Or try one of your home brewed favourites.
Fishery Rules
No night fishing. No matches. No pre booking required.
Facilities
Car park on the verge at the roadside. Access points for disabled anglers.

HEWENDEN RESERVOIR

Location (OS104:073335)
From Keighley take the A629 road towards Denholme. Turn left onto the B6144 to Cullingworth. Go straight through the village and in about ¾ mile turn right onto an unmade track. Go under the railway viaduct to the reservoir.
Fishery Controller
Central Division Angling Club.
Water and Stock
A 20 acre reservoir holding bream, carp, eels, perch, roach and tench. The pike are big and plentiful, as are the bream and tench.

Ticket Prices
Season tickets only.
Opening Times
All year from dawn to dusk.
Fishery Rules
No night fishing.
Facilities on Site
Small car park.

JENKINS LAKE

Location (OS349947)
From Northallerton, take the A167 towards Darlington. Just past the railway bridge turn left onto the B6271 to Yafforth. The entrance to the lake is about 1 mile on the right.
Fishery Controller
Andy Scaiff, Northallerton Angling Centre, 3 East Road, Northallerton (Tel: 01609 779140).
Water and Stock
One lake, approximately 1 acre, holding a good stock of coarse fish including bream, carp, chub, perch, roach, rudd and tench.
Ticket Prices
Annual membership covering this lake and Olde Mill Lake £40.00. Day tickets are £4.00 and an evening ticket (after 1700 hrs) is £2.50. All tickets from the Northallerton Angling Centre or the Richmond Angling Centre. *See Fishing Tackle Shops section.* Also obtainable from the Guisborough Angling Centre (Tel: 01287 630687) and the Aycliffe Angling Centre (Tel: 01325 301876).
Opening Times
All year, dawn until dusk.
Description
This is a good all round water. For the carp angler, there are fish in the range 1lb to 18lb, the tench man can expect fish ranging from 1lb to 5lb and the all rounder can expect big bags of roach and rudd. There's fairly easy access across a grass meadow to the lake which sits in a small hollow near to the River Wiske. A clump of trees is growing on one side but there's little protection from the wind. It's very well stocked and, although the water is cloudy, there is no difficulty finding the fish. The best baits to attract just about everything are bread, caster, maggots, and worms. The carp and

tench can be tempted on luncheon meat and sweetcorn. Access around the lake is generally good and all the sensibly placed fishing platforms are well constructed.

Fishery Rules

Night fishing for annual members only. No boilies, bloodworm or joker. No groundbaiting. Barbless hooks only.

Facilities on Site

Car park near the lake.

KILNSEY PARK TROUT FISHERY

Location (OS98:974677)

From the Skipton bypass take the B6160 Wharfedale road towards Grassington and continue to Kilnsey. The fishery is on the left, overlooked by Kilnsey Crag.

Fishery Manager

Any of the staff on site (Tel: 01756 752150).

Water and Stock

Three spring fed, clear water lakes. Two fly fishing waters holding large numbers of rainbow trout, averaging 3lb, with many others into double figures, and one small lake exclusively for the under 12s for 'fun fishing'.

Ticket Prices

Kilnsey Park Fly Fishing Club

Annual membership £235.00. One full or part day each week (Monday to Saturday) plus one Saturday evening. Discount in the restaurant. Limited membership.

Trout fly fishing lakes

Day ticket, from 0900 until 1700 hrs, £15.00 for 4 fish. Half day ticket, 0900 until 1300 hrs or 1300 until 1700 hrs, £11.50 for 2 fish. Evening ticket, 1800 until 2130 hrs (not available on Sunday or Monday), £11.50 for 2 fish. Rod hire £5.00 extra.

Children's Fishery

Hire of all equipment and bait £3.75. All fish caught must be kept and paid for at £1.65 per lb.

Opening times

All year from 0900 until 1730 hrs. Open for fishing until 2130 hrs during the summer months.

Description

Set right in the heart of Wharfedale and overlooked by the Dale's best known landmark, Kilnsey Crag, this is arguably the most scenic still water fishery in the area. A crystal spring, bubbling from the limestone strata, has been dammed to create a fishery and family centre. Two mature landscaped lakes, stocked with high quality rainbow trout, provide good sport for the fly fisherman whilst the family is off following the nature trail, pony trekking on the fells or playing in the adventure playground.

The fly fishing is good, particularly when there is a ripple on the water. With an average of about 3lb, and some fish reaching double figures, the hard fighting rainbows, from the fishery's own stock ponds, are well worth trying for. Buzzers are always worth a shot as, in season, are mayfly nymphs, Daddy-Long-Legs and sedges. Stocking takes place twice a week and the current record rainbow to date is 17lb 12oz. Access is very easy from the car park which is situated right alongside the lakes.

A small pond is set aside for the exclusive use of under 12s to enjoy their first experiences of catching trout. This is not a 'toy' lake. Fishing is with adult tackle under the supervision of an expert and the trout can reach 4lb. The water is very clear and the fish are easy to spot. This lake is open during the summer holidays, bank holidays and weekends from April to October from 1000 hrs.

Popular flies

Lures. Church Fry, Sweeny Tod, Baby Doll and Tadpole.

Wets. Black and Peacock Spider, Peter Ross, Butcher and Invicta.

Drys. Greenwell's Glory, Grey Duster, Daddy-Long-Legs (crane fly) and Black Gnat.

Nymphs. Buzzers, Corixa, Midge or Sedge Pupa and Mayfly (in season).

Fishery Rules

Fly fishing only using barbless or debarbed hooks.

Facilities on Site

E.A. licences for sale, toilets, hot drink making facilities, flies for sale, access for disabled anglers. Family facilities include the Daleslife Visitor Centre, a fun fishery for children, a small picnic area, a cold water aquarium and a coffee shop and restaurant.

KINGSLEY CARP WATER

Location (OS104:324566)

Take the A59 from Harrogate towards Knaresborough. In Starbeck, just before the railway level crossing, turn left into Kingsley Road. Continue onto Bogs Lane. The entrance to the lake is on the right, just after the railway bridge.

Fishery Controller

Sam Watson, 31 Camwell Road, Starbeck, Harrogate HG1 4PT (Tel: 01423 881180 or 886353).

Water and Stock

One lake of approximately $^1/_2$ acre holding carp, roach, rudd, perch and tench.

Ticket prices

Day ticket £5.50, early bird from 0700 hrs to noon, £3.50, and evening 1630 hrs until dusk £3.50. Concessions for senior citizen, disabled, young person (12-16), day £4.00, evening £3.00. Family rates: husband and wife, using same peg, £7.00 and family ticket (maximum 4 people on 2 pegs) £11.00. Tickets on site or from C. J. Fishing Tackle in Harrogate.

Opening Times

Open all year. Dawn to dusk.

Fishing the attractive Kingsley Carp Water at Starbeck, Harrogate

Description

Set in a woodland copse between a cycleway and a railway line, you'd would expect this lake to be noisy, whereas it is quiet and nicely secluded. Many of the willow trees surrounding this wedge shaped lake have been carefully trimmed and left to provide some bank cover. A solid path gives good access to all the bankspace. The water is quite clear and the average depth is about 5 feet from bank to bank. It's known locally for its good stock of carp, averaging about 5lb. They tend to prefer the narrow end away from the car parking area. Best baits to try are sweetcorn and meat, although bread is good in the summer months. Maggots are the favourite bait with local anglers trying to attract one of the big shoals of roach and rudd. Recently the lake has received a stocking of thousands of smallish rudd which tend to shoal in the centre of the lake. Access from the car park to the special fishing pontoons is easy for disabled anglers.

Fishery Rules

Barbless and microbarb hooks only. No boilies, bloodworm or jokers. All fish to be returned. No carp over 5lb to be kept in keepnets. Fishing only from designated pegs. Unhooking mats must be used when removing hooks from fish.

Facilities on Site

Car park by the lakeside.

KIPLIN HALL TROUT LAKE

Location (OS99:276975)

From the A1 at Brompton-on-Swale, take the B6271 road towards Bolton-on-Swale. Continue through the village passing Ellerton Lakes on your right. After 1½ miles turn right into Kiplin Hall. Follow the track towards the hall and then, as indicated, turn right to the lake.

Fishery Controller

Brian and Sonia Morland, Bellflask Cottage, Bellflask, East Tanfield, Ripon, North Yorks HG4 5LW (Tel: 01677 470716).

Water and Stock

One 25 acre lake, set in front of the hall, holding rainbow trout in the range 1lb to 5lb and a small head of native browns.

Ticket Prices

Day £15.00 for 4 fish, then catch and release is allowed.

Opening Times
Every day except Christmas Day, Boxing Day and New Year's Day. Fishing is from 0800 until 2000 hrs or dark, whichever is the earlier.
Description
This fishery will appeal to anglers who appreciate good fishing in pleasant surroundings. Overlooked by the splendid Jacobean Kiplin Hall, this 25 acre lake lies in a beautiful landscaped area bordered by Kiplin Beck. The easily accessible banks are flat and have been laid to grass. Sufficient room has been left between the edge of the water and the trees to permit snag-free back casting. Further landscaping is planned for the near future during which a castellated stone house, overlooking the lake, will be developed as a high class fishing lodge. The lake is shallow in the margins but soon shelves away to around 20 feet near the island. It's a rainbow trout water, but it is not the place to come if you're looking for overfed monster trout. A large stock of full tailed rainbows in the 1lb to 5lb bracket have been stocked as part of a plan to create a traditional fly fishery where small flies and fine leaders are the order of the day. But bear in mind that the lake is deep and big enough for the lively rainbows to make a fight of it, so regularly check your leader.
Popular Flies
Buzzers, in black, green or claret. Tiny goldheads tied in the popular patterns, Gold Ribbed Hares Ear, Mayfly nymph and Black and Peacock Spider. When there's a wind try a Daddy-Long-legs, Walkers Wake Fly or, in season, Mayfly.
Fishery Rules
Barbless hooks only. No boobies or Static Sinking Flies to be used. No wading or paddling in lake margins. No dogs. No firearms. Stay by the lake, Kiplin Hall is out of bounds.
Facilities on Site
Car park, fishing lodge and toilets.

KNARESBOROUGH LAGOONS

Location (OS104:362579)
From the centre of Knaresborough take the A59 road towards York. At the B6164 Wetherby Road traffic lights turn left. In about 500 yards turn right into Stockwell Lane. Under the railway bridge turn sharp left into the car park by the lagoons.

Wading out to the fish at Fewston Reservoir on opening day

Reaching for distance! A lure fisherman at Leighton Reservoir

Sitting comfortably at the edge of the deep gravel pit at Helwith Bridge Trout Fishery

Fishery Controller

At the time of writing, the fishing rights to this quality fishery are changing hands, but it will undoubtedly reopen at some time in the future. Check with the local fishing tackle shop, M.H. & C. Johnson, 2 Briggate, Knaresborough (Tel: 01423 863065).

Water and Stock

Two small ponds and one very large lake extending to 60 acres. They all hold bream, carp, perch, pike, roach, rudd and tench.

Ticket prices

Not available.

Opening Times

Currently closed.

Description

The biggest lake, at 60 acres, is a huge expanse of water which can be a little daunting at first sight. It's a mature gravel pit falling away in places to depths of over 20 feet but it also has extensive shallow margins. The water is clear and bankside vegetation is sparse but a few gallant willow bushes have grown along one side. Biggest of the varied stock of coarse fish are the carp which can reach 30lb, then the pike, reaching 20lb, and lastly the bream and tench which often tip the scales at 10lb. Because of the large shoals of small perch, roach and rudd constantly attacking the carefully laid-down big fish baits, this can be a frustrating water to fish. However, if you're after specimens it can also be a good water. Big pike waters are rare in Yorkshire and this is becoming an excellent one. When it reopens, try a plug or flashy spinner in the weedy margins for quick results or alternatively lay a small herring on one of the shallower gravel bars.

The other two ponds are much smaller and relatively shallow. They used to get overfished and consequently the fish were shy. Local anglers used flavoured boilies to good effect for the carp and tench and bread or maggots for the bream and smaller fish.

Fishery Rules

Not known.

Facilities on Site

Car park.

KNOTFORD LAGOONS

Location (OS104:225462)

From Otley take the A659 road towards Pool in Wharfedale. After approximately 1½ miles, turn left onto the old road running between the two lagoons. A car park has been provided on the left.

Fishery Controller

There are two lakes on the site. The smaller one belongs to Bradford No. 1 Angling Association for members only. The other, alongside the River Wharfe, belongs to the Leeds & District Amalgamated Society of Anglers and can be fished on a day ticket.

Water and Stock

Both lakes, of approximately 5 acres, hold much the same stock, bream, common carp, mirror carp, chub, perch, roach, tench and a few trout.

Ticket Prices

Season fee. *See Angling Clubs section.* Day ticket for the Leeds and District ASA lagoon £2.50 from Angling and Country Sports tackle shop in Pool Road, Otley (Tel: 01943 462770), Pool Bridge Filling Station (Tel: 0113 2842105) and the many fishing tackle shops in Leeds.

Opening Hours

All year from dawn to dusk.

Description

Two landscaped lakes, both flooded extinct gravel workings, holding much the same stock and both fishing equally well. Carp are the main quarry, the large numbers attracting anglers from miles around, so the lakes can get very busy on bank holidays. Day ticket fishermen on the Leeds and District ASA water can expect to hook common and mirror carp to about 10lb with many over 20lb and there are rumours of at least one wily old fish expected to tip the scales at over 30lb. And there are plenty of them: bags of between ten and twenty fish are not uncommon. Best baits are boilies, sweetcorn or luncheon meat. Floating bread crust thrown well out sometimes attracts the older fish that have grown wise to boilies. The north-west corner of the Leeds & District ASA lake, by the Yorkshire Water Treatment Plant, is favoured by local anglers. Try maggots, bread or worms for the numerous tench, perch and roach.

Fishery Rules

No night fishing, no carp to be retained in keepnets and no wading.

Mr Wakelin from Wakefield lands a nice carp from Knotford Lagoon

Facilities on Site
Car park near the lake (no parking in the field).

LAKESIDE FISHERIES

Location (OS99:212999)
From Catterick village take the A6136 north. Just over the Swale river bridge turn left onto the B6271 towards Richmond. Go through Brompton-on-Swale and on the outskirts, where the river meets the road, turn right into Parkgate Lane. Turn left into the caravan field and follow the road to the lake, which lie of the left.

Fishery Controller
Mrs J. Bake, Lakeside Fisheries, Parkgate Lane, Brompton-on-Swale (Tel: 01748 812405. Mobile 0421685414).

Water and Stock
Two small lakes holding a good stock of rainbow trout from 1$^{1}/_{2}$lb to 10lb plus and a few wild browns.

Ticket Prices
Day tickets £5.00, from the fishing hut. All fish taken must be purchased at £1.60 per pound. Anglers must take the first fish after

which catch-and-release is permitted.

Opening Times

All year from 0800 hrs until dusk. Closed on Tuesdays.

Description

It's almost like fishing in someone's garden at this pretty, well tended fishery. Access to the well tended grassy bank is very easy and a small car park is only yards from the water's edge. Because the water is crystal clear it's a good stalking fishery. Stocked regularly with quality rainbow trout, these miniature attractive lakes benefit from copious amounts of crystal clear water which brings in a constant supply of insect life. It's often easy to see the trout and casting directly to a feeding fish, with a tadpole for instance, will often induce a take. Leave your heavy sinking lines at home and use a floater or possibly a sink-tip. Natural fly life, in season, includes damsels, buzzers, may fly and pond olives. Try Black or Green Buzzers, a selection of Goldheads, Damsel nymphs and Montanas.

Fishery Rules

Barbless hooks only. One fly per cast. No boobys. Damaged trout to be killed and paid for. Trout must be killed quickly with a priest. No dogs. No spectators. Limit of 14 rods only.

Facilities on Site

Car park, extensively equipped fishing hut and tackle hire £3.00 per day.

LANGLANDS LAKE

Location (OS92:172053)

From Richmond take the road north towards Ravensworth. After about 4 miles turn left to Gayles. Go through Gayles and Dalton villages to Newsham. Turn left in Newsham towards Barningham. On the outskirts of the village turn right and continue down the long lane, keeping right half way down, to the fishery.

Fishery Controller

Jeff and Sue Wilkinson, Langlands Farm, Barningham, Richmond DL11 7ED (Tel: 01833 621317).

Water and Stock

One man-made lake holding rainbows averaging 3lb with some bigger grown-on fish up to about 8lb.

Ticket Prices

Day ticket £9.00, half day and evening £5.00 and father and son ticket £12.00. All fish taken must be purchased at £1.70 per pound. Eight rods per day maximum.

Opening Times

Open all year from dawn to dusk.

Description

A kidney shaped lake, excavated in a pretty setting alongside a stream, Langlands holds a generous stock of hard fighting rainbows. A car park leads directly onto the level grassy banks, so access is easy. A maximum of eight rods a day means that there's always space available to move around the lake in search of feeding trout. Casting is easy because of the lack of tree cover but the wind can be troublesome at times. When it is windy it's worth trying a Walker's Wake fly on the surface. Often skittering the fly in the ripple will induce a take. Floating lines or sink tips are all that are needed here. Try nymphs or buzzers. Black, brown or green are usually the best colours.

Fishery Rules

Barbless hooks only. Single fly. Size 10 maximum. No lures. No wading. No pets permitted on the farm. Access to the lake only, no access to farmland. A fishing return is required.

Facilities on Site

Car park and toilet.

LANGTON PONDS

Location (OS99:296962)

From the A1 at Brompton-on-Swale, take the B6271 towards Bolton-on-Swale. Follow this road to Great Langton. The ponds are on the right in the village.

Fishery Controller

Richmond and District Angling Society. *See Angling Clubs section.*

Water and Stock

Two small ponds holding a very large stock of coarse fish including bream, carp, eels, perch, pike, roach, rudd and tench.

Ticket prices

Season fees, *see Angling Clubs section*. Weekly tickets £15.00 adult, £7.50 junior and daily tickets £5.00 adult and £2.50 junior. From the Richmond Angling Centre and Gilsan Sports, Richmond.

Opening Times

All year from dawn until dusk.

Description

These very popular mature ponds sit in a landscaped garden area with plenty of trees to provide welcome shade in the summer months. Although cloudy, the water is fairly rich in aquatic life and able to support a huge stock of coarse fish. Bank access is fairly easy to all of the 40 pegs on each lake. The water tends to be weedy in places but the carp and tench seem to like the spaces between the patches of lilies. It's best to use strong tackle because the carp, which can run to 20lb, will head for the weed every time. Use larger baits when fishing for the carp and tench as the smaller roach and rudd tend to take casters and maggots very quickly. The tench average 3lb or 4lb, with some fish over 8lb. For the dedicated roach angler there are lots of fish in the 1lb to 1½lb bracket and they're fond of casters and hemp.

Fishery Rules

One rod only.

Facilities on Site

None.

LARKFIELD TARN

Location (OS104:215395)

From Leeds take the A65 towards Wharefedale. In Rawdon village turn right to Lakefield, then follow Canada Road to the Tarn.

Controller

Bingley Angling Club. *See Angling Clubs section.*

Water & Stock

A small pleasantly situated small tarn holding a good stock of coarse fish. Plenty of small roach, rudd and perch to be had.

Ticket Prices

Members only. *See Angling Clubs section.*

Opening Times

All year from dawn to dusk.

LEEMING RESERVOIR

Location (OS104:040341)

From Keighley take the A629 road to Denholme. Just through the village at Denholme Gate, turn right onto the B6141 Oxenhope Road. In about 3½ miles the reservoir is alongside the road on the left.

Fishery Controller
Bradford City Angling Association. *See Angling Clubs section.*

Water and Stock
A 22 acre supply reservoir holding a good stock of both brown and rainbow trout.

Ticket Prices
Day tickets £5.00 from The Lamb Inn, Denholme Road, Oxenhope (Tel: 01535 643061), and the fishing tackle shops in Bradford and Keighley.

Opening Times
March 15th to September 30th. Sunday 0900 hrs until dusk and weekdays 0700 hrs until dusk.

Description
This moderately sized Pennine reservoir may seem a little daunting at first but it does offer some excellent trout fishing for those who persevere. The fly fishing is particularly good on the few days when there is a near flat calm. Try the evenings though when the fish seem to come to the surface. A small black fly tied with white wings is a favourite. Most people fish with bait though, worms being the favourite, although some anglers prefer chrysalis. When the conditions are right, you can have a lot of fun on floating chrysalis. Fishing alongside the wall is good, but no fishing is permitted from the wall itself. A flashy spinner, deep down, can often interest a big trout. Generally the fish average about $^{3}/_{4}$lb but as always there are some much bigger wild and grown-on fish. You may be lucky and find one in excess of 4lb, but they are few and very shy.

Fishery Rules
No keepnets. No cereal baits. No trout less than 12 inches to be taken and only two in any one day. No fishing from the dam wall.

Facilities on Site
Small car park.

LEIGHTON RESERVOIR

Location (OS99:160785)
Situated midway between upper Nidderdale and Wensleydale on Masham Moor alongside the scenic road from Lofthouse to Masham. The road passes over a bridge on one arm of the water, close to the fishing office.

Fishery Controller

Mike Driver, Swinton Estate, The Estate Office, Swinton, Masham, Ripon, North Yorkshire (Tel: 01765 689224). Leighton Reservoir fishing hut (Tel: 01765 689024).

Water and Stock

There are two large reservoirs on site, Leighton and Roundhill, each approximately 105 acres. No fishing is permitted in Roundhill, the top reservoir. Leighton is regularly stocked with medium sized brown and rainbow trout, plus some browns to 5lb and rainbows to 10lb.

Ticket Prices

Season tickets range from £240.00 to £360.00 and are only obtainable from the Estate Office. Adult day tickets 0600 until 2200 hrs, or sunset, £12.00 for 4 fish. Evening tickets from 1700 hrs, £6.00 for 2 fish. Children, 10 years and under, accompanied by a ticket holder, fish free. Children 16 years and under, registered disabled and senior citizen tickets are £8.00 for 3 fish. Catch and release fishing is allowed after catching three fish. All short term tickets are issued from the fishing hut in the car park on the north side of the reservoir.

Opening Times

Fishing starts on the first Saturday in March and ends on the first Sunday in October. Dates are inclusive. Access to the water is between 0600 and 2200 hrs or sunset, whichever is earlier.

Description

This large tooth shaped reservoir is situated 800 feet above sea level, on the bleak side of Masham Moor and consequently suffers badly when strong winds blow. In common with most Dales reservoirs a deep valley has been dammed to produce a lake extending to 105 acres and at its deepest point nearly 100 feet deep. It is an upland reservoir, spring fed from numerous streams and the water can be peaty coloured although quite clear. The Swinton Estate runs an efficient put-and-take policy with a regular stocking throughout the season to maintain the generous stock of rainbows averaging 2½lb. There are also many fish in the 4lb bracket and some well into double figures. Because it was created by damming the small streams feeding the tiny River Burn, there are lots of small wild brown trout to be caught. They tend to be greedy and can be a nuisance especially in the area away from the wall. Fishing close to the dam-wall on the south side is popular and productive, as is the

Leighton Reservoir on a calm day.
Three anglers try their luck from the overflow

area by the overflow. In the past, large numbers of rainbows have been taken from here including the fishery record for rainbow trout, held by a Stockton angler, a beautiful grown-on fish of 18lb 4oz.

During windy conditions try a sedge or large bushy brown hackled fly, or a Daddy-Long-Legs, skimmed across the ripples. It's surprising how often a trout will be brought to the surface by this method and the fish are usually large so use a hefty leader and expect a savage take. Another popular method is to very slowly retrieve a large lure, anything black with a green or orange beard, along the stony bed near the wall. Patience is needed but the result can be worth the effort. Try to visit when an easterly wind blows and fish in the popular hot-spot beneath the wall, or better still go on one of those infrequent days when there is a flat calm.

Best Flies

Favourite lures are Dawson's Olive and Maid Marion although anything in black is good. Orange and yellow muddlers do well in the wind. Most of the nymphs are popular, Pheasant Tail, Damsel, PVC and in season Mayfly nymphs and Daddy-Long-Legs. For wet fly fishing try an Invicta, Peter Ross or an early March Brown.

Fishery Rules

Fly fishing only using barbless or de-barbed hooks. One rod only. No fish less than 10 inches to be taken. Fishermen must complete a daily return of catches. 'NIL' returns are also required as they are important for efficient stock management.

Facilities on site

Fishing hut, toilet and car park.

LINDA'S LAKE

Location (OS104:052389)

From Keighley take the A644 road towards Halifax. In about 2 miles, whilst travelling up the Worth Valley, turn right at a large signpost showing the Bronte Caravan Park. Travel down the hill to the lake.

Fishery Controller

Keighley Angling Club. *See Angling Clubs section.*

Water and Stock

One tiny lake containing most species of coarse fish, mostly small. It's a surprisingly attractive lake, popular with junior anglers.

Ticket Prices

Season tickets only. *See Angling Clubs section.*

Opening Times

During the coarse fishing season, 0830 hrs to dusk.

Fishery Rules

No cereal ground bait. No fishing between the viewing point and Waterfalls Lane Bridge.

Facilities on Site

Car park.

LINDLEY WOOD RESERVOIR

Location (OS104:215485)

From Otley take the B6451 road towards Summerbridge. Stay on this road and in about 3 miles it crosses the end of Lindley Wood reservoir.

Fishery Controller

Farnley Hall Estate Office, Farnley, near Otley (Tel: 01943 463031).

Water and Stock

One beautiful reservoir of approximately 120 acres holding brown and rainbow trout.

Ticket Prices

Season tickets only. Fees unknown. Apply to Estate Office between 0930 and 1300 hrs.

Opening times

Dawn to dusk during the trout fishing season.

Description

The lowest of the four reservoirs in the Washburn valley, this is the only one where the fishing rights are still in private hands. Farnley Hall Estate owns the riparian rights to the reservoir and the River Washburn from the reservoir outflow downstream to where it joins the River Wharfe. It's a put and take fishery, with the water kept well stocked with quality browns and rainbows averaging about 2lb. There are many grown-on fish in the 4lb and 5lb bracket and a few rainbows over the magical 10lb. The reservoir is quite shallow at the top end by the road bridge, a popular spot when there's enough water. Yorkshire Water have a policy of "running down" this reservoir in the summer months which means that it's often only about half full. But of course that means that all the fish are congregated in one half. It's the only reservoir where fly fishing from the wall is permitted and that's a good place to try. Or when the reservoir is full try dry fly near the road bridge at the top end. A large bushy sedge skittered across the surface in the wind under the bridge often brings results.

Best Flies:

Ace of Spades, Viva and Montana Nymph. Almost anything in black with green or orange brings results. Walker's Sedge and Daddy-Long-Legs are good when in season.

Fishery Rules

Fly fishing only.

Facilities on Site

Car parks by the B6451 road bridge and near the entrance to the reservoir house by the wall.

LUMLEY MOOR RESERVOIR

Location (OS99:224777)

From Ripon take the B6265 Pateley Bridge road. After approximately 4 miles at Risplith turn right to Grantley. About 1/2 mile through the village turn right to Lumley Farm. The reservoir is at the end of the track.

Fishery Controller

Ripon Angling Club. *See Angling Clubs section.*

Water and Stock

A typical Pennine reservoir of about 10 acres supporting a good head of wild and stocked brown trout. A pretty spot to fish. Try it when a south-easterly blows over the dam wall.

Ticket Prices

Season tickets only. *See Angling Clubs section.*

Opening Times

Dawn to dusk, during the trout fishing season.

MALHAM TARN

Location (OS98:895668)

From the A65 road between Hellifield and Gargrave take a left at Coniston Cold village onto the small road signposted Bell Busk. Follow the road through Aireton to Malham village. Take the road north leading to Malham Cove and after about 3 miles, at Water Houses, turn right into Malham Tarn Field Centre.

Fishery Controller

The Malham Tarn Field Centre on behalf of the National Trust and Field Studies Council (Tel: 01729 830331).

Water and Stock

One natural lake, over 153 acres, holding mainly wild brown trout and a few perch.

Ticket Prices

Day tickets, weekdays £6.00 for 4 fish. Boats £7.00 extra. Senior citizen and children under 16 £3.00. Weekends and bank holidays, £6.00 for 4 fish. Boats £12.00. No concessions. Fishing is permitted only from one of four boats which must be booked in advance. Maximum of three anglers to a boat.

Opening times

Trout season May 1st to September 30th. Perch fishing from July 1st to October 31st.

Fishing is from 0900 until 2100 hrs or sunset whichever comes first.

Description

Malham Tarn is one of only two truly natural lakes in the Yorkshire Dales. It is a delightful place to fish, not only because of its spectacular setting but also because it is at the centre of a nature reserve and wildlife conservation area. In order to protect the wildlife's habitat access to the lake's bank is not permitted, nor is fishing allowed in the small bays. Fishing is only allowed from a boat and as there are only four available, the tarn is very much underfished. But be warned, the water is very exposed and when strong winds blow across the top of the Pennines fishing from a boat can be difficult. The water is fairly shallow, but extremely rich in aquatic life so it supports a huge stock of small wild brown trout that breed in the numerous streams feeding the lake. The lake is not artificially stocked so all the fish are wild. Large bags of browns are not uncommon with the fish averaging about 1/2lb although the occasional 3lb fish has been recorded.

Be prepared for the weather and wear the buoyancy aids provided. Remember, during the day in summer it can be hot and sunny, but in early and late season it can get very cold. But it's great fishing. After a day on the exposed water of Malham Tarn you cannot fail to feel invigorated and may also have a few wild browns for the pot!

Popular flies

Wets. Reservoir types - Black & Peacock Spider, Red Tag, Butcher, Peter Ross and Mallard & Claret.

Drys. Any time - Hawthorn, Black Gnat (with white wings) and Greenwell's Glory. In season - Daddy-Long-Legs, Mayfly and Sedges.

Nymphs. Buzzers are favourite in red, black, or green.

Lures. Any of the popular flashy types will catch trout but they also attract the perch.

Fishery Rules

Boat fishing only. Fishing by fly and worm. No spinning, ground baiting or live baiting permitted. Under 16s must be accompanied by an adult. All fish caught must be recorded. Limit 4 fish over 11 inches. Anglers must not land anywhere except at one of the boathouses. Use of lead weights is prohibited.

Facilities on site

Car parking, toilets, accommodation.

MARAN LAKES

Location (OS105:487501)

From the A1, take the B1224 road from Wetherby towards York.

After about 4 miles, just after Bilton village, turn right into Marston Wyse Trout Farm.

Fishery Controller

Mr M. J. And Mrs A. Rhodes, Marston Wyse Trout Farm, Long Marston, York YO5 8NH (Tel: 01904 738383 or 0800 137660, Pager 01426 697078).

Water and Stock

Currently 4 lakes totalling 5 acres holding mainly rainbow trout averaging 1¾lb. Some fish to 10lb, and a few browns.

Ticket Prices

Day ticket £15.00 for 3 fish including catch and release. Half day £10.00 for 2 fish including catch and release, sporting tickets, 5 hours £6.00 and 2½ hours £4.00.

Opening Times

Open all year. Dawn to dusk.

Description

This intelligently constructed complex of lakes looks set to become popular with anglers who need easy access, open backcasting space, uncrowded banks and lively trout. The wind can be a bit of a problem but there is plenty of space to move and get it at your back. All the lakes have been designed in a variety of shapes, each one different from its neighbour, so there is a quiet corner for everyone. Lake number 4, a catch and release water holding only rainbows in double figures, will appeal to those anglers searching for big fish. Don't forget to use strong leaders! Excavated in 1997, the complex and surrounding area need time to mature. A continuing programme of work will ensure that further lakes are opened as required. The fish certainly appear to have settled into their new surroundings well. Some notable bags to date include one angler who landed 73 rainbows in 5 hours of fishing, another who had 41 fish in 2½ hours and yet another who had three rainbows in three casts for 28lb! The fishery record rainbow stands at 10lb 8oz. Without doubt, the most popular flies are goldheads tied as Hares Ear and Damsel and Green Nymph. Buzzers are also very popular in black or green.

Fishery Rules

Barbless hooks only. No boobies or tandems. Maximum 2 flies. Please keep to permanent pegs. No night fishing. Children under 14 must be accompanied by an adult.

Facilities on Site

Car park close to lakes and toilets.

NUNROYD POND

Location (OS104:198414)

Situated in Nunroyd Park alongside the A65 between Yeadon and Guiseley in West Yorkshire. Turn into the park and the lake is on the right near the main car park.

Fishery Controller

Airborough and District Angling Association. *See Angling Clubs section.*

Water and Stock

One tiny lake containing small bream, chub, crucian carp, gudgeon, roach, rudd and tench. There are 20 fishing pegs and 3 purpose built stages for disabled anglers.

Ticket Prices

Season tickets only. *See Angling Clubs section.*

Opening Times

All year from dawn to dusk.

Fishery Rules

No night fishing. Barbless hooks only.

Facilities on Site

Car park. Good access for wheelchair disabled anglers.

THE OAKS FISHERIES

Location (OS99:451762)

From the A1, take the A168(T) towards Topcliffe. About 1/2 mile after passing over the River Swale, turn right towards Dalton. Pass through the village on the road towards Sessay. Two hundred yards after crossing the main railway line turn left by the first bungalow. Continue down the track and then turn left again to the lakes.

Fishery Controller

Mrs Rachel Kay, The Oaks, Sessay, Thirsk, North Yorkshire YO7 3BG (Tel: 01845 501321).

Water and Stock

Three lakes of various sizes holding a large stock of most coarse fish.

Ticket Prices

Adult day tickets £6.00, under 14s accompanied by an adult £4.00. Available on the bank. Half day, after 1600 hrs, £4.00.

Opening Times

Most of the year, 0700 hrs until dusk.

Description

This is a fishery for the pleasure angler looking to catch some good carp and tench. There are three intelligently designed lakes in the development, each one an interesting shape. They've been excavated in a small copse and much of the bankside vegetation has been trimmed and left in place to add to the attractiveness of the site. Willow lake, the largest of the group, holds specimen common and mirror carp in excess of 20lb and a good stock of tench. The water is fairly shallow in the margins, shelving away to between 10 and 12 feet near the central wooded island. There's a limit of sixteen rods permitted on this lake. The Oaks is a match lake, 35 pegs, teeming with smaller fish including, bream, carp, perch roach rudd and tench. It's an attractive lake with a crescent shaped island reaching out into the middle. All the usual match baits, maggots, pinkies and squats, will take fish. And finally, there are more carp and tench to be had by a maximum of twenty anglers on Firs Lake. Carp to 10lb and lots of good tench all feed freely on the usual baits. Pork luncheon meat is popular along with bread, but it's a good place to try your home made concoction. There are gravel paths around the site to make access to all the lakes easy and the car park is very close. Access for disabled anglers is good particularly to Willows lake where fishing stages have been specially constructed.

Fishery Rules

One ticket for one rod. No night fishing. No ground baiting. No keepnets, except during matches. Barbless hooks only. Excess baits must be taken away.

Facilities on Site

Car park and toilets.

OAK TREE LEISURE ANGLING

Location (OS100:547653)

From York, take the A19 north towards Easingwold. At the Tollerton crossroads, turn right towards Huby, the lakes are 1 1/2 miles on the right.

Fishery Controller

Mr Tony Bowes, Tumbledown Cottage, Sutton on Forest, York YO6 1DT (Tel: 01347 810686).

Water and Stock

There are two lakes on site, one a specimen lake of $1^{1/2}$ acres and the other a match fishing lake of $1^{1/4}$ acres, both holding a large stock of coarse fish including barbel, bream, carp, chub, ide, orfe, roach, rudd and tench.

Ticket Prices

Day tickets, adult £5.00, junior 16 and under £3.00, senior citizen £3.00 and half day, after 1500 hrs, £3.00.

Opening Times

First Sunday in March to the end of November, 0700 hrs until dusk.

Description

This is a good venue for the dedicated carp angler. The T shaped specimen lake holds common carp, best fish 22lb, ghost carp to 10lb, grass carp to 19lb and crucians to $2^{1/2}$lb, and is a good place to try out your home brewed favourite bait. Boilies and bean baits are banned. However, bread and luncheon meat are always good for the carp. Apart from carp, there are lots of other coarse fish to be caught from one of the 38 fishing pegs around the lake. The tench, running to 6lb, are worth a try, but if you're not tempted by the usual coarse fish species, try for an ide. It's Scandinavian, a cross between a roach and a chub, and that's just what it looks like. Best baits tend to be maggot, corn, bread or caster. For the match fisherman the star shaped lake, with 39 pegs, is interesting and productive. Its shape means that there's always a place to get out of the wind and there's a good variety of coarse fish, ranging from a few ounces to over 6lb, to be caught. The normal match baits are the best. Try bread, caster, corn, maggots, pinkies or squats. Solid pathways have been constructed around all the flat bankside giving easy access. Disabled anglers should be able to reach the pegs near the car parks with little difficulty.

Fishery Rules

No method feeders to be used. No keepnets, except during matches. Barbless hooks only, not microbarbs. 1kg of groundbait only. No boilies or bean baits.

Facilities on Site

Two car parks, toilets, very easy access for disabled anglers.

OLDE MILL LAKE

Location (OS99: 348936)

From Northallerton, take the A167 towards Darlington. Just past the railway bridge turn left onto the B6271 to Yafforth. Turn left facing the entrance to Jenkins Lake and, in about 3/4 mile, turn right immediately by the railway bridge. Turn first left and the lake is at the bottom of the lane.

Fishery Controller

Andy Scaiff, Northallerton Angling Centre, 3 East Road, Northallerton (Tel: 01609 779140).

Water and Stock

One small lake, approximately 1/2 acre, holding King Carp only.

Ticket Prices

Annual membership covering this lake and Jenkins Lake £40.00, from Northallerton Angling Centre, Richmond Angling Centre, *See Fishing Tackle Shops section,* the Guisborough Angling Centre (Tel: 01287 630687) and the Aycliffe Angling Centre (Tel: 01325 301876).

Opening Times

All year from dawn until dusk.

Description

This small lake is something of an oddity. It's unusual to have a water dedicated to carp, and King Carp at that, but that's all that has been stocked. And it's the answer to a dedicated carp angler's prayers. There are plenty of fish in the range 1lb to 15lb and they are hard fighters, so be sure you use strong tackle. Best baits are bread, luncheon meat and sweetcorn. Try a floating crust when you see the bigger fish rolling in the sunshine. Otherwise sweetcorn laid on the bottom should do the trick. Access is good around all the bankside.

Fishery Rules

No night fishing.

Facilities on Site

Car park.

PROSPECT FARM POND

Location (OS104:253548)

From Harrogate take the A59 Skipton Road. At the first roundabout take left onto the B6161 road to Otley. In about 1 1/4 miles turn right into Penny Pot Lane. Pass the Army Apprentices College Barracks and in approximately 1 mile, turn left over a cattle-grid, onto the signposted farm road.

Fishery Controller

Mr Walmsley, Prospect House Farm, Penny Pot Lane, Harrogate (Tel: 01423 504166).

Water and Stock

One small man-made pond holding bream, carp, perch, roach, rudd, tench and the odd wild trout.

Ticket prices

Day ticket £3.00 obtainable, prior to fishing, from the farmhouse.

Opening Times

All year from dawn to dusk.

Description

This picturesque small pond, lying in a secluded valley close to Oak Beck, offers quiet fishing in lovely surroundings. Thanks to a liberal stocking policy the water contains a lot of fish, mainly coarse, but there are a few trout. None of the fish are particularly large but they are plentiful and they have good appetites. The lake's banks are attractively landscaped and one side is tree lined providing some shade in the hot summer months. There's easy access to the entire bankspace which can accommodate up to fifteen anglers. With an overall depth of about 6 feet the lake is easy to fish. Expect heavy bags of small carp, perch, roach and rudd to float fished maggot or casters. Cars can be driven right down to the lakeside.

Fishery Rules

Barbless hooks only. No keepnets if the weather is too hot.

Facilities on Site

Car park at the lakeside.

QUEEN MARY'S PONDS

Location (OS99:305749)

Take the A6108 Masham Road from Ripon. After about 1 mile turn right into Park Lane, near the golf course, and follow the track for 1¼ miles to the car park near the lakes.

Fishery Controller

Bradford No.1 Angling Association. *See Angling Clubs section.*

Water and Stock

Four varied small ponds, the largest of which is noted for its huge carp, bream, roach and tench. The smaller ponds hold perch, pike and tench.

Ticket Prices

Season tickets and members permits only. *See Angling Clubs section.*

Opening Times

During the coarse fishing season. Fishing is allowed one hour either side of sunrise and sunset.

Description

These are four irregularly shaped ponds located in marshy ground alongside the River Ure. In summer the area is somewhat overgrown and the lakes themselves weedy, but the fishing is still good. Carp fishermen will be interested in the bigger ponds that hold carp over 20lb as well as some hefty bream and good stock of perch and roach. Try a floating crust for the carp. It's exciting fishing and seems to do well here. The smaller ponds are primarily pike venues. The fish are not big but they are plentiful and scavenge freely in the weedy margins. Best methods are dead-bait laid in the margins or a flashy spinner.

Fishery Rules

Thirty members and guests only per day.

Facilities on Site

Car park.

RACECOURSE LAKE

Location (OS99:329695)

From the centre of Ripon take the B6265 road towards Boroughbridge. The racecourse is on the right on the outskirts of the town. Cars can be taken down to the side of the lake.

Fishery Controller

Ripon Piscatorials. *See Angling Clubs section.*

Water and Stock

A long featureless lake, with islands to break the monotony, located in the centre of the racecourse. It contains bream, carp, roach, rudd, tench and a few trout.

Ticket Prices

Season ticket. *See Angling Clubs section.* Day ticket £4.00 from Ripon Angling Centre, North Street (Tel: 01765 604666).

Opening times

Open all year except on a few race meeting days.

Description

This oddly positioned lake, right in the centre of Ripon racetrack, is one of the best coarse fishing lakes in the area. It's a featureless lake set in a flat and uninteresting area and it can be difficult to fish on windy days. But don't be put off, it's a great venue for carp fishermen. Mirrors and commons to 25lb are prolific and they seem to like the more traditional baits, bread crust or boiled potato. However, they'll also take boilies as will the bream which seem to do well in the shallow water. There are large shoals that roam around the islands - interest one of these and a bag of 60lb to 70lb is the likely result. The lake also teems with perch, roach and rudd. They are small, but big bags can be had if you locate one of the big shoals. Try maggots or casters for these fish and you'll have a good day.

Rules

No night fishing.

Facilities on Site

Car parking area.

RASKELF LAKE

Location (OS100:476715)

From Boroughbridge take the road to Brafferton. Turn left in the village towards Raskelf. In about 4 miles, just over the railway bridge, turn right to the lake.

Fishery Controller

Bradford No.1 Angling Association. *See Angling Clubs section.*

Water and Stock

A small lake holding most varieties of coarse fish.

Ticket Prices

Season tickets only. *See Angling Clubs section.*

Opening Times

Open all year, sunrise to sunset.

Facilities on Site

None.

RAYGILL TROUT FISHERY

Location (OS103:944456)

The fishery is situated in a disused quarry near the village of Lothersdale approximately 5 miles south-west of Skipton. From the village, with the Hare and Hounds pub on the right, take the road towards Colne. In about 1 mile, at The Fold, turn left into a potholed

Playing an acrobatic rainbow in the quarry lake at Raygill Trout Fishery

unmarked road leading to a caravan site. The fishery lies about $^1/_2$ mile down on the left.

Fishery Manager and Owner

Bernard Clement, 1 Raygill Cottage, Lothersdale, Nr Skipton, North Yorkshire BD20 8HH (Tel: 01535 632500).

Water and Stock

Four lakes each containing large stocks of brown and rainbow trout running well into double figures.

Ticket Prices

Top Lake. Prices to be announced.

Upper Lake. £2.00 an hour or £12.00 for a full day (6 hours plus). Catch and release or any fish taken to be purchased for £1.75 per lb. Boats are available for £3.00 per session.

Lower lakes. Full day £14.00 for 3 fish, OAP/junior £9.00 for 2 fish, half day (5 hours) £9.00 for 2 fish.

Opening times

Every day except Christmas Day from 0830 hrs until dusk.

Description

Raygill fishery lies in a former quarry site nestling in picturesque but little-known Lothersdale close to Skipton. There are currently three lakes, one of 8½ acres, set in the old quarry, one of 3½ and one of 1 acre lying in a landscaped area overlooked by the fishing hut. Fly fishing only is permitted with dry flies, wet flies and lures all acceptable. Because of the prolific fly life in the surrounding countryside there is nearly always a good rise particularly in the morning or evening. Daily rod averages of approximately five fish are normal with many regular fishermen achieving two and three times that catch rate. The fish are ferocious. Strong tackle is needed if you're looking to catch these hard fighting trout which, when hooked, make a fly reel scream and will often strip line down to the backing.

Another lake, soon to be opened, promises to be an excellent venue for those seeking large trout. It will hold both browns and rainbows with an average size in excess of 10lb and, because all fish caught in this lake must be carefully returned to the water, it will soon become a noted venue for monster fish.

The upper quarry lake is a crystal clear spring fed water which teems with the insect life necessary to sustain the high level of stocks it contains. In places the lake is over 40 feet deep so fish have plenty of room to move. When hooked they go deep and far away, so use a strong point. Typically over 5lb breaking strain. There are fish in this lake over 20lb and no doubt some which could exceed the British rod caught record, but they tend to be well down in the deep water. The water is so clear and deep at the fringes that very large trout often cruise right up to the bank seeming to look you straight in the eye! That can be frustrating on quiet days. In common with most Pennine venues, fishing is difficult on some days because of the strong winds. It doesn't seem to worry the fish, though, and a surface ripple is often better than a flat calm when dry fly or nymph fishing.

Below the fishing hut the area has been landscaped to include two lakes both of which hold double-figure browns and rainbows. The largest lake, some 20 feet deep, and sheltered from the worst of the winds, is popular. Fishing in the shallower smaller lake is often better in the evening when the sun's gone off the water.

The fishery record for rainbow trout is 21lb and for brown 15lb 5oz, but there are bigger fish to be had for those who persevere.

Popular flies
Lures. The flashy types - Sweeney Todd, Zonkers, Appetizers, Muddlers, Montanas and Gold Heads in yellow, white, orange or black.
Wets. Reservoir types - Black & Peacock Spider, Red Tag, Butcher, Peter Ross and Mallard & Claret.
Drys. Any time - Hawthorn, Black gnat (with white wings) and Greenwell's Glory. In season - Daddy-Long-Legs, Mayfly and Sedges.
Nymphs. Buzzers are favourite in red, black, or green. Also Pheasant Tail, G.R.H.E and tin head nymphs.
Fishery Rules
Fly fishing only using barbless or debarbed hooks. All brown trout to be returned carefully to the water. No knotted landing nets.
Facilities on Site
Tackle and flies for sale, boats and casting tuition. To book a lesson telephone Ken Wharton on 01756 752387.

RIPLEY CASTLE LAKE

Location (OS99:281608)
Ripley village sits on the A61 Harrogate to Ripon road just north of where it crosses the River Nidd. Turn into the village and then take a left by the church. The Estate Office is clearly marked on the right.
Fishery Controller
Steve Atkinson, Ripley Estate Office, Ripley, near Harrogate (Tel: 01423 770152) between 0900 hrs and 1700 hrs.
Water and Stock
One 5 acre lake holding bream, carp, chub, perch, roach, rudd and tench.
Ticket Prices
Season tickets only, £50.00, from the Estate Office. The Castle owners reserve the right to close the lake for occasional events.
Opening times
Open all year. Fishing is permitted from 0600 until 2200 hrs.
Description
This beautiful landscaped lake built in the shadow of Ripley Castle offers really good coarse fishing. There are 25lb carp, chub to 4lb, perch to 3lb, roach to 2lb and tench to 6lb. Formed by damming a small tributary of the River Nidd, Thornton Beck, the lake gets a

constant supply of fresh water. Normally it is clear but, after heavy rain, it can be coloured. It's a popular venue for carp anglers although night fishing is not permitted. The water holds carp to 23lb, which feed freely on maggot, caster, luncheon meat, or alternatively traditional bread crust or even potato chunks will tempt fish. Maggots or casters usually account for good bags of roach, some over 2lb, rudd and perch to 3lb. Luncheon meat or sweetcorn are worth a try for the tench.

Fishery Rules

Maximum 30 rods. Boilies and nut baits are not allowed. One rod only and no carp rigs. Unaccompanied children under 16 not allowed. No night fishing.

Facilities on Site

Car parking, toilets and gift shop.

ROBERT'S POND

Location (OS104:052389)

From Keighley centre take the road towards Skipton. In about 1/2 mile, at the start of the new trunk road, the lake is on the left.

Fishery Controller

Keighley Angling Club. *See Angling Clubs section.*

Water and Stock

One very popular tiny lake, in what used to be the river bed, containing a good head of bream, carp, chub, pike, roach and tench.

Ticket Prices

Season tickets only. *See Angling Clubs section.*

Opening Times

All year, dawn to dusk.

Fishery Rules

No night fishing.

Facilities on Site

None.

ROECLIFFE BRICK PONDS

Location (OS99:386659)

From Boroughbridge take the Roecliffe Road. After passing under the A1 by-pass bridge take first left. The lakes are on the right.

Fishery Controller

Boroughbridge and District Angling Club. *See Angling Clubs section.*

Water and Stock
A handful of small ponds holding a good stock of coarse fish.
Ticket Prices
Season tickets only. *See Angling Clubs section.*
Opening Times
All year from dawn to dusk.
Fishery Rules
No dogs. No night fishing.
Facilities on Site
None.

ROGER'S POND

Location (OS99:329691)
Roger's Pond is located at the southern end of the Ripon Racecourse Lake. From the centre of Ripon, take the B6265 road towards Boroughbridge. Turn into the racecourse grounds on the right on the outskirts of the town. Follow the left bank of the long Racecourse Lake down to the end where you will find Roger's Pond.
Fishery Controller
Bradford No.1 Angling Association. *See Angling Clubs section.*
Water and Stock
One small lake holding bream, carp, perch, roach, and some tench.
Ticket prices
Season tickets. *See Angling Clubs section.*
Day tickets £4.00 from the Ripon Angling Centre, North Street (Tel: 01765 604666).
Opening Times
Dawn to dusk during the coarse fishing season.
Description
This tiny lake, situated on Ripon Racecourse, is somewhat dominated by its much bigger neighbour. However because of its size and the large numbers of fish it holds, it is preferred by many fishermen. The bream and tench are the main quarries here with corn, worms and meat baits all popular. Maggots, hemp and bread will attract the roach and perch. As the lake is surrounded by flat land it is badly affected by the wind. Try to pick a day when it's calm.
Fishery Rules
No fishing on race meeting days.
Facilities on Site
Car park near the lake.

ROLEITH FISHERY

Location (OS99:377881)

From the A1, take the A684 through Morton-on-Swale and then turn right onto the A167. In about 2½ miles, in South Otterington, turn left. Then in approximately ½ mile, just before the railway bridge, turn left into Station Farm.

Fishery Controller

Keith and Carol Bowe, Roleith Fishery, Station Farm, South Otterington, Northallerton, North Yorkshire DL7 9JB (Tel: 01609 780263).

Water and Stock

One lake of approximately 1 acre holding a good head of coarse fish including bream, crucian carp, perch, roach and tench.

Ticket Prices

Season ticket £70.00, day ticket £5.00 and half day £3.00.

Opening Times

Open all year, except Christmas Day. 0700 hrs until sunset every day.

Description

This small attractive lake sits in a hollow about ¼ mile across a meadow from the farm. When the ground is dry, cars can be taken to the bankside. A main railway line runs on an embankment closeby. The lake is "tooth" shaped with trees and shrubbery, on the two longest sides, affording protection from the wind. Twenty solid fishing stages have been constructed and access around the entire bankspace is easy. The fish, which grow-on well here, are not massive but they are plentiful. Tench in excess of 4lb have been taken on sweetcorn. Heavy bags of crucian carp, in the 1lb to 2lb bracket, have been landed by anglers using cheese paste a favourite bait here. They like the deeper water near the toilet shed, except when they frolic in the reedy margins taking advantage of the sunshine. Maggots, hemp and casters are popular baits for the roach and perch. Bream, a recent addition to the water, should do well. Disabled anglers by appointment.

Fishery Rules

Barbless or microbarb hooks only. No keepnets. Groundbait limited to 1kg per peg, remaining bait not to be thrown into the water. No dogs. All fish to be returned.

Fishing for carp on the point at Roleith Fishery near Northallerton

Facilities on Site
Car park, toilets and rod hire. Light refreshments usually available.

ROUNDHAY PARK LAKE

Location (OS104:335375)
From the centre of Leeds, take the A58 Wetherby road. In Beechwood, turn left onto Princess Way and then immediately right into Park Avenue. Follow this road to the official car park.

Fishery Controller
Leeds and District Amalgamated Society of Anglers. *See Angling Clubs section.*

Water and Stock
One large lake holding bream, carp, chub, perch, pike, roach, rudd, tench and a few trout.

Ticket Prices
Season fee: *See Angling Clubs section.* Day tickets, adult £1.50, juniors 50p, from the Lakeside Cafe and the many fishing tackle shops in Leeds.

Opening Times
All year. The park opens at 0700 hrs and closes one hour after sunset.
Brief description
Waterloo Lake is an attractive water set in landscaped grounds providing excellent fishing on the outskirts of the city. Most people use maggots to tempt one of the large shoals of smaller fish, typically roach rudd and perch, but some set up carp rigs and try the proprietory baits for the bigger fish which average 6lb to 7lb. A favourite spot is near the old waterfall. The pike grow to be fairly large and double figure fish are common. Try laying a dead sprat in the deeper water. There are also some good trout to be had. Fishing with white maggots on a float rig is a good method for the trout.
Fishery Rules
No night fishing. Keepnets are only permitted between October 1st and March 14th. Trout under 10 inches to be returned. Three trout only to be taken in any one day. Bloodworm, joker and feedworm are banned. No fishing in the small upper lake.
Facilities on Site
Car park, cafe and toilets.

ROYDS HALL DAM

Location (OS104:147286)
From Bradford city centre, take the Huddersfield Road to Odsal Top. Continue along the A641 until it becomes Woodside Road. The dam is on the right.
Fishery Controller
Bradford No.1 Angling Association. *See Angling Clubs section.*
Water and Stock
A small ex-mill dam holding most kinds of coarse fish.
Ticket Prices
Day tickets, adults 70p and juniors 35p from Wibsey Angling, High Street, Wibsey.
Opening Times
Open all year from sunrise until sunset.
Description
This surprisingly attractive typical stone mill dam contains an impressive stock of bream and roach. Most anglers visit here for the bream - they are not big but if you can interest one of the large shoals, you'll have a good day. As always, the best baits are maggots and

bread, although some of the newer concoctions will attract the fish. There are also some nice roach, up to 2lb, which seem to like hemp seed. Access is a bit difficult in places where the stonework has crumbled, but otherwise it's good.

Fishery Rules

No night fishing.

Facilities on Site

None.

SANDWATH LAKE

Location (OS105:555371)

From Tadcaster take the A162 south towards Sherburn in Elmet. In Barkston Ash village turn left to Church Fenton then left again just before the railway bridge and the lake is on your left.

Fishery Controller

Leeds and District Amalgamated Society of Anglers. *See Angling Clubs section.*

Water and Stock

One pretty lake of 2½ acres teeming with bream, carp, chub, perch, pike, roach, rudd and tench. Reaching up to 6lb, the tench are worth a try. Use sweetcorn.

Ticket Prices

Season fee: *See Angling Clubs section.* No day tickets.

Opening Times

All year from dawn to dusk.

Fishery Rules

Gates must be kept locked at all times.

Facilities on Site

Large car park.

SCARHOUSE RESERVOIR

Location (OS99:067770)

From Pateley Bridge follow the road up Nidderdale passed Gouthwaite Reservoir to Lofthouse. Just outside the village, on the road to Middlesmoor, take a right turn into Yorkshire Water grounds and then follow the scenic road up the valley to the car park.

Fishery Controller

Nidderdale Angling Club. *See Angling Clubs section.*

Water and Stock

There are two 180 acre reservoirs on site. Fishing is not permitted in the top reservoir, Angram, but it is allowed in Scar House which holds a large stock of wild brown trout supplemented annually with a stocking of local browns up to 14 inches.

Ticket Prices

Day ticket £6.00 for 2 fish, junior £3.00. Available from the Post Offices in Glasshouses, Lofthouse (Tel: 01423 755203), Pateley Bridge (Tel: 01423 711201) and Summerbridge (Tel: 01423 780248). Also from the Reception at the Riverside Caravan Park, Pateley Bridge (Tel: 01423 711383) and The Royal Oak, Dacre Banks (Tel: 01423 780200).

Opening times

Open April 1st to September 30th from 0800 hrs to one hour after sunset, or 2100 hrs whichever is the latest.

Description

Situated high on the slopes of Great Whernside in Upper Nidderdale, Scar House Reservoir used to be one of the most inaccessible fishing sites in the Yorkshire Dales. All that changed when the old reservoir road was opened to visitors enabling cars to be taken to within a few hundred yards of the water's edge. Because of its lovely setting, this is without doubt a most attractive water to fish, but it can be wild. But any angler who is prepared to brave the prevailing winds will be rewarded with some exciting fishing for wild brown trout. Fishing is usually best on the right-hand side, when viewed from the dam wall, where a number of hillside streams have created small bays favoured by brown trout. The Scottish reservoir wet flies do well here as do the Yorkshire wets, fished fairly well down towards the bottom. Lures are also productive, almost anything in black will do. On the surface try an orange Muddler in the wind channels. Worm fishing, minnow and spinning are also permitted.

Popular flies

Dry. Early March Brown, Mayfly, Greenwell's Treacle Parkin or Sturdy's Fancy.

Wet. Snipe and Purple, Partridge and Orange or Invicta.

Lures. Virtually anything flashy in black or white.

Fishery Rules

No wading. No fishing from the dam wall. No keepnets. No hooks larger than size 12 except size 10 for mayfly. No lead shot. Cars must be left in the car park. Fishing returns notes to be left in the box in the car park.

Facilities on Site
Car parking and toilets.

SEMERWATER LAKE

Location (OS98:920872)
In Bainbridge take the road south for about 2 miles to Countersett. In the village turn left to Stalling Busk. Semerwater is on your right. There's a car park at the end of the lake.near the River Bain outflow.

Fishery Controller
Mr C. Metcalfe, Low Blean Farm, situated about 100 yards beyond the car park on the left (Tel: 01969 650295).

Water and Stock
A shallow glacial lake of approximately 100 acres holding large shoals of bream, some perch, roach and trout.

Ticket prices
Day ticket £3.50 for the south and east sides from Low Blean Farm, *see above*. Fishing on the other banks belongs to the Wensleydale Angling Club, *see Angling Clubs section*.

Opening times
Open all year from dawn until dusk.

Description
Nestling in a natural amphitheatre of rolling moorland, Semerwater possesses characteristics more akin to the Lake District than North Yorkshire. Its water is very clear and mostly shallow with an overall depth of 3 to 4 feet, although in some places the bottom does shelve away to 20 feet. In winter, after heavy rain, when the streams crashing down the fellsides of Raydale are swollen, Semerwater floods. It can virtually double its volume very quickly.

Strangely, despite the fact that the diminutive River Bain flowing through the lake is as famous for its wild brown trout fishing, Semerwater is a great bream water. The fish are not large, typically 1lb to 2lb, but they are there in large numbers. Indeed catches exceeding 100lb used to be common, but respectable sized bags over 60lb are now the order of the day. Maggots and small red-worms are best. Try using a quiver ledger rig just over the edge of one of the deeper shelves. The roach fishing is good too. Caught on the right day fish over 2lb can be expected. Small perch can be troublesome. On occasion water-skiers also use the water.

An attractive fishing peg at Hessay Pond

A boatful of anglers sets out towards the middle of the upper lake at Raygill Trout Fishery

Fishing near the picnic site at Stack Point on the vast Swinsty Reservoir

Fishery Rules
No night fishing. No camping in the car park.
Facilities on Site
Car parking.

SETTLER DAM

Location (OS104:215395)
From Keighley take the A650 to Stockbridge. In about 1/2 mile, turn left into Swine Lane and follow the road to Morton. The dam is in the village, on the left where the Otley Road crosses Bradup Beck.
Controller
Bingley Angling Club. *See Angling Clubs section.*
Water & Stock
A tiny dam built to serve a long gone mill. Its clear water holds plenty of smallish trout and coarse fish. Maggots are the best bait. Restricted fishing space.
Ticket Prices
Members only. *See Angling Clubs section.*
Opening Times
All year from dawn until dusk.
Fishery Rules
No night fishing.
Facilities on Site
None.

SHELF DAM

Location (OS104:149290)
From Bradford city centre take the Huddersfield Road to Odsal Top. Follow the Halifax Road A6036. Turn left into Shelf and then right again into Cock Hill Lane. The lake is on the right.
Fishery Controller
Bradford No.1 Angling Association. *See Angling Clubs section.*
Water and Stock
A tiny mill dam holding plenty of bream, carp, perch, roach and tench.
Ticket Prices
Season tickets only. *See Angling Clubs section.*
Opening Times
Open all year from sunrise until sunset.

Facilities on Site
None.

SHIELD FLY FISHING LAKE

Location (OS99:244908)
From Bedale take the Crakehall road. In the village turn right immediately over the bridge into Hackforth Road. In about 1/4 mile take the second lane on the right and continue down the track to Burtree Farm.
Fishery Controller
Shield Lake Fly Fishing Club, Mrs M. Shield, Burtree Farm, Crakehall, Bedale DL8 1LB (Tel: 01677 422833).
Water and Stock
Two lakes: one, about 1 1/2 acres, is stocked with mainly rainbow trout and a few browns, the other is a coarse fishing water holding bream, carp, chub, roach and tench.
Ticket prices
Trout fishing. Season ticket £130.00, day ticket £6.00 and evening tickets £4.00. All prices are for 2 fish which must be paid for at an additional £2.00 each.
Coarse fishing. Day ticket £5.00, evening £3.00 and juniors £3.00.
Opening Times
Trout fishing. From mid March to November 30th. 0700 until 2130 hrs.
Coarse fishing. All year. 0700 until 2130 hrs.
Description
An S shaped lake, with islands, excavated alongside a small stream, Shield's Lake is situated in a quiet hollow about 1/2 mile beyond the farm. The clear water, spring fed, is liberally stocked with nice full tailed rainbow trout averaging 1lb to 2lb with some bigger grown-on fish. There's lots of aquatic life present in the lake and washed in from the an underground spring, so the fish put on weight fairly quickly. On the right day, the fish are lively surface feeders, so nymphs or dry flies do well. Try buzzers in the surface film, or a Grey Duster, Ginger Quill or Greenwell's dry. Deeper in the water, Butcher's, G.R.H.E. nymphs, Pheasant Tail nymph and anything black will take fish.

A recent addition to this fishery, the coarse fishing pond looks set to become a favourite with anglers seeking to catch quality fish in pleasant surroundings. The pond has been nicely created near an underground spring from which it gets ample clean water. It is oval in shape with a string of islands joined by timber bridges. There are plenty of bream, common, crucian and mirror carp, chub, roach and tench to be had. Most of the proprietory baits do well but it's probably best to stick to the old favourites, bread, maggots and sweetcorn.

Fishery Rules

Trout lake: No lures. Barbless hooks or microbarb only. Maximum 7 rods. Coarse lake: Carp over 2lb not to be kept in keepnets or carp sacks, groundbait may only be used via a feeder or pole cup.

Facilities on Site

Car park.

SHIPTON LAKE

Location (OS105:553595)

Situated just off the A19(T) York to Northallerton Road at Shipton-by-Benningbrough.

Fishery Controller

Bradford City Angling Association. *See Angling Clubs section.*

Water and Stock

One small lake holding bream, carp, perch, pike, roach, rudd, tench and trout. Most of the fish are fairly small except the carp which can reach 10lb.

Ticket Prices

Season tickets only. *See Angling Clubs section.*

Opening Times

Open all year, 24 hours a day.

Fishery Rules

None.

Facilities on site

Car park inside main gate.

SILSDEN RESERVOIR

Location (OS104:046477)

From the A629(T) Airedale trunk road take the A6034 for Silsden and Addingham. About 1½ miles past Silsden on the long climb up Cringles Hill the reservoir lies to the left.

Fishery Controller

Bradford Waltonians' Angling Club. *See Angling Clubs section.*

Water and Stock
A small sheltered reservoir, on the edge of Cringles Moor, holding native brown trout.
Ticket prices
Season tickets only. *See Angling Clubs section.*
Opening Times
Dawn to dusk during the trout fishing season.
Fishery Rules
Fly fishing only.
Facilities on Site
Small car parking area.

STAVELEY LAKES

Location (OS99:358626)
From Boroughbridge take the A6055 road towards Knaresborough. After about 2 miles turn right towards Staveley. Go through the village and turn right to Copgrave and the lakes lie on your right.
Fishery Controller
Bradford City Angling Association. *See Angling Clubs section.*
Water and Stock
Two lakes, one of 3 acres and the other about 1$^{1}/_{2}$ acres, both holding a good head of coarse fish. There are seven varieties of carp, silver and common bream, chub, dace, eels, perch, roach, rudd, tench and a few trout. The carp run to 25lb and the tench to 4lb.
Ticket Prices
Season tickets only. *See Angling Clubs section.*
Opening Times
All year.
Fishery Rules
No keepnets between 15th March and 15th June inclusive. No night fishing. No spinning. No live bait. One rod only. Access to the fishing is via a locked gate, keys are available from the Membership Secretary.
Facilities on Site
Car park.

SUGDEN END RESERVOIR

Location (OS104:044373)
From Keighley take the A644 road towards Halifax. After a climb of

about $2^1/_2$ miles up the Worth Valley, take a left at the first roundabout and continue on the A644 towards Halifax. After a further 100 yards turn right onto a dirt road leading to this small reservoir.

Fishery Controller

Keighley Angling Club. *See Angling Clubs section.*

Water and Stock

A small attractively sited reservoir containing perch, roach tench and brown trout.

Ticket Prices

Season ticket. *See Angling Clubs section.* Day ticket £3.50 obtainable in Keighley from Willis Walker, 100 Cavendish Street (Tel: 01535 602928), K.L. Tackle, 131 Mornington Street (Tel: 01535 667574) and other local dealers.

Opening Times

Open all year from dawn to dusk.

Description

An attractive mixed fishery situated on the edge of Haworth Moor. The land rises steeply to one side but access is easy to all banks. A maximum of 25 anglers per day are permitted which is about right for its size, although it's rare to see more than a handful of people fishing. The best fishing is for brown trout and perch which tend to be larger and more numerous than the roach and tench. Most local anglers use maggots and small redworms but many of the new proprietory baits also do well.

Fishery Rules

No night fishing.

Facilities on Site

Car park near the lake.

SUNNYDALE RESERVOIR

Location (OS104:101434)

The reservoir is tucked away in a tiny glen above East Morton village some 4 miles from Bingley. Follow Morton Lane which is signposted from the A65 in Crossflats. In East Morton village take the road to Menston and Otley. At the top of the steep hill in the village take left onto Green End Road. In about 600 yards turn left into Upwood Lane and then right, via the five-bar gate, onto the track leading a further $^3/_4$ mile to the reservoir.

Fishery Controller

Bingley Angling Club. *See Angling Clubs section.*

Water and Stock

A small and very pretty reservoir containing a fine stock of roach and trout. Stocked annually with American Brook and rainbows to 2lb.

Ticket prices

Season ticket. *See Angling Clubs section.* Day tickets £3.50 for 2 fish, from The Pantry and Sub-Post Office, 7 Main Road, East Morton, facing the bus terminus (Tel: 01274 563560).

Opening times

From the start of the trout season to December 31st, 0600 until 2200 hrs.

Description

Sunnydale is a lovely little reservoir hiding in a small remote valley above the village. Its clear water is spring fed from Bradup Beck. After heavy rain the water turns peaty brown. The area is thickly wooded making access difficult and it's virtually impossible to cast a fly from about 3/4 of its banks. It's a pity that access is difficult because the fish rise freely especially on a sunny evening when the water has warmed up. A few fishing platforms and spaces have been created but it's unlikely that more than half a dozen anglers could fish at any one time. Claim one of these positions near the wall and it's possible to have a very good day here. Most anglers use a floating rig baited with worm.

Fishery Rules

All baits are permitted except spinning. Anglers caught fishing without a ticket will be charged double. Trout size limit 12 inches.

Facilities on Site

Limited car parking.

TANFIELD LODGE LAKE

Location (OS99:259777)

West Tanfield is on the A6018 Ripon to Leyburn road in Wensleydale. In the village take the Leyburn road and at the roundabout turn left. At the top of the village, turn left again and follow the track to Tanfield Lodge. After a further 1/4 mile turn left to Tanfield Lodge and the lake is on the left down this road.

Fishery Controller

Mr Bourne-Arton, Tanfield Lodge Lake, Tanfield Lodge, West Tanfield (Tel: 01677 470385).

Water and Stock

A gin-clear 11½ acre lake holding approximately 4,000 brown and rainbow trout, averaging 1½lb, with some fish over 10lb.

Ticket Prices

Day ticket £9.00 for 4 fish, junior under 15 £4.50 for 2 fish, evening ticket (1700 hrs to dusk) £4.50 for 2 fish. Catch and release is permitted after reaching limit. Tickets must be obtained before fishing from the fishing hut in the car park.

Opening Times

Fishing from the third week in March until the first Sunday in October, from 0800 hrs to sunset.

Description

In common with most lakes formed in ex-gravel workings, the water at Tanfield Lodge is gin-clear making this a great stalking water. It's a big lake which can be a bit daunting at first sight but it has been carefully landscaped to give access to most of the banks. On the left a peninsula encloses a small area which is a popular hot spot. Although the depth drops to over 30 feet, fish can still be spotted in the margins and are generally bigger than they seem, so use a strong leader. There are some shallow shingle areas but the deepest water, a favourite for those using sinking lines, is to the right of the path down from the fishing hut. Some of the bigger fish come from this spot but they are not easy to catch. The water teems with aquatic fly life so the stocked fish grow-on quickly. They also run hard and far when hooked and they have a long way to go, so check fly line backing before fishing, you'll probably need it! There's a lot of surface life so it's worth trying nymphs or dry fly and casting to a rise. The water is stocked every two weeks with top quality browns and rainbows. The fishery records stand at, rainbow 10lb and brown 8lb.

For the surface feeders try hoppers, Daddy-Long-Legs, Walker's Wake fly and may flies in season. Buzzers always do well in the surface film here. Anything in green or black will take fish. Gold heads are popular, as are all the flashy types or lures.

Fishery Rules

No animals to be brought to the fishery. No visitors permitted on the banks. No wading. No season tickets. No fish less than 10 inches to be taken. Fishing returns are required.

Facilities on Site

Car park at the lake. Disabled anglers may take their car down to the lakeside. Fishing hut and toilet.

TEAPOT DAM

Location (OS104:025405)

From Keighley, take the road alongside the Central Library to Braithwaite. Continue through the village to Laycock and then turn left to Goose Eye. In about 50 yards where the road crosses Newsholme Beck, the dam is a short distance on the left, through the woods.

Controller

Bingley Angling Club. *See Angling Clubs section.*

Water & Stock

One of the area's numerous attractive small dams holding a good stock of coarse fish.

Ticket Prices

Members only. *See Angling Clubs section.*

Opening Times

All year from dawn to dusk.

Fishery rules

No fires. No night fishing. No spinning.

Facilities on Site

None.

THORNTON STEWARD RESERVOIR

Location (OS99:181881)

From Leyburn take the A684 road towards Bedale. About 1½ miles after passing through Constable Burton turn right to Finghall village. Take a left in the village to Thornton Steward and go straight over the next crossroads. The reservoir is on the right after a further 500 yards.

Fishery Controller

Yorkshire Water, Recreations Department, 32/34 Monkgate, York YO3 7RH.

Water and Stock

A man-made reservoir of about 35 acres stocked with rainbow trout.

Ticket Prices

Day ticket £9.00 for 4 fish. Concessionary tickets for state pensioners, disabled anglers, and unaccompanied children under 15 £8.00 for 4 fish, and evening tickets, from 1600 hrs, May 1st until August 31st, £6.00 for 2 fish. Children under 15 years old fishing with a parent or grandparent may fish free. In this case, a single limit of 4 fish applies. All tickets from Mrs Hainsworth, Hargill House, Finghall (Tel: 01677 450245).

Opening times

Daily from the Saturday preceding March 25th to November 30th inclusive. No brown trout to be taken after September 30th. Fishing is permitted from 0800 hrs until dusk.

Description

Situated in lovely upper Wensleydale scenery, this is a surprisingly unattractive concrete bowl trout fishery operated by Yorkshire Water. A small sailing club, with a base in the south-west corner, also uses the reservoir, but the boats rarely interfere with the fishing. The western side, exclusive to anglers, is usually the best, especially when a westerly winds blows. Wind can be a problem but take advantage of it and use yellow or orange muddler in the ripple. Or try skittering a Walker's Wake Fly across the water. When they are in season a Daddy-Long-Legs can be deadly. For those flat calms a small Black Gnat should bring a rise. Black, green or claret buzzers, nymphs and goldheads are also productive when retrieved very slowly. As for lures, chenille always does well, try black with a flash of fluorescent green or orange. The water is kept well stocked with fish averaging 1lb to 1½lb but there are fish reaching 10lb, so use a strong leader. The bigger browns like to cruise low in the water. Try a Black or a Grey Ghost deep down and retrieve it slowly. Feel for the take, it could be very gentle but once hooked the browns tend to run a long way.

Fishery Rules

Fly fishing only. Use barbless hooks. Size limit of takeable fish - 10 inches or over.

Facilities on Site

Car park.

THORPE PERROW LAKE

Location (OS99:256857)

From Bedale take the B6268 Masham road. In about 1$^{1}/_{2}$ miles, at a crossroads, turn right towards Well. The lake is about 500 yards on your right.

Fishery Controller

Richmond and District Angling Society. *See Angling Clubs section.*

Water and Stock

One coarse lake of approximately 2$^{1}/_{2}$ acres holding mainly carp and roach.

Ticket Prices

Season fees. *See Angling Clubs section.* Day tickets £5.00 from the Richmond Angling Centre, 8 Temple Square, Cravengate, Richmond (Tel: 01748 822989).

Opening Times

All year from dawn to dusk.

Description

This lovely little lake, in a wooded setting, is a brilliant carp venue. The fish are very big, running to over 25lb, and numerous. They'll also fall to most of the popular baits although boilies are banned. Try floating crust near the weedy area when the weather is hot and there's a flat calm. It's not an easy method but it is satisfying. Roach are the other main quarry here. They tend to be fairly small but there are lots of them so heavy catches are possible. Maggots and hemp do well for the roach.

Fishery Rules

No boilies. No night fishing.

Facilities on Site

Car park.

THORPE UNDERWOOD LAKES

Location (OS105:4575910)

From its junction with the A1, take the A59 towards York. In about 3 miles turn left onto the B6265 road towards Boroughbridge. Then in 1$^{1}/_{2}$ miles take a right to Thorpe Underwood at a sign indicating Queen Ethelburga's College. Follow this road for $^{3}/_{4}$ mile and the fishery lies on the left at the Thorpe Underwood Water Meadows.

Fishery Controller

Mr David Almond, Thorpe Underwood Water Meadows, Thorpe

Underwood, York YO5 9TA (Tel: 01423 331080).

Water and Stock

Two lakes, one stocked with rainbow trout and one with bream, carp (ghost, common and mirror), roach, rudd and tench.

Ticket Prices

Day tickets. Trout: day £15.00 for 3 fish, 5 hours £10.00 for 2 fish, 2½ hours £5.00 for 1 fish. Catch and release is permitted after limit is reached. Coarse: day £5.00. All tickets can be purchased on the bank.

Opening Times

Open all year from 0600 until 2200 hrs.

Description

This purpose built fishery, excavated in water meadows, provides excellent fishing for both trout and coarse fish. Currently there are two lakes on the site, one holding rainbow trout averaging about 1½lb with some reaching 10lb, and an attractive 40 peg coarse lake offering some really interesting carp fishing. Excavations are still continuing, although the work doesn't interfere with the fishing, to develop the site into a premier fishery. There are plans to excavate a predator lake, holding big pike, a specialist carp lake and another lake holding big coarse fish of all species.

Trout anglers will find that the old water meadows are a breeding ground for all types of insect life much of which finds its way into the fishing lakes. Try the standard patterns of dry fly, such as a Greenwell's or Pond Olive, for the free rising rainbows. Most nymphs are good, particularly black or olive buzzers, when retrieved slowly through the surface film. Open bank space makes casting easy. One side has been planted with trees but they are far enough back. This tends to be the favourite side. Carp enthusiasts should try floating bread crust a method very popular with some regulars. It can be deadly and it is a fun way to take fish. Be careful, though, as the takes can be vicious. Boilie enthusiasts will find that red or yellow flavoured balls will catch fish.

Fishery Rules

No night fishing. No ground baiting. No keepnets. Use barbless hooks only. Maximum 10 fishermen.

Facilities on Site

Toilets, 9 disabled pegs suitable for wheelchair access and a car park.

THORPE UNDERWOOD No.1 LAKE

Location (OS100:470600)

From the A1, take the A59 east. Follow the signs for R.A.F. Linton-on-Ouse to Thorpe Underwood. Turn right by the Nurses Home and follow the road to the river and lake.

Fishery Controller

Bradford No.1 Angling Association. *See Angling Clubs section.*

Water and Stock

Not to be confused with the lakes at Thorpe Underwood Water Meadows, this is one of two small lakes by the riverside. It holds a variety of coarse fish including bream, rudd and tench.

Ticket Prices

Season tickets only. *See Angling Clubs section.*

Opening Times

Open all year, sunrise to sunset.

Facilities on Site

None.

THRUSCROSS RESERVOIR

Location (OS104:155575)

From the A65 Skipton to Harrogate road, turn left at Blubberhouses immediately opposite the church. Follow this small scenic road for about 1$^{1}/_{2}$ miles up the Washburn Valley to the reservoir.

Owner

Yorkshire Water, 32/34 Monkgate, York YO3 7RH.

Water & Stock

A huge, very deep reservoir holding native and stocked brown trout. Currently used by a sailing club.

Ticket Prices

No fishing.

TONG PARK LAKE

Location (OS104:165403)

From Shipley take the A6038 road towards Otley. In about 3 miles turn left into Roundwood Road. Take the first right into Langley Lane and then right again into Hollins Head. At the top of this road turn behind the new houses at the Paddock. Follow the unmade track across a field and down into the valley. The lake is dead ahead.

Fishery Controller

Saltaire Angling Association. *See Angling Clubs section.*

Water and Stock

An attractive ex-mill dam which used to supply water to the mill in the village. Stocked with native browns to 2lb and rainbows to 4lb.

Ticket Prices

Season fees. *See Angling Clubs section.* Day ticket £5.00 for 2 fish, from the Hon. Sec. or from the fishing tackle shops in Shipley and Keighley.

Opening Times

March 25th to the end of October from dawn to dusk.

Description

This is a surprising pretty small lake nestling in a tiny valley, alongside a stream, on the edge of Baildon Moor. It is spring fed, quite clear and contains lots of small wild brown trout plus an annual stocking of both browns and rainbows of about 12 inches. The water is deepest near the long dam wall and fairly shallow in the area to the right. Fishing is by fly and worm only and the fly fishing is invariably better in the early morning or late evening. Local patterns do well for these free rising fish although most of the bigger trout are taken by local youngsters using float fished or ledgered worms. There's good access to all the banks and plenty of back casting space.

Fishery Rules

Fly and worm fishing only. No fish less than 11 inches to be taken. Barbless hooks only.

Facilities on Site

A small car parking area at the lakeside.

WHINNY GILL RESERVOIR

Location (OS103:998511)

Situated on Skipton Moorside within the town boundary. From the roundabout at the bottom of Skipton High Street take Newmarket Street. Go straight ahead at the mini roundabout onto Shortbank Road. In about 1/2 mile turn right into Greatwood Avenue. Then immediately left into Whinny Gill Road. The reservoir is at the end.

Fishery Controller

Skipton Angling Association. *See Angling Clubs section.*

Water and Stock

A small reservoir of about 6 acres holding bream, perch, roach, rudd and trout.

Ticket Prices

Season ticket. *See Angling Clubs section.*

Day ticket £4.00 for 2 trout. Available from the Hon. Sec., the Paper Shop, Main Street, Embsay (Tel: 01756 792810), the Esso Garage on Keighley Road, Skipton (Tel: 01756 793953), K. L. Tackle in Keighley, and Jackson's Fishing Tackle, Earby.

Opening times

Every day 0700 hrs to one hour after sunset. March 25th to October 31st. In future it may stay open all year.

Description

An uninteresting concrete bowl mixed fishery situated on the edge of a housing estate. The best fishing is for perch and roach with bags of 3lb and 4lb not uncommon. There are a few good sized bream but they are difficult to tempt. The trout tend to be large, record brown 5lb 4oz and rainbow 5lb, but they're not easy to find. The trout fishing is better at nearby Embsay Reservoir. Fishermen at Whinneygill should be careful. The water is deep, reaching 30 feet in places and the reservoir's concrete collar can be very slippery when wet.

Fishery Rules

Fishing by fly, minnow and spinning only. No fishing from the dam wall. Maggots are banned.

Facilities on Site

Car parking.

WHITEFIELD RESERVOIR

Location (OS104:023430)

From Keighley take the A629 old Skipton Road towards Steeton. In the village, about 100 yards past the traffic lights, turn left into Barrows Lane to Whitely Head. After 1 mile turn right into Intake Lane. The reservoir is $^1/_2$ mile across the field on the left.

Fishery Controller

Keighley Angling Club. *See Angling Clubs section.*

Water and Stock

A small reservoir holding a good head of carp, roach, perch and tench. Despite the long walk to get to the water's edge, it is popular with locals.

Ticket Prices

Season tickets only. *See Angling Clubs section.*

Opening Times

During the coarse fishing season. Dawn to dusk.

Fishery Rules

No carp to be kept in nets.

Facilities on Site

None.

THE WILLOWS

Location (OS105:535540)

Follow the A59 from the A1 junction towards York. After passing the crossroads signposted to Moor Monkton, the entrance, marked by a large sign decorated with a picture of a carp, is approximately 1¾ miles on the left.

Fishery Controller

Cath Gallagher, The Willows, Willow Close, Hessay, Moor Monkton, York YO5 8JU (Tel: 01904 738206).

Water and Stock

One 2½ acre garden pool heavily stocked with bream, carp, chub, golden orfe, perch, roach, rudd and tench.

Ticket Prices

Day tickets £5.00, obtainable on site. Tickets must be bought before starting to fish. Because the lake is sometimes matchbooked, it's advisable to book in advance at weekends.

Opening Times

All year from dawn until dusk.

Description

Set in a mature 7½ acre garden well planted with trees and shrubs, this is a big carp water. The best fish recently was a fine 30lb and the top bag of ten carp weighed in at 98lb. They fell to the new favourite bait, boilies, offered in a variety of flavours.

Another lake speciality, for those big fish, is trout pellet paste, mixed with marmite or something similar. But it's not just a carp water. Some 15 years ago the lake received a huge stocking of most types of coarse fish. Large mixed bags of bream, roach, rudd and perch are often taken by anglers using the old faithful method of maggots on a waggler rig. All baits are permitted so it's a good place to try one of your home brews! A continuing policy of bank maintenance has ensured that all the 21 fishing pegs are easily accessible and attractive. Bankside trees and shrubs provide some shade on the hottest days and some protection from the worst of the wind.

Because the lake is occasionally used for match fishing it's always a good idea to check first.

Fishery Rules

No carp to be kept in nets. No night fishing. Barbless hooks only. Children under 14 must be accompanied by an adult. No pets. Fish from the permanent pegs only.

Facilities on Site

Toilet and car park close to the lake.

WINTERBURN RESERVOIR

Location (OS98:945602)

From Gargrave take the road to Hetton. After the Angel pub in the village, turn left and in about 1/2 mile the reservoir is straight ahead.

Fishery Controller

Bradford Waltonians' Angling Club. *See Angling Clubs section.*

Water and Stock

A huge Pennine reservoir situated between Malhamdale and Wharfedale holding a good stock of wild brown trout. It's not an easy fishery, particularly on windy days.

Ticket Prices

Season tickets only. *See Angling Clubs section.*

Fishery Rules

Fly fishing only.

Facilities on Site

Car park.

WOODLAND LAKES

Location (OS99:390803)

From Ripon take the A61 road towards Thirsk. On the outskirts of Carlton Miniott village turn right onto a signposted single track road to the fishery. Willowgarth Lake lies on the right in about 1/2 mile and the others are at the end of the track.

Fishery Controller

Robin or Melanie Fletcher, Woodland Lake Fishery, Carlton Miniott (Tel: 01845 522827 or mobile 0831 824870).

Water and Stock

Five, soon to be eight, varied lakes holding a variety of coarse fish. There are carp (mirror, ghost and koi), barbel, bream, chub, rudd, golden orfe, golden rudd and golden tench.

Ticket prices

Adult day ticket, £6.00 evening ticket, after 1600 hrs £4.00, senior citizen or accompanied junior under 16 years old £4.00. Ladies sharing a ticket peg fish free. All tickets are available at the lakeside.

Opening Times

March 15th to December 15th from 0600 until 2100 hrs or dusk.

Description

Thoughtfully designed for the fisherman these five attractively sited landscaped lakes offer 170 flat comfortable pegs and the chance to catch some really different fish. Each irregularly shaped lake has been designed with peninsulas and islands to create lots of interesting fishing spots. There's easy flat access from the car park to the gravel paths around each lake and the fishing positions are all solidly made and clearly marked. Currently the biggest carp are about 18lb, the tench, the bream and the barbel all reach about 9lb. It can be a surprise to catch one of the golden orfe or rudd but they do make the day interesting and will fall to the usual baits. Luncheon meat, corn, maggots and caster are all good baits. A local speciality is trout pellet paste. Ground pellets mixed with marmite or other "secret" ingredients seem to attract fish in these waters.

Fox Covert Lake, near the car park, is popular but it tends to be a late starter. It's better in the evenings. Silver Birch Lake, surrounded by birch trees, is good when the sunlight is strong. Cock Pheasant and Kingfisher Lakes are productive for most of the day as is Willowgarth Lake which is situated away from the others. This is a well run fishery that even has a snack bar in the car park.

Three further lakes, very recently opened for fishing, increase the peg numbers to over 200.

Fishery Rules

Only barbless hooks permitted - no microbarbs. Two rods allowed. No keepnets. No boilies, bloodworm or jokers. No groundbaiting. No dogs. No night fishing.

Facilities on Site

Toilets, car parks and a good snack bar, open every day until November and then weekends only.

A quiet corner of Woodland Lakes

YEADON TARN

Location (OS104:215415)

From Bradford take the main A658 road towards Harrogate. In Yeadon turn left into the High Street. In approximately 500 yards, turn right into cemetery Road. The Tarn is a few hundred yards up this road on the right.

Fishery Controller.

Airborough and District Angling Association. *See Angling Clubs section.*

Water and Stock

One lake of about 1/2 acre holding plenty of bream, carp, gudgeon, perch, roach and tench.

Ticket Prices

Day tickets, adult £2.50, juniors £1.25, obtainable in Yeadon from Cliffe Court News, Yeadon High Street, C. Rowe, Newsagent, 103 High Street and Yeadon News, Fountain Crossroads. Also from Watercraft Products in Greengates, Angling and Country Sports in Otley and the fishing tackle shops in Leeds.

Opening Times

All year from dawn to dusk.

Description

This is a really good coarse fishing venue. Access is very easy. There are tarmac paths around the tarn, the surrounding parkland is well maintained and there are 80 purpose built fishing platforms. Disabled access to the specially constructed platforms is also very easy. The water contains a large stock of bream averaging 2lb, carp averaging 6lb and tench up to 4lb. A few 25lb carp have been caught here and there are rumours of a fish over 30lb. The carp fishing is best in the warmer weather when the fish move into the bay near the Boys Club. Bread flake is a good bait then. At other times most fishermen use maggots. A sailing club also uses the lake but boats don't interfere with the angling. It's situated close to the end of the main runway at the Leeds/Bradford Airport, but the occasional noise doesn't seem to affect the fish.

Fishery Rules

No night fishing. No live/dead bait, spinners, plugs or lures to be used. No fishing from the sailing jetties.

Facilities on Site

Toilets and car park.

Canals

LEEDS AND LIVERPOOL CANAL

Over 127 miles long this trans-Pennine canal was a huge engineering achievement when it finally opened to high acclaim in 1816, after a building period of some 46 years. Raising heavy cargo boats from sea level to top of the Pennines would present engineering problems even today, but in the eighteenth century, when the work began, it was considered to be impossible. The perseverance and skill of those engineers, and the navvies who actually did the digging, lives on in this monument to their ingenuity and determination. Today the waterway is one of the North's important coarse fisheries.

With considerable effort and expertise British Waterways lovingly tends to the needs of this fine waterway, keeping it in tiptop condition to be used by anglers, boaters, walkers and cyclists, all of whom gain great pleasure from its presence.

Coarse fish form the main stock although there are still some trout to be caught in the Gargrave area. Bream, chub, dace, eels, gudgeon, pike, roach and rudd all abound in the canal in various sections. Many anglers are happy to catch small fish in large numbers and this is where the Leeds and Liverpool Canal scores over some coarse fisheries. There are huge shoals of bream, roach and rudd, throughout most of the canal's length, of a size to satisfy the increasingly popular method of pole fishing.

Another big advantage of canals is that they are easily accessible, particularly in urban areas where roads and canals run side-by-side competing for the level ground.

The canal follows a surprisingly rural path as it climbs out of Leeds from its hiding place behind the Railway Station. Its water is often very clear and the fishing for dace, roach and rudd is excellent. At Rodley it begins to reach out into the countryside clinging to the south side of the River Aire. Shipley used to be a large industrial town with sprawling woollen mills using the canal for transport. But today the mills have gone leaving the waterway to pass peacefully on through Saltaire to one of the seven wonders of the waterways, Bingley's Five-Rise locks. The fishing all along this stretch is brilliant with big bags of roach being the order of the day. Bread and casters are good baits to tempt these fish and also the dace. There are many jack pike to be taken along the weedy margins. Above Bingley the canal takes to the northern hillside of Airedale leaving it exposed to the strong winds. On the quieter days try for the shy carp which tend to shoal in the section by Keighley Golf Club and on the Skipton side of Silsden.

Boats are attracted to the popular tourist town of Skipton but don't let them put you off the fishing. It's good, right in the centre, at the junction with the Springs Branch, the short dead-end canal to the castle. Between Gargrave and Foulridge over the top of the Pennines the canal cuts through some of the most spectacular scenery in Yorkshire. The fishing is excellent in Marton Pool, near East Marton, where the canal follows the contours of the hillside weaving in and out of small valleys and almost doubling back on itself at times. There's great fishing for bream, roach, rudd and tench to be had over several miles all along this stretch and numerous places to escape from the prevailing wind.

A lot of the fishing rights are leased from British Waterways by angling clubs, most of whom in turn permit fishing for the modest cost of a day ticket. The water not currently let to fishing clubs, or which cannot be made available for some other reason, may also be fished as part of a new scheme called 'Waterways Wanderers'. For a modest fee, a ticket holder in this scheme can fish hundreds of miles of canal bank on dozens of canals throughout the country. Some angling clubs have an agreement with British Waterways, which they call "Waterways Anglers Together" whereby their fully paid-up members may fish BW Wanderers lengths free of charge.

Waterways Wanderers twelve month tickets cost just £15.00 for an adult and £7.50 for a junior, OAP or disabled person. **Monthly tickets** are £7.50 for an adult and £4.00 for a concession, and **daily tickets** cost £2.00 for an adult and £1.50 at the concession rate.

All permits for this area and further information from:

John Harding, 34 Nantwich Road, Tarporley CW6 9UW (Tel: 01829 732748).

Barry Tuffin, Maesbury Wharf Cruisers, Maesbury, Oswestry Shropshire (Tel: 01691 670849).

Regional Fisheries Manager, BW Northwest, Navigation Road, Northwich Cheshire CW8 1BH (Tel: 01606 74321).

LEEDS AND LIVERPOOL CANAL TOWPATH FISHING SITES FROM LEEDS TO FOULRIDGE TUNNEL

(Bridges on the canal are numbered and easily identifiable in descending order from bridge 226 in Leeds canal basin to Liverpool. Fixed somewhere to each bridge is a white oval plaque with black numbering stating the bridge number. As new bridges are built across the canal, the number is suffixed with a letter.)

LEEDS TO RODLEY

Railway Bridge 225H, about 200 yards above Leeds Office Lock, to Kirkstall Brewery Bridge (excluding Spring Garden lock no.6 to bridge 225F) approximately 1 mile, is controlled by the Leeds and District Angling Association. Contact Mr Dennis Lemmon (Tel: 0113 2645500).
Day tickets £2.00 or £1.00 for juniors, from local fishing tackle shops.

Bridge 225F to Spring Garden lock no.6, over 1/3 mile, is controlled by Armley Angling Supplies (Tel: 0113 2790738).
Day tickets £1.50 on the bank or from the shop.

Kirkstall Bridge 222 to Newlay Locks, approximately 1 1/2 miles, is controlled by Crown Leisure Angling Association. Contact Mr J. Gains (Tel: 01926 334508).
Day tickets £1.50 on the bank.

Newlay Locks to Thornhill Bridge 214B, about 2 miles, is available to BW Wanderers permit holders.
Day tickets from British Waterways. *See above.*

RODLEY TO SHIPLEY

Rodley Swing Bridge 217, by the boatyard, to Horsforth Road Bridge 216A, a few hundred yards, is controlled by Rodley Boats Angling Club. Contact Mr Colin Snowden (Tel: 0113 2576132).
Day tickets £1.50 from boatyard alongside the swing bridge.

Horsforth Road Bridge 216A to Calverley Lodge Swing Bridge 215, nearly 1/2 mile, is controlled by the Listerhills Old Boys Angling Association. Contact Mr Edward Harrison (Tel: 01274 503141).
Day tickets £1.50 from local fishing tackle shops.

Thornhill Bridge 214B, Apperley Bridge to Idle Swing Bridge 212, about 2/3 mile, is controlled by the Idle and Thackley Angling

Association. Contact Mr Charles Hardaker (Tel: 01274 615016).
Day tickets £1.50 from local fishing tackle shops.

Idle Swing Bridge 212 to Field Locks at Thackley, approximately 1 mile, is controlled by the Unity Angling Association (Tel: 01274 720072).
Day tickets £2.00 from the bailiff on the bank or Watercraft Products fishing tackle shop, Greengates, Bradford.

Field Locks at Thackley to Oddies Swing Bridge 210, nearly 1½ miles, is available to BW Wanderers ticket holders.
Day tickets from British waterways. *See above.*

SHIPLEY TO SKIPTON

Oddies Swing Bridge 210 to Dowley Gap Bottom Lock, about 3 miles through Shipley and Saltaire, is controlled by the Saltaire Angling Association. Contact Mr A. D'Arcy (Tel: 01274 588694).
Day tickets £2.00, junior and ladies £1.00 from local fishing tackle shops.

Dowley Gap Locks, approximately 3 miles through Bingley to Swine Lane Bridge is controlled by the Bingley Angling Association. Contact Mr Ian Ward (Tel: 01274 567422).
Day tickets £2.00, junior, ladies and senior citizen £1.00, from local fishing tackle shops. No bloodworm or joker to be used.

Swine Lane Bridge 198 to Lodge Hill Bridge 194, nearly 3 miles through Stockbridge, is controlled by the Marsden Star Angling Society. Contact Mr J. Hartley (Tel: 01282 603362).
Day tickets £2.00 from local fishing tackle shops.

Lodge Hill Bridge 194 to Hamblethrope Swing Bridge 183, about 6 miles through Kildwick and Silsden, is controlled by the Keighley Angling Club. Contact Mr Dennis Freeman (Tel: 01535 663695).
Day tickets £2.00, juniors £1.00 from fishing tackle shops in Keighley and district.

Hamblethrope Swing Bridge 183 to Bank Newton Top Lock, over 12 miles through Skipton and Gargrave, is available to BW Wanderers ticket holders.
Day tickets from British Waterways. *See above.*

SKIPTON TO FOULRIDGE

Bank Newton Top Lock to Park Bridge 151A at Salterforth, about 6

miles, is controlled by the Marsden Star Angling Society. Contact Mr J. Hartley (Tel: 01282 603362).
Day tickets £2.00 from local fishing tackle shops.

Park Bridge 151A at Salterforth to Foulridge Tunnel, about 3 miles, is available to BW Wanderers / Waterways Anglers Together ticket holders. Also fished by members of the Keighley AC.
Day tickets £2.00, £1.00 for juniors, from Keighley fishing tackle shops and British Waterways. *See above.*

RIPON CANAL

Extending only 2 miles from the River Ure, via three locks, to Ripon town centre, this canal is a fine coarse fishery. To find it from Ripon Market Square, take the B6265 road towards Boroughbridge. In less than 1/2 mile, cross over the tiny River Skell and then in about 100 yards the canal runs alongside the road on your right.

The water is usually gin clear but it can get churned up by a regular procession of boats, especially in the summer, to and from Ripon Marina at Littlethorpe. Although viewed by some as a nuisance the boats do keep the weed under control and occasionally stir up the fish. Bream, carp, chub, eels, perch, pike and roach are all plentiful. In recent years the Ripon Piscatorials, who control the fishing, have boosted the fish population with a massive restocking of some 28,000 coarse fish. In general the fishing is better in the early morning or late evening when the boats are not moving.

Carp anglers will be pleased to learn that night fishing is allowed as are all the usual baits. Generally local anglers tend to use maggots and casters but when fishing for the big bream and carp, small boilies, around 12mm, are good. The pike are small, rarely reaching double figures, but it is worth trying a dead bait in the weedy margins for this predator.

The riparian rights are owned by the Ripon Canal Fisheries. Fishing is open all year.
Day tickets, £2.00 and £1.00 for children, can be had from the Ripon Angling Centre and C. J. Fishing Tackle in Harrogate. Full members of the Ripon Piscatorial Association may fish the canal free of charge.

Angling Clubs

Angling clubs and societies are an essential part of the sport. If it was not for the hard work, often unrewarded, of club officials, many of the fishing waters listed in this guide would be the preserve of exclusive syndicates and not available to the casual angler. The listing below is the most comprehensive ever produced for this area. It is as complete as possible from the information provided. Some of the clubs catalogued are massive, holding the rights to fishing on hundreds of waters throughout northern England, whilst others are tiny, having the rights to one water only. In other words they cater for all anglers. Those people who like to fish the same water, getting to know it year by year, may wish to join one of the very small clubs, whilst roving anglers, wanting more of a challenge, will probably wish to join one of the big boys and try their skill on a variety of waters. Many clubs are dedicated to game fishing only, others are aimed at the coarse fishermen and some offer mixed fishing opportunities. Some clubs favour river fishing and others still waters. Some are expensive and some are not. Many offer weekly and day tickets and some don't. However, in a number of cases the annual fee is so small that a visiting angler will often find it cheaper to take out a season ticket rather than buy a number of day tickets. This comprehensive listing has been produced to help you decide which is the best way for you to gain access to the waterside.

If you telephone any of the contacts listed, please remember that their official position is a labour of love. They have other things in their lives besides fishing. Try to phone when they are not busy and please be patient. And when writing for information always enclose a stamped self addressed envelope for the reply.

ACCRINGTON AND DISTRICT FISHING CLUB
Mr A. Balderstone, 42 Townley Avenue, Huncoat, Lancs. BB5 6LP (Tel: 01254 233517).
Rivers: Greta, Ribble and Wenning.
Still waters: None in the area.
Membership: Open.
Season fees: £155.00.

Day tickets: £9.00 for Mitchell's House Reservoir in Lancashire (not in this guide).

ADDINGHAM ANGLING ASSOCIATION
Mr H. Sunderland, 51 Moor Park Drive, Addingham, West Yorks. LS29 OPU (Tel: 01943 830043).
Rivers: Wharfe.
Still waters: None.
Membership: Waiting list.
Season fees: Adult £70.00 plus £50.00 joining fee. Junior £10.00, intermediate 16-18s £35.00.
Day tickets: £6.00

AIRBOROUGH AND DISTRICT ANGLING CLUB
Mr D. M. Scott, 6 Harley Green, Leeds 13 (Tel: 0113 2356437).
Rivers: Ouse and Wharfe
Still waters: Nunroyd Pond and Yeadon Tarn.
Membership: Open.
Season fees: Adult £7.00, juniors £3.00, ladies, senior citizen and disabled £5.00. Associate members £13.00.
Day tickets: Adult £2.50, junior £1.25 for Yeadon Tarn.

APPLETREEWICK BARDEN AND BURNSALL ANGLING CLUB
Mr J. G. H. Mackrell, 'Mould Greave' Oxenhope, Keighley, West Yorks. BD22 9RT (Tel: 01535 642325).
Rivers: Wharfe.
Still waters: Barden Reservoirs.
Membership: Open
Season fees: £455.00 plus £200.00 joining fee.
Day tickets: River Wharfe, £18.00, half price for juniors. Weekly ticket £90.00.

BAINBRIDGE ANGLING ASSOCIATION
See Wensleydale Angling Association.

BARROWFORD ANGLERS'
Mr J. Davis, 2 Barrowford Road, Colne (Tel: 01282 867558).
Rivers: Ribble.
Still waters: None.

Membership: Closed.
Season fees: Not known.
Day tickets: No.

BENTHAM ANGLING ASSOCIATION
Mr M. Ramsay, 18 Mount Pleasant, Bentham via Lancaster LA2 7HL (Tel: 015242 62041).
Rivers: Wenning.
Still waters: None.
Membership: Open
Season tickets: £55.00 plus £10 joining fee.
Day tickets: No. Weekly tickets £25.00 and £10.00 for juniors.

BINGLEY ANGLING CLUB
Mr R. Heaton, 34 Daleview Road, Longlee, Keighley, West Yorkshire BD21 4YF (Tel: 01535 211856).
Rivers: Aire, Swale and Wharfe. Newsholme Dean Beck.
Still waters: Coppice Pond, Larkfield Tarn, Leeds and Liverpool Canal, Settler Dam, Sunnydale Reservoir and Teapot Dam.
Membership: Open.
Season fees: Adult £17.00, entrance fee £5.00. Junior, ladies and senior citizens £8.50.
Day tickets: For some waters. Prices vary between £3.50 and £1.00.

BIRSTWITH PRIVATE ANGLING CLUB
Mr P. D. Lowndes, Prospect House, Kirbey Overblow, Nr. Harrogate, North Yorks. HG3 1HQ (Tel: 01423 872605).
Rivers: Nidd.
Still waters: None
Membership: Closed
Season fees: Not known.
Day tickets: No.

BLACK OX ANGLING CLUB
Mr R. M. Wright, 5 Lascelles Lane, Northallerton (Tel: 01609 776850).
Rivers: Bedale Beck.
Still waters: None.
Membership: Open
Season fees: All categories £5.00 plus £1.00 joining fee.
Day tickets: No.

BOROUGHBRIDGE AND DISTRICT ANGLING CLUB
Mr M. Burgess, 1 Bungalow, Littlethorpe Road, Ripon HG4 1TZ (Tel: 01765 690715).
Rivers: Ure.
Still waters: Aldborough Pond and Roecliffe Brick Ponds.
Membership: Open.
Season fees: Adult £20.00, 16 to 18s and senior citizen £10.00 and juniors £4.00. All plus small entrance fee.
Day tickets: £3.00 for some waters. Not on Sunday.

BOSTON SPA ANGLING CLUB
Mr A. Waddington, The Cottage, 17 The Village, Thorpe Arch, Wetherby LS23 7AR (Tel: 01937 842664).
Rivers: Wharfe.
Still waters: None.
Membership: Open only for anglers living within 3½ miles of Boston Spa.
Season fees: Not known.
Day tickets: £2.00.

BOWLAND GAME FISHING ASSOCIATION
Mr B. Hoggarth, 1 Moorfield Road, Leyland, Preston, Lancs. PR5 3AR (Tel: 01772 424018).
Rivers: Aire, Hodder, Lune, Rawthey, Ribble and Wenning.
Still waters: Parsonage Reservoir in Lancashire.
Membership: Waiting list. Prospective members must be proposed and seconded by a member.
Season fees: £315.00 plus £500.00 entrance fee.
Day tickets: Members' guests only.

BRADFORD CITY ANGLING ASSOCIATION
Mr S. Gunn, 18 Long House Drive, Denholme, Bradford BD13 4NG (Tel: 01274 835173).
Rivers: Aire, Swale, Ure, Wharfe.
Still waters: Doe Park Reservoir, Leeming Reservoir, Shipton Lake and Staveley Lake.
Membership: open.
Season fees: Adult £26.00 plus £10 joining fee, disabled £13.00, senior citizen £9.50 and junior £7.00.

Day tickets: £3.00 for some waters.

BRADFORD NO.1 ANGLING ASSOCIATION
General Secretary, Mr H. M. Foster, 6 Moorclose Lane, Queensbury, Bradford BD13 2BP (Tel: 01274 815326).
Tickets Officer: Mr D. B. Arnett, 49 Templers Way, Bradford BD8 OLW (Tel: 01274 546556).
Rivers: Aire, Calder, Derwent, Nidd, Ouse, Rye, Swale, Ure and Wharfe.
Still waters in the area of this guide: Chellow Dene Reservoir, Harold Park Lake, Knotford Lagoon, Queen Mary's Ponds, Raskelf Lake, Royds Hall Dam, Shelf Dam, Thorpe Underwood Lake and Willow Hall Dam.
Membership: Waiting list.
Season fees: Adult £24.00, entrance fee £18. Ladies and juniors £9.00 and Senior Citizen £5.50.
Day tickets: Adults 70p, juniors 35p for Harold Park Lake and Royds Hall Dam only.

BRADFORD WALTONIANS' ANGLING CLUB
Mr H. J. B. Swarbrick, 43 Hawksworth Drive, Manston, Ilkley, West Yorks. LS29 6HP (Tel: 01943 875989).
Rivers: None.
Still waters: Chelker and Silsden Reservoirs.
Membership: Waiting list.
Season fees: Not known.
Day tickets: No.

BRITISH WATERWAYS WANDERERS
Mr J. Harding, 34 Nantwich Road, Tarporley, Cheshire CW6 9UW (Tel: 01829 732748).
Mr Barry Tuffin, Maesbury Wharf Cruisers, Maesbury, Oswestry, Shropshire (Tel: 01691 670849).
Regional Fisheries Manager, British Waterways North East, Navigation Road, Northwich, Cheshire CW8 1BH (Tel: 01606 74321).
Leeds and Liverpool Canal plus many other canals throughout the UK.
Membership: Open.
Season fees: Adult £15.00, junior, senior citizen and disabled £7.50.

Day tickets: Adult £2.00, concession £1.50. Monthly tickets, adult £7.50, concession £4.00.

CASTLEFORD AND DISTRICT SOCIETY OF ANGLERS CLUBS
Mr R. Holmes, 1 Hope Street, East Castleford, West Yorks.
Rivers: Derwent, Nidd, Ouse, Rye, Wharfe.
Still waters: None.
Membership: Open.
Season fees: Not known.
Day tickets: Yes.

CRAKEHALL ANGLING CLUB
Mr D. Capstick, Mastile Lane, Crakehall, Bedale (Tel: 01677 422802).
Rivers: Bedale Beck.
Still waters: None.
Membership: Village residents only.
Season fees: Not known.
Day tickets: No.

FEDERATED ANGLERS (PRESTON)
Mr P. A. Mayor, 27 Shirley Lane, Longton, Preston, Lancs. PR4 5WJ (Tel: 01772 613606).
Rivers: Ribble and tributaries.
Still waters: None
Membership: Waiting list.
Season fees: Not known.
Day tickets: No.

HARROGATE ANGLING ASSOCIATION
Mr A. Eccles, 17 Fawcett Lane, Leeds LS12 4PG (Tel: 0113 263 3667).
Rivers: Nidd.
Still waters: None.
Membership: Closed.
Season fees: Not known.
Day tickets: No.

HARROGATE AND CLARO CONSERVATIVE ANGLING ASSOCIATION
Mr M. G. Cooke, 1 Kirkham Road, Bilton, Harrogate HG1 4EL (Tel:

(Tel: 01423 566901).
Rivers: Nidd.
Still waters: Farnham Lakes.
Membership: Open.
Season fees: Coarse fishing £70.00 plus £45.00 joining fee. Trout fishing £55.00 extra.
Day tickets: No.

HARROGATE FLY FISHERS

Mr A. Gillmartin, 40 St Claire Road, Otley LS21 1DE (Tel: 01943 464467).
Rivers: Nidd.
Still waters: None
Membership: Waiting list.
Season fees: £185.00 plus £200.00 entrance fee.
Day tickets: No

HAWES AND HIGH ABBOTSIDE ANGLING ASSOCIATION

Mr G. Phillips, Holmlands, Appersett, Hawes, North Yorks. DL8 3LN (Tel: 01969 667362).
Rivers: Ure and Cotterdale, Duerley, Hardraw, Snaizeholme and Widdale Becks.
Still waters: None.
Membership: Open
Season fees: £48.00, junior or senior citizen £24.00. No joining fee.
Weekly tickets: £24.00 (50% reduction for over 65 and 12 to 16s)
Day tickets: £8.00 (concessions as above)
Grayling only tickets (after 30th September): Season £10.00, week £5.00 (concessions as above).

HUBY ANGLING CLUB

Mr L. Magee, 4 Park Square, Pool in Wharfedale LS21 1LB.
Rivers: Wharfe.
Still waters: None.
Membership: Write to the Hon. Secretary for information.
Season Fees: Not known.
Day tickets: No.

IDLE AND THACKLEY ANGLING ASSOCIATION
Mr C. T. Hardaker, 24 Park Avenue, Thackley, Bradford DD10 0RT (Tel: 01274 615016).
Rivers: Aire, Swale and Wharfe.
Still waters: Leeds and Liverpool Canal.
Membership: Open.
Season fees: Adult £13.00, senior citizen £7.50, junior £6.00 plus £1.00 joining fee.
Day ticket: £1.50 for canal fishing only.

ILKLEY AND DISTRICT ANGLING ASSOCIATION
Mr B. Moore, 50 Valley Drive, Ilkley, West Yorkshire LS29 8PA (Tel: 01943 430606).
River: Wharfe.
Still waters: Two lagoons at Ben Rhydding, Ilkley.
Membership: Open.
Season fees: Adult £38.00, plus £38.00 joining fee. Junior and senior citizen £19.00, plus £19.00 joining fee.
Day tickets: £6.50 for River Wharfe.

INGLETON ANGLING ASSOCIATION
Mr N. W. Capstick, 2 Bower Cottage, Uppergate, Ingleton (Tel: 015242 41026).
Rivers: Doe, Greta and Twiss.
Still waters: None.
Membership: Open.
Season fees: Non-residents. Adult £45.00, junior £30.00 plus £10.00 joining fee. Concessions for residents.
Day tickets: Non residents £8.00 and weekly £35.00 for most waters.

KEIGHLEY ANGLING CLUB
Mr D. Freeman, 62 Eelview Street, Keighley, West Yorkshire BD20 6AY (Tel: 01535 663695).
Rivers: Aire and Worth.
Still waters: Leeds and Liverpool Canal, Linda's Lake, Robert's Pond and Sugden End Reservoir.
Membership: Open.
Season fees: Senior £20.00, 18-16s £10.00, ladies £10.00, juniors under 16, £6.50 and senior citizens £6.00.

Day tickets: River and canal £2.00, junior £1.00. Sugden End £3.50 and junior £2.00.

KILNSEY ANGLING CLUB
Mr E. Wood, Moorside Cottage, Ogden, Halifax HX2 8XP (Tel: 01422 244720).
Rivers: Wharfe and Skirfare.
Still waters: None.
Membership: Full.
Season fees: Adult £420.00 plus £75.00 entrance fee.
Day tickets: £20.00. Weekly tickets £100.00.

KIRKBY FLEETHAM ANGLING CLUB
Mr R. Ball, 12 Village Way, Kirkby Fleetham, Northallerton (Tel: 01609 748738).
Rivers: Swale
Still waters: None
Membership: Local membership only.
Season Fees: Not known.
Day tickets: No.

KILNSEY PARK FLY FISHING CLUB
See still water entry for Kilnsey Park in Wharfedale

KNARESBOROUGH ANGLERS' CLUB
Mr C. J. Lister, 7 Dragon Avenue, Harrogate, North Yorkshire HG1 5DS (Tel: 01423 562796).
Rivers: Nidd.
Still waters: None.
Membership: Waiting list. Applications in writing only to the Club Secretary.
Season fees: £170.00 Joining fee £200.00.
Day tickets. No.

KNARESBOROUGH PISCATORIALS
Membership Secretary, Mr M. Johnson, 2, Briggate, Knaresborough HG5 8GH (Tel: 01423 863065).
Rivers: Nidd, Ouse, Swale and Wharfe.
Still waters: None.

Membership: Open.
Season fees: Senior £55.00 plus £18.00 joining fee. Concessions approximately third of seniors' fee.
Day tickets: No.

LANCASHIRE FLY FISHING ASSOCIATION
Mr J. Winnard, Manor House, Grunsagill, Long Preston, North Yorks. (Tel: 01729 840491).
Rivers: Hodder, Lune, Ribble and Wenning.
Still waters: None.
Membership: Very short waiting list.
Season fees: £250.00, concession £125.00. Joining fee £250.00.
Day tickets: No.

LEEDS AND DISTRICT AMALGAMATED SOCIETY OF ANGLERS
Hon. Secretary, Mr D. Taylor, Leeds and District ASA, Becket Street, Leeds LS9 7TB (Tel: 0113 2482373).
Rivers: Aire, Costa, Derwent, Nidd, Ouse, Rye, Seven, Swale, Ure and Wharfe.
Still waters: Aire and Calder Canal, Blacker Dam, Ferrybridge Complex, Kippax Pond, Knotford Lagoon, Leeds and Liverpool Canal, Roundhay Park Lake and Sandwath Lake.
Membership: Open
Season fees: £31.00, ladies £15.00, senior citizen £6.00, intermediate £9.00 and junior £5.00.
Day tickets: Knotford Lagoon £2.50, Roundhay Park £1.50, junior 50p and all other waters £2.00, junior £1.00.

LINTON THRESHFIELD AND GRASSINGTON ANGLING CLUB
Mr J. A. Birdsall, River End, Wood Lane, Grassington, North Yorks. BD23 5LU (Tel: 01756 753093).
Rivers: Wharfe.
Still waters: None.
Membership: Waiting list. Typically three or four seasons. Apply by letter to Hon. Secretary.
Season fees: Trout, not known. Grayling (outside trout season) £20.00.
Day tickets: £16.00, weekly £55.00. Grayling day £4.00.

LISTERHILLS OLD BOYS ANGLING ASSOCIATION
Mr E. Harrison, 8 Lime Street, Bradford BD7 3HQ (Tel: 01274 503141).
Rivers: Aire.
Still waters: Leeds and Liverpool Canal and Eccleshill Lake.
Membership: Open.
Season fees: Adults £9.00, junior and lady £4.50, senior citizen and disabled £3.00.
Day tickets: Adults £1.50, juniors 75p for canal only.

LONG PRESTON ANGLING CLUB
Mr J. Ketchell, 2 The Coach House, Bishopdale Court, Settle BD24 9EB
Rivers: Ribble.
Still waters: None.
Membership: Waiting list approximately 1 year.
Season fees: £50.00 plus £90.00 joining fee. Juniors may accompany full members.
Day tickets: No.

MANCHESTER ANGLERS' ASSOCIATION
Mr F. Fletcher, 7 Alderbank Close, Kearsley, Bolton, Lancs. BL4 8JQ
Rivers: Lune and Ribble.
Still waters: Newhouses Tarn, Ribblesdale and a variety of lakes in Lancashire.
Membership: Short waiting list.
Season fees: £180 plus a £100 entrance fee. Juniors half price.
Day tickets: Members guest tickets only.

MARSDEN STAR ANGLING SOCIETY
Mr J. Hartley, 3 Duerden Street, Nelson, Lancs. (Tel: 01282 603362).
Rivers: Aire.
Still waters: Leeds and Liverpool Canal and various lakes in Lancashire.
Membership: Open.
Season fees: Adult £18.00, junior or lady £9.00 and senior citizen or disabled angler £7.00.
Day tickets: £2.00.

MASHAM ANGLING CLUB
Mr A. R. Proud, 38 Park Street, Masham HG4 4HN (Tel: 01765 689361).
Rivers: Ure.
Still waters: No.
Membership: Waiting list. Usually about 2 to 2½ years.
Season fees. £125.00 plus £30.00 joining fee.
Day tickets: Members' guest tickets only.

MIDDLESBROUGH ANGLING CLUB
Mr J. Herbert, 10 Walworth Grove, Acklam, Middlesbrough (Tel: 01642 825604).
Rivers: Swale.
Still waters: None.
Season fees: Not known.
Day tickets: No.

NIDDERDALE ANGLING CLUB
Mr T. Harpham, P.O. Box 7, Pateley Bridge, Nr. Harrogate, North Yorks. HG3 5XB.
Membership Secretary, Mrs B Breckon (Tel: 01423 711633).
Rivers: Nidd.
Still waters: Scar House Reservoir.
Membership: Open.
Season fees:

Local members:	Adult £31.00 plus nomination fee £10.00.
	14-17s £20.00 plus nom. fee £2.00.
	Junior £13.00 plus nom. fee £2.00.
	Senior Citizen (after 5 years' membership) Free.
Other members:	Adult £54.25 plus nom. fee £10.00.
	14-17s £34.00 plus nom. fee £2.00.
	Junior £23.00 plus nom fee £2.00
	Senior Citizen (after 5 years' membership) £33.
Day tickets:	Adult £8.00, junior £5.00 for most of River Nidd.
	Adult £6.00, junior £3.00 for Scar House Reservoir.

OTLEY ANGLING CLUB
Mr T. Windross, 43 Newall Carr Road, Otley, West Yorkshire (Tel: 01943 466041).

Rivers: Wharfe.
Still waters: None.
Membership: Otley residents only.
Season fees: Not known.
Day tickets: No.

PADIHAM AND DISTRICT ANGLING SOCIETY
Mr J. W. Whitham, Pendleside, Lingmoor Drive, Burnley BB12 8UY (Tel: 01282 411340).
Rivers: Calder, Hodder and Ribble.
Stillwaters: None.
Membership: Open.
Season fees: £375.00 plus £200.00 joining fee.
Day tickets: No.

PRINCE ALBERT ANGLING SOCIETY
Hon. Secretary, Mr J. A. Turner, 15 Peckshill Drive, Macclesfield, Cheshire SK10 3LP (Tel: 01625 422010).
Membership Secretary, Mr C. Swindells, 37 Sherwood Road, Macclesfield SK11 7RR (Tel: 01625 427078).
Rivers: Dee, Greta, Rawthey, Ribble and Wenning.
Still waters: None in the area.
Membership: Long waiting list.
Season fees: £60.00 plus £60.00 joining fee.
Day tickets: No.

RIBBLE FISHERIES ASSOCIATION
Mr C. J. Heap, 81 Moorland Road, Langho, Ribblevalley BB6 8HA (Tel: 01254 249157).
This is not a fishing club. The RFA is a consultative organisation. Amongst other things its purpose is to monitor abstraction/discharge, discuss all matters relating to the well-being of the river, and take action as necessary to protect the interests of anglers.

RICHMOND AND DISTRICT ANGLING SOCIETY
Mr P. Bennett, 7 Pilmoor Close, Richmond, North Yorkshire (Tel: 01748 824894).
Rivers: Swale.
Still waters: Great Langton Lakes and Thorpe Perrow Lake.

Membership: Open.
Season fees: Adult, inc. trout, £25.00, coarse only £20.00. Senior citizen £15.00, 17s £15.00, 15s and under £10.00, 11s and under £5.00.
Weekly tickets: £15.00, £7.50 juniors and day tickets £5.00, £2.50 juniors for most waters.

RIPON ANGLING CLUB
Mr R. Trees, 43 College Road, Ripon HG4 2HE (Tel: 01765 602277).
Rivers: Laver, Skell and Ure.
Still waters: Lumley Moor Reservoir.
Membership: Open. Prospective full members require a proposer and a seconder.
Season fees: £185.00 (full) £35.00 (rivers only). Joining fee £60.00 (full). No concessions.
Day tickets: £5.00 (two only per day) for rivers only.

RIPON FLY FISHERS
Mr C. Clarke, 9 Moorside Avenue, Ripon HG4 1TA (Tel: 01765 601677).
Rivers: None.
Still waters: Six lakes, stocked with brown and rainbow trout, within a 10 mile radius of Ripon.
Membership: Waiting list.
Season fees: £135.00 plus £50.00 joining fee.
Day tickets: No.

RIPON PISCATORIAL ASSOCIATION
Mr S. Looney, 'Cornerstones', 2 Hell Wath Grove, Redwell Heath, Ripon HG4 2JT (Tel: 01765 602112).
Rivers: Laver and Ure.
Still waters: Racecourse Lake, Ripon Canal and Ure Bank Pond.
Membership: Open.
Season fees: £45.00, accompanied junior £5.00 and senior citizen (after 5 years' full membership) £5.00. Local members £38.00, £2.00 and £5.00 respectively.
Day tickets: £4.00 and £2.00 juniors for all waters. Weekly tickets £12.00.

RODLEY BOATS ANGLING CLUB
Mr C. Snowden, Rodley Boat Centre, Rodley, Leeds (Tel: 0113 2576132).
Rivers: None.
Still waters: Leeds and Liverpool Canal.
Season fees: Not applicable.
Day tickets: £1.50

SALTAIRE ANGLING ASSOCIATION
Mr A. D'Arcy, 68 Grosvenor Road, Shipley (Tel: 01274 588694).
Rivers: Aire and Wharfe.
Still waters: Leeds and Liverpool Canal and Tong Park Lake.
Membership: Open.
Season fees: Adult £16.00, lady, junior, disabled and senior citizen £8.00.
Day tickets: For Tong Park Lake £5.00, River Aire and the L & L Canal £2.00, junior and ladies £1.00.

SEDBERGH AND DISTRICT ANGLING ASSOCIATION
Mr G. Bainbridge, El-Kantara, Frostrow, Sedbergh, Cumbria LA10 5JL (Tel: 015396 20044).
Rivers: Clough, Dee, Rawthey and Lune.
Still waters: None.
Membership: Waiting list, currently 2 to 3 years.
Season fees: Adult £110.00 plus a joining fee of £50.00. Concessions for local residents.
Day tickets: (March 15th to August 31st) £10.00. Weekly tickets: £50.00, late season (mid September to October 31st) £100.00.

SETTLE ANGLERS' ASSOCIATION
Mr A. Butt, Garris Lodge, Rylestone, Skipton, North Yorkshire (Tel: 01756 730391).
Rivers: Ribble.
Still waters: None.
Membership: Waiting list
Season fees: Adult £85.00 plus £250.00 joining fee.
Day tickets: £15.00, weekly £50.00.

SKIPTON ANGLING ASSOCIATION
Mr R. Noble, 3 Uplands, Skipton, North Yorks. BD23 1BJ (Tel: 01756 795222).
Rivers: Aire.
Still waters: Embsay and Whinnygill Reservoirs.
Membership: Open.
Season fees: Adult £40.00 plus £15.00 joining fee. Senior Citizen £25.00 (after one full year's membership). Junior £12.00.
Day tickets: £7.00, juniors £4.00, for Embsay Reservoir and £4.00 for Whinnygill Reservoir and the River Aire.

STAINCLIFFE ANGLING CLUB
Mr B. Wilcock, 25 Malvern Road, Nelson, Lancashire BB9 8JR (Tel: 01282 692921).
Rivers: Ribble.
Still waters: None.
Membership: Closed. Small club. Very limited membership.
Season fees: Not known.
Day tickets: No.

TADCASTER ANGLING AND PRESERVATION SOCIETY
Mr R. A. Emmott, 3 Ingleby Drive, Tadcaster (Tel: 01937 833843).
Rivers: Wharfe.
Still waters: None.
Membership: Long waiting list for outside (country) members.
Season fees. Local members, adult £15, junior £7.50. Country members, £20.00 plus £10.00 joining fee.
Day tickets: £2.00.

THIRSK ANGLING CLUB
Mr C. Weaver, 2 Garden Cottages, South Crescent, Sowerby, Thirsk (Tel: 01845 524633).
Rivers: Swale and Cod Beck.
Still waters: None.
Membership: Open.
Season fees: Adult £25.00, junior, disabled and senior citizen £10.00.
Day tickets: £4.00 and £3.00 for parts of Cod Beck and Swale lengths.

UNITY ANGLING CLUB
Mr E. K. Mann, 19 Busfield Street, Bradford, West Yorks. BD4 7QX (Tel: 01274 720072).
Rivers: Aire.
Still waters: Boroughbridge and Leeds and Liverpool Canals and Dye House Pond, Bradford.
Membership: Open.
Season fees: Adult £10.00, junior £7.00, senior citizen and lady £5.00.
Day tickets: £2.00 for the Leeds and Liverpool Canal.

WENSLEYDALE ANGLING ASSOCIATION
Mrs P. A. Thorpe, Grange Farm, High Birstwith, Harrogate HG3 2JT (Tel: 01423 771307).
Rivers: Bain and Ure.
Still waters: Lake Semerwater.
Membership: Open
Season fees: £27.00 juniors, 10 to 16s half price.
Day tickets: £6.00 and weekly tickets £12.00. Juniors half price.
Grayling tickets (not during the trout season): Season £7.50, day £3.00.

WETHERBY AND DISTRICT ANGLING CLUB
Mr P. Broxham, 1 Eel Mires Garth, Wetherby LS22 7TQ (Tel: 01937 585764).
Rivers: Nidd and Wharfe.
Still waters: Waplington Pond.
Membership: Waiting list.
Season fees: Adult £20.00 plus £5.00 joining fee. Junior £3.00 plus £1.00 joining fee. Concession for senior citizens.
Day tickets: £2.00 for stretches of the River Wharfe.

YORK AND DISTRICT AMALGAMATION OF ANGLERS
Mr D. Dalton, 11 Swinsty Court, Green Lane, Clifton, York YO3 6ZP (Tel: 01904 692046).
Rivers: Derwent, Foss, Nidd, Ouse, Rye and Severn. Barton Hill Beck.
Still waters: Aire and Calder Canal, Burn Road Pond, Claxton Brick Ponds, Hemingbrough, Moor Monkton Lagoon, Park View Lake and Sand Hutton Gravel Pits.
Membership: Open

Season fees: Adult £25.00, senior citizen and disabled £12.50, junior, 10 to 16s £10.00.
Day tickets: £3.00 for most waters.

YORKSHIRE COPPER WORKS ANGLING CLUB
Mr I. M. Jeffs, 36 Hellena Street, Kippax, Leeds (Tel: 0113 2871585).
Rivers: None.
Still waters: Copper Works Pond, Stirton.
Membership: Long waiting list.
Season fees: Not known.
Day tickets: No.

YORKSHIRE FLY FISHERS' CLUB
Hon. Secretary, Margaret House, 2 Devonshire Crescent, Leeds LS8 1EP (Tel: 0113 2370099).
Rivers: Ribble and Ure.
Still waters: None.
Membership: Waiting list.
Season fees: Not known.
Day tickets: No.

Fishing Tackle Shops

Many fishermen now buy their tackle by mail order and in doing so unwittingly subscribe to the loss of local tackle shops. Unfortunately for the visiting angler the closure of local fishing tackle shops means that their fishing owners, usually a mine of local information, are no longer in a position to offer advice on the best places to fish and what tackle to use. Not surprisingly most of the establishments listed below are situated in the major towns because that's generally where people live and work. However they're not far from the Dales boundary. Some of the shops stock a huge range of fishing tackle whilst others are not so big. Some specialise in game fishing, others in coarse fishing and some cater for the match anglers. In every case I have given an idea of the shop's specialism. A listing of fresh baits refers to a selection of maggots, casters, squats, pinkies, worms, cooked hemp amongst other things, and preserved baits are usually boilies, canned sweetcorn or one of a multitude of modern delights. Some shops also stock frozen sprats for pike fishing and others sell prawns or shrimps for salmon fishing. Fishing tackle shops are generally a good source for buying visitors' tickets. Many also hold season membership books for angling clubs so you can join on the spot and be at the water's edge in the shortest possible time.

Please give your trade to the local fishing tackle shops.

BENTHAM

Village Pet Supplies, Station Road, High Bentham (Tel: 015242 62546)

Open 0930 to 1700 hrs. Monday, Wednesday and Friday. Closes at 1230 Tuesday and Saturday. Closed all day Thursday. Game tackle, mainly lines, spinning gear and flies. Fly tying materials. No baits. No club season books. Day tickets: Bentham AA and Ingleton AA stretches of Rivers Greta and Wenning.

BOROUGHBRIDGE

The Rod and Back Pack, 5 Horsefair, YO5 9LF (Tel: 01423 324776)

Open 0800 to 1730 hrs. Monday to Saturday, closed Thurdsay p.m. Sunday 0745 to 1030 hrs. Game and coarse tackle. Limited flies and tying materials. Fresh and preserved baits. Club season books: Bradford City AA, Idle and Thackley AA. Day tickets: For the above waters plus Boroughbridge and District AC, Boroughbridge Social AC and Brickyard Carp Fishery. Arranges fishing tickets and accommodation for visiting angling groups.

BOSTON SPA

Lower Wharfe Angling Centre, 236 High Street (Tel: 01937 844260) Open, Summer - Monday to Friday, 0700 to 1730 hrs, Saturday 0600 to 1700 hrs and Sunday 0600 to 12.00 hrs. Winter - Monday to Friday, 0830 to 1730 hrs, closes Wednesday at 1230. Saturday 0730 to 1700 hrs and Sunday 0700 to 1200 hrs. Large stock of coarse and game tackle, some sea. Flies and tying materials. Fresh and preserved baits including frozen pike baits. Club season books: Bingley AC, Boston Spa AC, Leeds and District ASA and York and District AA. Day tickets: For all the above listed clubs where applicable plus Tadcaster Angling and Preservation Society and Wetherby and District AC. Also Outwood Angling Centre, 559 Leeds Road, Wakefield. Specialising in match tackle.

BRADFORD

Richmonds, 110 Morley Street, BD7 1AF (Tel: 01274 721042)
Open 0900 to 1700 hrs, Monday to Saturday (to 1800 hrs on Friday) except Wednesday. Mainly coarse but some game and sea tackle. Flies. Fresh and preserved baits. Club season books: Bradford City AA, Bingley AC, Saltaire AA, Listerhills Old Boys AA, Keighley AC, Marsden Star AS, Idle & Thackley AA, Unity AC, Spenborough AA, Dean Clough AA and Ryburn AC. Day tickets: For all the above listed clubs' waters where applicable plus the Leeds and Liverpool Canal.

Watercraft Products, 899 Harrogate Road, Greengate (Tel: 01274 620173)
Open 0900 to 1730 hrs. Monday to Saturday (closes 0800 hrs on Friday). Large range of game, coarse and sea tackle. Massive range of flies and tying materials. Fresh and preserved baits including frozen pike and sea bait. Club season books: Airborough and District AA, Bingley AC, Bradford City AA, Idle and Thackley AA, Leeds and District ASA, Listerhills OBAA, Marsden Star AS, Saltaire AA, Skipton AA and Unity AC. Day tickets: For all the above listed

clubs waters where applicable plus Bradford No.1 AA. Runs fly tying and fly casting courses individually or in conjunction with local college. Mail order fly tying materials.

Westgate Anglers, 63 Westgate, BD1 2RD (Tel: 01274 729570)
Open 0900 to 1730 hrs Monday to Saturday. Game, coarse and sea tackle. Flies and tying materials. Fresh and frozen baits including frozen pike baits. Club season books: Bradford No.1 AA, Bradford City AA, Keighley AC, Bierley AC, Saltaire AA, Leeds & Dist. ASA, Listerhills Old Boys AA, Unity AC and Bingley AC. Day tickets: For all the above listed clubs' waters where applicable plus local still waters.

West Park Angling, 572 Thornton Road, BD8 9NF (Tel: 01274 548289)
Open 0900 to 1800 hrs Monday to Saturday. 0900 to 1230 hrs on Bank Holidays. Game, coarse and sea tackle. Some flies and tying materials. Fresh and preserved baits including frozen pike baits. Club season books: Bradford City AA, Bradford No.1 AA, Bierley AC, Bingley AC, Idle and Thackley AA, Keighley AC, Marsden Star AS, Saltaire AA. Day tickets: For all the above listed clubs' waters where applicable.

Wibsey Angling Centre, 208 High Street, Wibsey (Tel: 01274 604542)
Open 0900 to 1730 hrs Monday to Saturday. Game, coarse and sea tackle. Some fly tying materials. Fresh and frozen baits including frozen pike baits. Clubs season books: Bingley AC, Bradford City AA, Bradford No.1 AA, Keighley AC, Leeds and District ASA and Saltaire AC. Day tickets: For all the above listed clubs' waters where applicable.

EARBY

Jackson's Fishing Tackle Shop, 27 Albion Street, Nr. Colne, BB8 6QA (Tel: 01282 843333)
Open 0900 hrs to 1800 hrs Monday to Friday. Saturday 0900 to 1700 hrs and Sunday 0900 to 1200 hrs. Mainly game, some coarse and sea tackle. Comprehensive range of flies and tying materials. Fresh and preserved baits including pike, sea baits and prawns. Club season books: Marsden Star AS, Keighley AC and Bradford City AA. Day tickets: For all the above listed clubs' waters where applicable plus Black Moss FFC, Colne Water AC and Skipton AA.

GUISELEY

Lock Stock & Barrel, 84 Otley Road, LS20 8BH (Tel: 01943 879938) Open 0900 to 1730 hrs Monday to Saturday. Game and coarse tackle. Flies and leaders. Fresh and preserved baits. Club season books: Airborough AC, Idle and Thackley AA, Leeds and District ASA and Saltaire AA. Day tickets: For all the above listed clubs' waters where applicable plus Ilkley and District AA, River Wharfe.

HARROGATE

C. J. Fishing Tackle, 182 Kings Road, HG1 5JG (Tel: 01423 525000) Open 0830 to 1800 hrs Monday to Saturday. 0900 to 1200 hrs on bank holidays. Game, coarse specialist sea tackle. Comprehensive range of flies and tying materials. Fresh and preserved baits including frozen pike baits. Club season books: Leeds and District ASA, York and District ASA, Bradford City AA and Knaresborough Anglers' Club (River Nidd only). Day tickets: For all the above listed clubs' waters where applicable plus Harrogate and Claro, Ure at Boroughbridge, Ripon Canal and Kingsley Carp Water.

Linsley Bros. Ltd, 55 Tower Street, HG1 1HG (Tel: 01423 505677) Open 0900 to 1730 hrs Monday to Saturday. Specialist game fishing tackle. Comprehensive range of flies and tying materials. Specialist spinning tackle. Club season books: No. Day tickets: Various local waters.

Orvis Company Inc, Parliament Street, HG1 2QU (Tel: 01423 561354)

Open 0930 to 1730 hrs Monday to Saturday. Game tackle only. Extensive range of flies and materials. Club season books: No. Day tickets: No. Casting tuition by A.P.G.A.I. instructor and guiding service on Yorkshire river network. Mail order catalogue.

KEIGHLEY

Fish People, 37 Aireworth Road, Stockbridge, BD21 4DN (Tel: 01535 680195)

Open 1000 to 1900 hrs Tuesday to Friday, 1000 to 1700 hrs on Saturday and Sunday. Open on Bank Holiday Mondays. Game and coarse tackle. Limited flies and tying materials. Fresh and frozen baits. Club season books: Bingley AC, Keighley AC and Marsden Star AC. Day tickets for all the above listed clubs' waters where applicable.

K. L. Tackle, 131 Mornington Street, Rear of 131 North Street (Tel: 01535 667574)
Open 0900 to 1730 hrs Monday to Friday, Saturday 0900 to 1700 hrs. Big range of coarse, game and sea tackle. Flies and tying materials. Fresh and preserved baits including frozen pike and sea bait. Club season books: Bingley AC, Bradford City AA, Keighley AC, Marsden Star AC and Saltaire AC. Day tickets for all the above listed clubs where applicable plus Skipton AC, Embsay and Whinny Gill Reservoirs and River Aire.

Willis Walker Sports, 109 Cavendish Street, BD21 3DG (Tel: 01535 602928)
Open 0900 to 1730 hrs Monday to Saturday. Game and coarse tackle. Flies. Fresh and mixed bait. Club season books: Bradford City AA, Bradford No.1 AA, Bingley AC, Keighley AC, Marsden Star AC and Saltaire AC. Day tickets for all the above listed clubs' waters where applicable.

KNARESBOROUGH

M. H. & C. Johnson, 2 Briggate, HG5 8BH (Tel: 01423 863065)
Open 0900 to 1730 hrs, Thursday 0900 to 1230 hrs. Closed Sunday. Game, coarse and sea tackle. Flies and tying materials. Fresh and preserved baits including frozen pike baits. Club season books: Bradford City AA, Knaresborough Anglers' Club, Knaresborough Piscatorials, York and District AA. Day tickets: For all the above listed clubs' waters where applicable plus Harrogate and Claro Conservative AA, and Ripon Canal.

LEEDS

Abbey Match Anglers, 38 Commercial Road (Tel: 0113 274 4562)
Open 0830 to 1730 hrs Monday through Thursday, 0830 to 1800 hrs Friday and Saturday. 0630 to 0830 hrs on Sunday during the summer. Specialist in match and coarse tackle. All fresh and preserved baits. Club season books: Aireborough & District AA, Fox & Hounds AC, Idle & Thackley AA and Leeds and District ASA. Day tickets: For all the above listed clubs' waters where applicable.

Armley Angling Centre, 14 Branch Road, Armley, LS12 3AQ (Tel: 0113 279 0738)
Open 0800 to 1800 hrs Monday to Saturday in summer and 0830 to

1700 hrs in winter. Coarse and sea tackle. No fly materials. All fresh and preserved baits except pike and sea baits. Club season books: Leeds and District ASA and Airborough AC. Day tickets: For all the above listed clubs waters where applicable.

Barry's of Goole Ltd, 19 Cardinal Road(Tel: 0113 270 3662)
Open 0830 to 1700 hrs on Monday, 0900 to 1700 hrs Tuesday through Thursday, 0900 to 1730 hrs on Friday and 0730 to 1730 on Saturday. Game, coarse and sea tackle. Some flies and tying materials. Fresh and preserved baits including frozen pike and sea baits. Club season books: No. Day tickets: No.

Bob's Tackle Shop, 1a Chapel Lane, Garforth, LS25 1EG (Tel: 0113 286 7112)
Open 0830 to 1730 hrs Monday to Friday in summer, and 0630 to 0845 hrs on Sunday during the coarse fishing season. Coarse tackle only. Fresh and preserved baits. Club season books: Leeds and District ASA and Allerton Bywater AC. Day tickets: For all the above listed clubs' water where applicable.

E. & J. Fishing Tackle, 20 Middleton Park Road, LS10 3ST (Tel: 0113 276 0034)
Open 0830 hrs to 1730 hrs Monday to Friday. Coarse tackle only. Fresh baits. Club season books: Allerton Bywater AC, Leeds and District ASA, Spenborough AC and Wakefield AC. Day tickets: For Leeds and District ASA waters

Eric's Angling Centre, 401 Selby Road, LS15 7AY (Tel: 0113 264 6883)
Open 0900 to 1730 hrs Monday to Saturday. Game, coarse and sea tackle. Specimen match tackle. No fly tying materials. Fresh and preserved baits and frozen pike baits. Club season books: Leeds and District ASA and York & District AA. Day tickets: For the above listed clubs where applicable.

Headingly Angling Centre, 58 North Lane, Headingly, LS6 3HU (Tel: 0113 278 4445)
Open 0830 to 1730 hrs Monday to Saturday. Open until 1900 hrs on Friday. Sundays, June to September, 0630 to 1000 hrs. Bank Holiday Mondays 0800 to 1300 hrs. Mainly coarse and game tackle, some sea. No fly tying materials. Fresh and frozen baits. Club season books: Aireborough AA, Fox & Hounds AC, Idle & Tackley AA, Leeds & District ASA and Listerhills OBAA. Day tickets: For all the above

listed clubs where applicable.

J. T. Rodgers, 12 Barwick Road, Crossgates, LS15 7QG (Tel: 0113 264 1195)
Open 0800 to 1700 hrs Monday to Saturday except, until 1730 hrs on Friday and until 1400 hrs on Wednesday. Mainly coarse tackle, some fly and sea. Fly tying materials. Fresh and frozen baits. Club season books: Allerton Bywater AC, Bradford City AA and Leeds & District ASA. Day tickets: For all the above listed clubs where applicable and Wetherby and District AC.

Kirkgate Anglers, 95 Kirkgate, LS2 7DJ (Tel: 0113 243 4880)
Open 0900 to 1715 hrs Monday to Saturday. Sunday 0630 to 1000 hrs from June to October. Game, coarse and sea tackle. Flies and tying materials. Fresh and preserved baits. Club season books: Leeds and District ASA, York and District AA and Bradford City AA. Day tickets: For all the above listed clubs' waters where applicable plus Boston Spa.

Marsh Fishing Tackle, 292 Upper Town Street, Bramley (Tel: 0113 255 9530)
Open Monday, Tuesday and Thursday 0900 to 1730 hrs. Wednesday 0900 to 1300 hrs. Friday and Saturday 0900 to 1730 hrs. Sunday 0630 to 0830 hrs. Game, coarse and sea tackle. Flies and some materials. Fresh and preserved baits including frozen dead baits. Club season books: Aireborough & District AA, Bradford No.1 AA and Leeds and District ASA. Day tickets: For all the above listed clubs' waters where applicable.

The Tackle Box, 22 Cross Hills, Kippax, LS25 7JP (Tel: 0113 286 1435)
Open 0900 to 1730 hrs Tuesday to Saturday. Mainly coarse tackle, some game and sea. Few flies. Fresh and preserved baits including frozen dead-baits. Club season books: Allerton Bywater AC, Castleford and District AS, Leeds and District ASA and Wheatsheaf AC. Day tickets: For Castleford and Leeds club waters. Mail order coarse fishing tackle.

LEYBURN

Gilsan Sports, 2 High Street (Tel: 01969 623942)
Open 0900 to 1730 hrs Monday to Saturday. Also Sunday 1000 to 1600 hrs in summer. Game, coarse and sea tackle. Flies and tying

materials. Fresh and preserved baits. Club season books: No. Day tickets: River Swale at Marrick Priory.

NELSON

Boyces, 44 Manchester Road (Tel: 01282 614412)
Open 0900 to 17.30 hrs. Closed half day on Tuesday. Game, coarse and sea tackle. Flies. Fresh and preserved baits plus frozen coarse and sea baits. Club season books: Bradford City AA and Marsden Star AS. Day tickets: For all the above listed clubs' waters where applicable plus the Leeds and Liverpool Canal and some lakes in Lancashire.

Fly & Tackle, 59 Cross Street (Tel: 01282 614417)
Open 1300 to 1800 hrs on Monday, Wednesday, Thursday and Friday. 0900 to 1700 on Saturday. Specialist game tackle but some coarse and sea. Professional fly tier. Big selection of flies and materials. Club season books: Marsden Star AS. Day tickets: For Marsden Star AS water and other waters in Lancashire.

NORTHALLERTON

Northallerton Angling Centre, 3 East Road, DL6 1ND (Tel: 01609 779140)
Open, summer 0730 to 1700 hrs, winter 0830 to 1700 hrs, Monday to Saturday. Game, coarse and sea tackle. Flies and tying materials. Fresh and frozen baits. Club season books: No. Day tickets: Jenkins Lake.

OTLEY

Angling & Country Sports, 36 Cross Green, LS21 1HD (Tel: 01943 462770)
Open 0900 to 1730 hrs Monday to Friday (closes 1300 hrs on Wednesday), 0830 to 1730 hrs on Saturday and 0730 to 0930 hrs on Sunday. Game and coarse tackle. Flies and tying materials. Fresh baits. Club season books: Airborough & District AC, Leeds and District ASA, Listerhills OB AA and Saltaire AA. Day tickets: For the above listed clubs' waters where applicable plus Ilkley and District AA waters on the Wharfe.

RICHMOND

Gilsan Sports, 5 Market Place (Tel: 01748 822108)
Open 0900 to 1730 hrs Monday to Saturday. Also Sunday 1000 to

1600 hrs in summer. Game, coarse and sea tackle. Flies and tying materials. Fresh and preserved baits. Club season books: Richmond and District AS. Day tickets: Richmond DAS water and Swale at Marrick Priory.

Richmond Angling Centre, 8 Temple Square, Cravengate, DL10 4ED (Tel: 01748 822989)
Open 0900 to 1700 hrs Monday to Saturday. Big range of game and coarse tackle. Large selection of flies and tying materials. Fresh and preserved baits including frozen sea and pike baits. Club season books: Richmond and District AS. Day tickets: Richmond and District AS waters, Langton Pond and Jenkins Lake.

RIPON

Ripon Angling Centre, 59 North Street, HG4 1EN (Tel: 01765 604666)
Open 0830 to 1730 hrs Monday to Saturday, 0900 to 1200 hrs on Sunday and bank holidays. Game and coarse tackle, some sea. Flies and tying materials. Fresh and preserved baits. Club season book: Ripon Piscatorials. Day tickets: For Ripon Piscatorials, Ripon AC waters Ripon Canal, Brickyard Fishery, Rogers Pond, Racecourse Lake and rivers.

SHIPLEY

Shipley Angling Centre, 23 Westgate (Tel: 01274 595726)
Open 0915 to 1715 hrs. Closed Wednesday and Sunday. Game, coarse and sea tackle. Flies and tying materials. Fresh and preserved baits. Club season books: Airborough AC, Bradford No. 1 AA, Bradford City AA, Bingley AC, Idle and Thackley AA, Keighley AC and Saltaire AA. Day tickets: For all the above listed clubs' waters where applicable plus Leeds and Liverpool Canal and local still waters.

THIRSK

Thirsk Anglers' Centre, 7 Sowerby Road, Sowerby, YO7 1HR (Tel: 01845 524684)
Open 0845 to 1730 hrs Monday to Saturday. Mainly game and coarse tackle, some sea. Flies and tying materials. Fresh and preserved baits including frozen pike dead-baits. Club season books: Thirsk AC and Idle and Thackley AA. Fly fishing instruction. Day tickets:

Thirsk AC on River Swale.

YORK

Acomb Fishing Tackle, 227 Hamilton Drive West, Acomb, YO2 4PL (Tel: 01904 785237)
Open 0830 to 1730 hrs Monday to Thursday, 0730 to 1800 hrs on Friday and Saturday. Coarse fishing tackle. No flies or tying materials. Fresh and frozen baits. Club season books: Leeds and District ASA, Wheatsheaf AC, York and District AA and York AA. Day tickets: For all the above listed clubs where applicable except Wheatsheaf AC. Operates mail order service.

Anglers Corner, 41 Huby Court, Walmgate Bar (Tel: 01904 629773)
Open 0830 to 1730 hrs Monday to Saturday. Gam, coarse and sea tackle. No flies or materials. Fresh, preserved baits and frozen pike and sea baits. Club season books: York and District AA. Day tickets: York and District AA water.

Hooks & Tackle, 40 Huntington Road, YO3 7RE (Tel: 01904 610357)
Open 0900 to 1730 hrs Monday to Saturday. 0730 to 1200 hrs on Sunday. Coarse, sea and specialist game tackle. Flies and tying materials. Fresh and preserved baits and shrimps. Club season books: York and District AA. Day tickets: York and District AA and local still waters. Specialises in hand built trout and salmon fly and coarse rods.

Mitre Pets Aquarium & Fishing Tackle, 212 Shipton Road, YO3 6RZ (Tel: 01904 654841)
Open from June 16th, 0730 to 1730 hrs Monday to Friday, 0730 to 1130 hrs on Sunday. November to June, opens at 0900 hrs. Coarse, game and sea tackle. Flies and tying materials. Fresh and preserved baits. Club season books: Bradford City AA, Leeds & District ASA and York and District AA. Day tickets: For all the above listed club waters where applicable.

York Tackle Shop, 13 Hull Road, YO1 3JL (Tel: 01904 411210)
Open 0830 to 1730 hrs Monday to Friday, 0800 to 17.30 hrs on Saturday and 0730 to 0930 hrs on Sunday. Game, coarse and sea tackle. Some flies and materials. Fresh and preserved baits. Club season books: Goole and District AA, Leeds and District AA, York and District AA and York AA. Day tickets: For all the above listed clubs' waters where applicable.

Maps of Day Ticket Fishery Locations

NORTH-WEST AREA:

1. Blackburn Farm, trout fishery.
2. Lake Semerwater, coarse fishery.
3. Helwith Bridge, trout fishery.
4. Kilnsey Park, trout fishery.

NORTH-EAST AREA:

1. Lakeside Trout Fisheries, trout fishery.
2. Broken Brae Lake, coarse fishery.
3. Ellerton Park Lake, coarse fishery.
4. Catterick Lakes, coarse fishery.
5. Kiplin Hall Lake, trout fishery.
6. Langton Ponds, coarse fishery.
7. Jenkins Lake, coarse fishery.
8. Roleith Fishery, coarse fishery.
9. Thornton Steward Reservoir, trout fishery.
10. Thorpe Perrow Lake, coarse fishery.
11. Leighton Reservoir, trout fishery.
12. Bellflask Fishery, trout fishery.
13. Tanfield Lodge Lake, trout fishery.
14. Woodland Lakes, coarse fishery.
15. Scar House Reservoir, trout fishery.
16. Brickyard Carp Fishery, coarse fishery.
17. The Oaks Fisheries, coarse fishery.
18. Racecourse Lake and Rogers Pond, coarse fisheries.

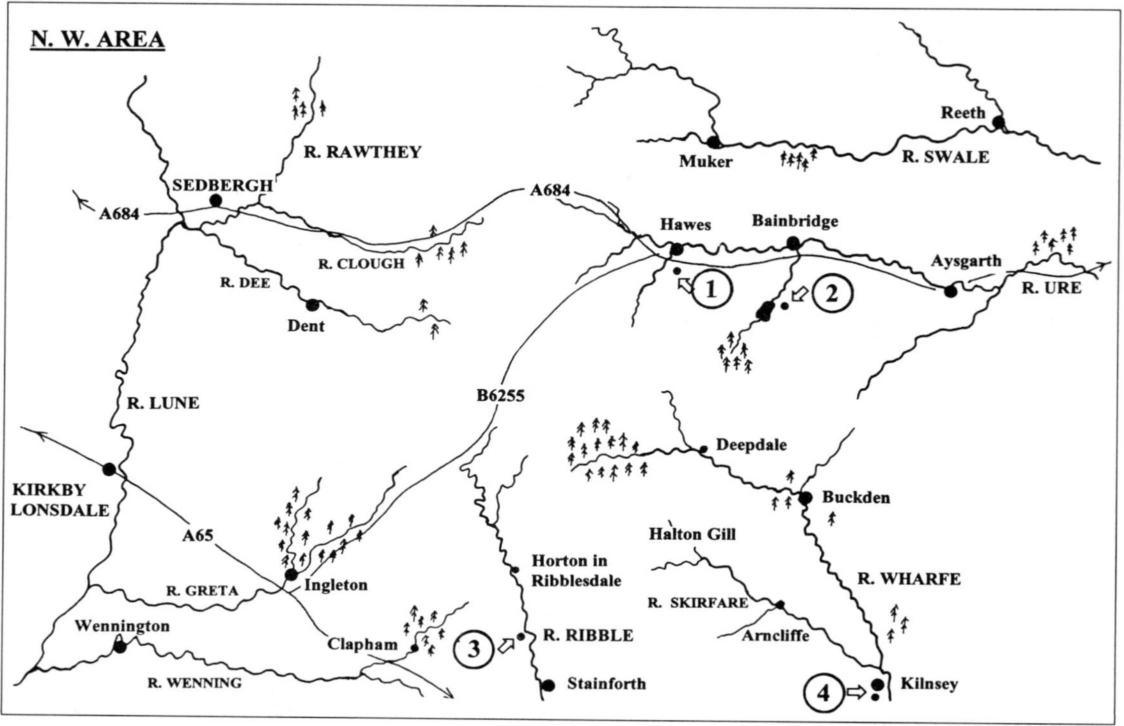
N. W. AREA
R. RAWTHEY
Muker
Reeth
R. SWALE
SEDBERGH
A684
A684
Hawes
Bainbridge
Aysgarth
R. URE
R. CLOUGH
R. DEE
Dent
1
2
R. LUNE
B6255
Deepdale
Buckden
KIRKBY LONSDALE
A65
Halton Gill
Horton in Ribblesdale
R. WHARFE
Ingleton
R. GRETA
R. SKIRFARE
Wennington
R. RIBBLE
Arncliffe
Clapham
3
R. WENNING
Stainforth
4
Kilnsey

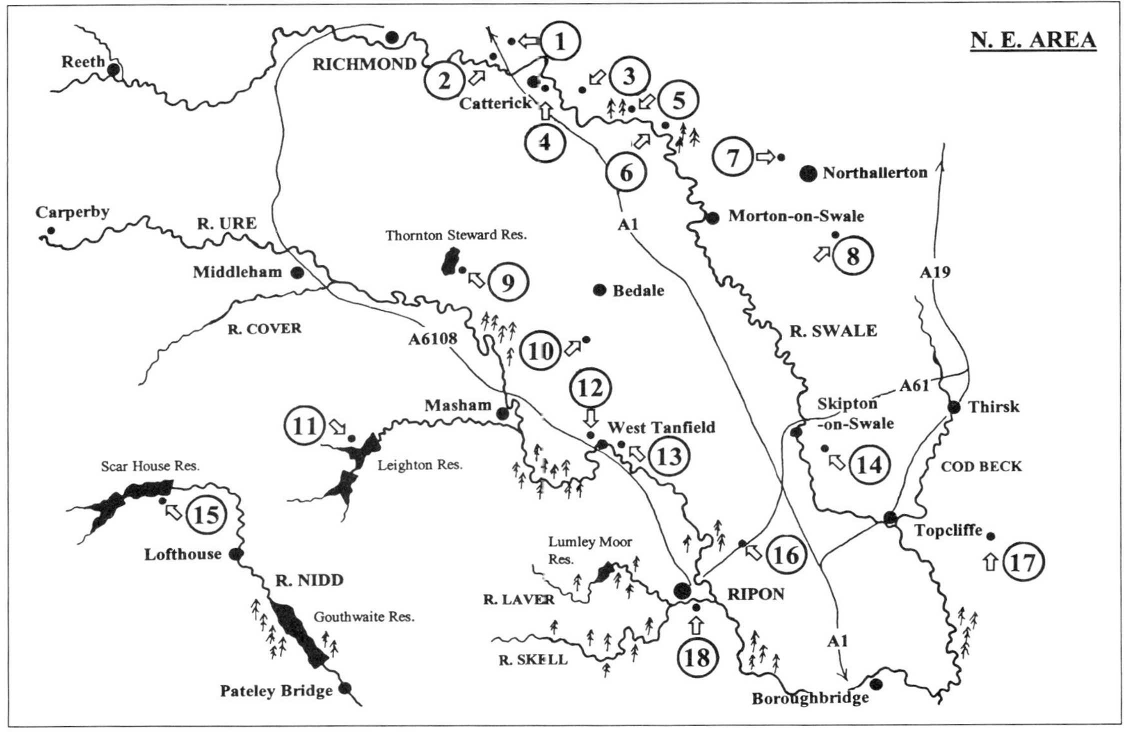
N. E. AREA
Reeth
RICHMOND
1
2
Catterick
3
5
4
6
7
Northallerton
Carperby
R. URE
A1
Morton-on-Swale
Thornton Steward Res.
8
Middleham
9
Bedale
A19
R. COVER
A6108
10
R. SWALE
12
A61
Masham
Skipton
-on-Swale
Thirsk
11
West Tanfield
13
14
Leighton Res.
COD BECK
Scar House Res.
15
Topcliffe
Lumley Moor
Res.
16
17
Lofthouse
R. NIDD
R. LAVER
RIPON
Gouthwaite Res.
A1
18
R. SKELL
Pateley Bridge
Boroughbridge

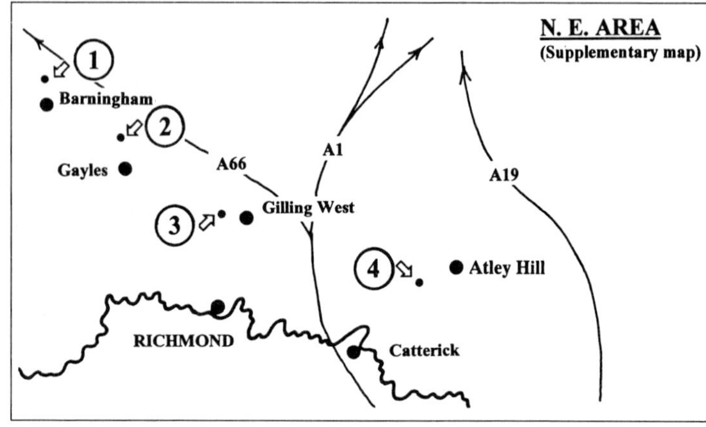

NORTH-EAST AREA (Sup):
1. Langlands Lake, trout fishery.
2. Dalton Fields Lake, trout fishery.
3. Crab Tree Angling Lake, trout fishery.
4. Green Lane Ponds, coarse fishery.

SOUTH-WEST AREA:
1. Malham Tarn, trout fishery.
2. Coniston Hall Trout Fishery.
3. Embsay Reservoir, trout fishery.
4. Whinneygill Reservoir, trout and coarse fishery.
5. Raygill, trout fishery.
6. Foulridge Reservoir, coarse fishery.
7. Leeming Reservoir, trout fishery.
8. Doe Park Reservoir, coarse fishery.
9. Sugden End Reservoir, trout and coarse fishery.
10. Sunnydale Reservoir, trout fishery.
11. Tong Park Lake, trout fishery.

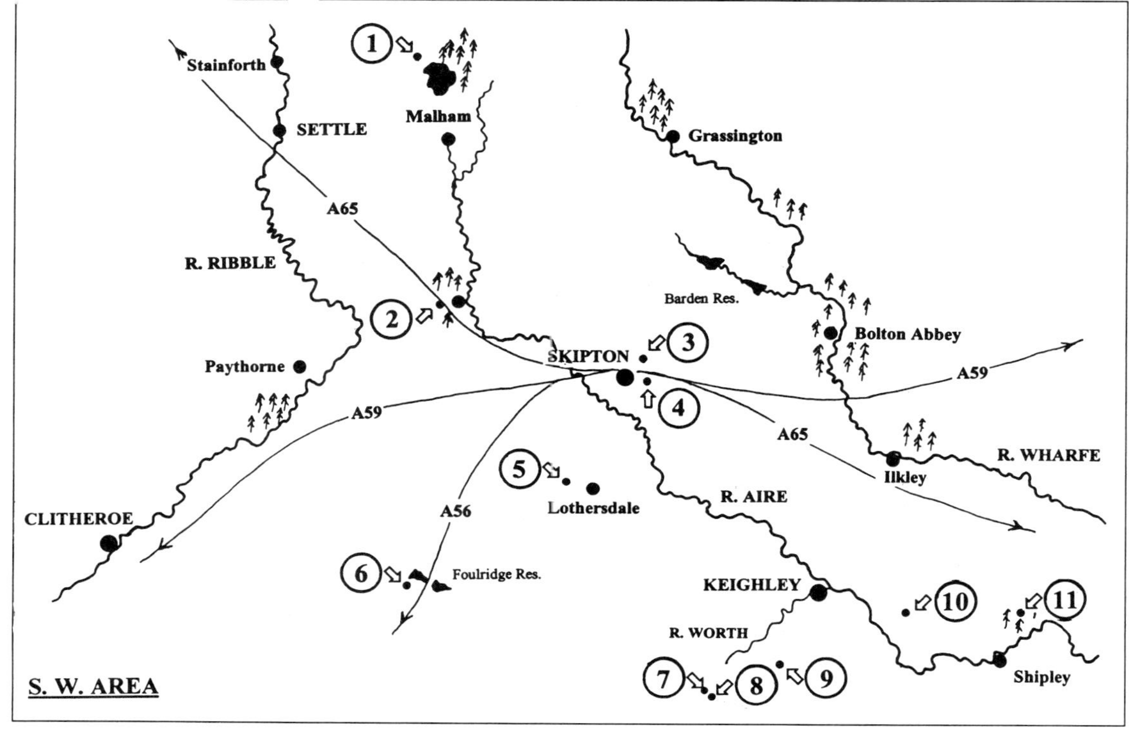
Stainforth
SETTLE
1
Malham
Grassington
A65
R. RIBBLE
2
Barden Res.
Bolton Abbey
SKIPTON
3
Paythorne
A59
4
A59
A65
R. WHARFE
5
Ilkley
A56
Lothersdale
R. AIRE
CLITHEROE
6
Foulridge Res.
KEIGHLEY
10
11
R. WORTH
7
8
9
Shipley
S. W. AREA

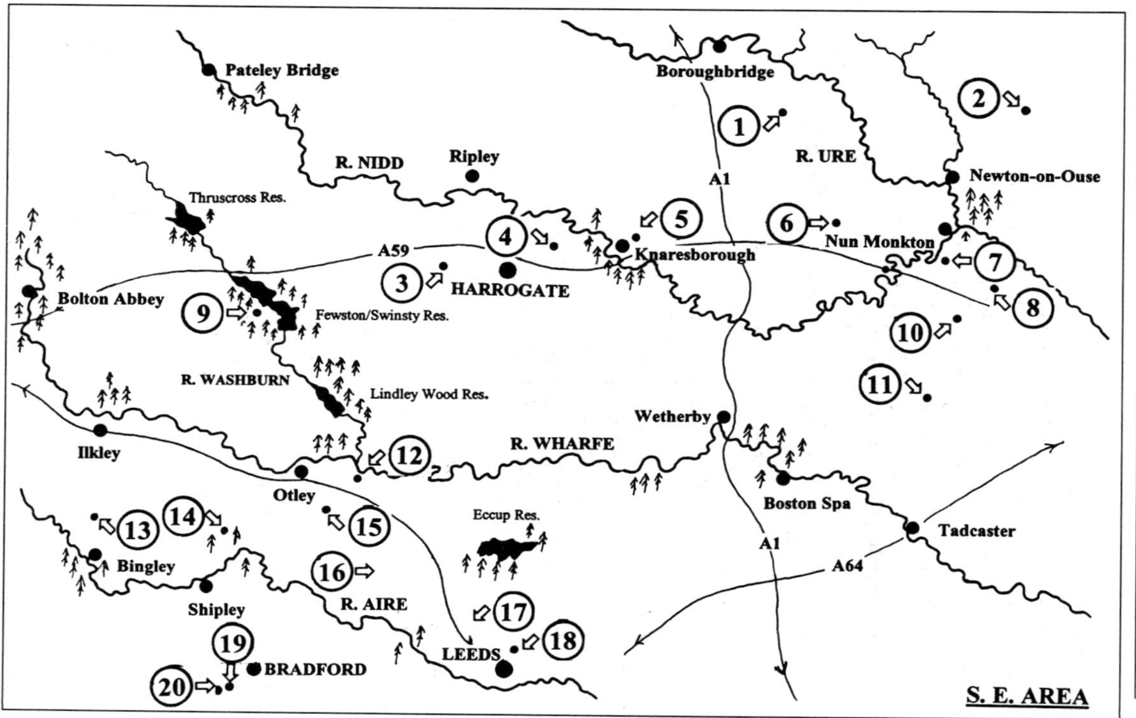
Pateley Bridge
Boroughbridge
R. NIDD
Ripley
R. URE
A1
Newton-on-Ouse
Thruscross Res.
Knaresborough
Nun Monkton
A59
HARROGATE
Bolton Abbey
Fewston/Swinsty Res.
R. WASHBURN
Lindley Wood Res.
Wetherby
Ilkley
R. WHARFE
Otley
Boston Spa
Eccup Res.
Tadcaster
A1
A64
Bingley
Shipley
R. AIRE
LEEDS
BRADFORD
S. E. AREA
1
2
3
4
5
6
7
8
9
10
11
12
13
14
15
16
17
18
19
20

SOUTH-EAST AREA:

1. Grafton Meres, coarse fishery.
2. Oak Tree Leisure Angling, coarse fishery.
3. Prospect Farm Pond, coarse fishery.
4. Kingsley Carp Water, coarse fishery.
5. Farmire Trout Fishery.
6. Thorpe Underwood Lake, coarse fishery.
7. Carpvale Pool, coarse fishery.
8. The Willows, coarse fishery.
9. Fewston and Swinsty Reservoirs, trout fishery.
10. Hessay Pond, coarse fishery.
11. Maran Lakes, trout fishery.
12. Knotford Lagoon, coarse fishery.
13. Sunnydale Reservoir, trout fishery.
14. Tong Park Lake, trout fishery.
15. Yeadon Tarn, coarse fishery.
16. Billing Dam, trout fishery.
17. Clayton Ponds, coarse fishery.
18. Roundhay Park Lake, coarse fishery
19. Harold Park Lake, coarse fishery.
20. Royds Hall Dam, coarse fishery.

Index

* * *

PRINTED BY
CARNMOR PRINT & DESIGN, PRESTON. U.K.